D0983815

WITHDRAWN

MAINE STATE LIBRARY

Using Literature to Help
Troubled Teenagers
Cope with Abuse Issues

Recent Titles in
The Greenwood Press "Using Literature to Help Troubled Teenagers" Series

Using Literature to Help Troubled Teenagers Cope with Family Issues
Joan F. Kaywell, editor and series editor

Using Literature to Help Troubled Teenagers Cope with Societal Issues
Pamela S. Carroll, editor

Using Literature to Help Troubled Teenagers Cope with Identity Issues
Jeffrey S. Kaplan, editor

Using Literature to Help Troubled Teenagers Cope with Health Issues
Cynthia Ann Bowman, editor

Using Literature to Help Troubled Teenagers Cope with End-of-Life Issues
Janet Allen, editor

Using Literature to Help Troubled Teenagers Cope with Abuse Issues

Edited by Joan Kaywell

The Greenwood Press "Using Literature
to Help Troubled Teenagers" Series

Greenwood Press
Westport, Connecticut • London

618.928582 U85 2004

Using literature to help
troubled teenagers cope
with abuse issues.

Library of Congress Cataloging-in-Publication Data

Using literature to help troubled teenagers cope with abuse issues / edited by Joan Kaywell.
 p. cm. — (The Greenwood press "Using literature to help troubled teenagers" series)
Includes index.
 ISBN 0–313–30715–6
1. Teenagers—Substance use—Prevention—Bibliography. 2. Teenagers—Drug use—
Prevention—Bibliography. 3. Substance abuse—Prevention—Bibliography. 4. Drug abuse—
Bibliography. I. Kaywell, Joan F. II. Series.
RJ506.D78U86 2004
618.92′858223—dc22   2004005919

British Library Cataloguing in Publication Data is available.

Copyright © 2004 by Joan Kaywell

All rights reserved. No portion of this book may be
reproduced, by any process or technique, without the
express written consent of the publisher.

Library of Congress Catalog Card Number: 2004005919
ISBN: 0–313–30715–6

First published in 2004

Greenwood Press, 88 Post Road West, Westport, CT 06881
An imprint of Greenwood Publishing Group, Inc.
www.greenwood.com

Printed in the United States of America

The paper used in this book complies with the
Permanent Paper Standard issued by the National
Information Standards Organization (Z39.48–1984).

10   9   8   7   6   5   4   3   2   1

Copyright Acknowledgments

The author and publisher gratefully acknowledge permission to reprint the following:

"What Is Love" by Beverly J. Wilson. Reprinted with the permission of the author.

"The Summer of Fifth Grade" by Joey Baughman. Reprinted with the permission of the author.

"The Last Closet" by Kayla Rigney as published in Diana Ressler's *The cauldron: Untitled: No boundaries,* Vol. 32, p. 59. Copyright © 2001 by Kayla Rigney. Reprinted with the permission of the author.

Excerpts of journal entries written by Dunedin High School students Jessica Kuligowski, Jenna Fitzgerald, Scott Sorset, Eryn Needy, Tracy Owens, and Takeisha Forley. Reprinted with the permission of the authors.

Excerpts of journal entries written by Pasco-Hernando Community College students Karla Kruzell, Leslie Moruia, Michael Kumicich, Anesta Boia, and Mark Nugent. Reprinted with the permission of the authors.

The comments of Leslie Hibbs and Vicki, which have been printed with their permission.

"A Bruised Butterfly" by April Templeton. Reprinted with the permission of the author.

The poem "Chinese Handcuffs" by Casey Smith. Reprinted with the permission of the author.

This book is dedicated to my son Stephen Matthew Kaywell,
my greatest gift from God,
and to all the courageous survivors who are determined
to break the cycle of abuse and create a new and
healthier generation.

Contents

Series Foreword   *Joan F. Kaywell*   ix

Acknowledgments   xvii

Introduction   xix

PART I Neglect   1

CHAPTER 1 Understanding the Parentified Child by
             Reading Margaret Haddix's *Don't You Dare
             Read This, Mrs. Dunphrey*   13
             Sue Street and Joan F. Kaywell

CHAPTER 2 A Reader's and Counselor's Response to Heather
             Quarles's *A Door Near Here*   29
             Jessica Pawelkop-Muroff and Leah Armstrong

PART II Emotional Abuse   43

CHAPTER 3 Escaping the Emotional Hold Using Chris
             Crutcher's *Ironman* as a Springboard for
             Discussion   49
             Joan F. Kaywell and Sue Street

CHAPTER 4 Han Nolan's *Born Blue:* Using Self-Expression
             to Heal the Wounds of Emotional Abuse
             and Neglect   69
             Danielle Lyons and Candace Odierna

CHAPTER 5 Without Witches and Wizards: Surviving
           Emotional Abuse and Neglect through
           Journaling on James Deem's *3 NBs of*
           Julian Drew   79
           Nicole Schaefer-Farrell and Eileen Kennedy

PART III Physical Abuse   91

CHAPTER 6 *Staying Fat for Sarah Byrnes:* A Counselor
           Picks Up Where Crutcher Leaves Off   111
           Sue Street and Joan F. Kaywell

CHAPTER 7 Precocious Teacher Encounters Professional
           Social Worker: Conversations toward
           Understanding Physical Abuse through
           Chris Crutcher's *Whale Talk*   127
           Shannon D. Dosh and Carolyn T. Royalty

PART IV Sexual Abuse   145

CHAPTER 8 Winning the Battle for Self after the Big Lie
           in Chris Crutcher's *Chinese Handcuffs*   165
           Joan F. Kaywell and Sue Street

CHAPTER 9 Voices of Healing: How Creative Expression
           Therapies Help Us Heal, Using Laurie Halse
           Anderson's Novel *Speak* as a Springboard
           for Discussion   185
           Diane Ressler and Dr. Stan Giannet

CHAPTER 10 Finding Strength in Friendship in Jacqueline
            Woodson's *I Hadn't Meant to Tell You This* 207
            Leslie Hibbs and Tom McDevitt

CHAPTER 11 A Therapeutic Teacher's Reader Response to
            Beatrice Sparks's *Treacherous Love*   215
            Terry Burkard Plaia and Judith M. Bailey

Index   231

About the Editor and Contributors   251

Series Foreword

The idea for this six-volume series—addressing family issues, identity issues, social issues, abuse issues, health issues, and death and dying issues—came while I, myself, was going to a therapist to help me deal with the loss of a loved one. My therapy revealed that I was a "severe trauma survivor" and I had to process the emotions of a bad period of time during my childhood. I was amazed that a trauma of my youth could be triggered by an emotional upset in my adult life. After an amazing breakthrough that occurred after extensive reading, writing, and talking, I looked at my therapist and said, "My God! I'm like the gifted child with the best teacher. What about all of those children who survive situations worse than mine and do not choose education as their escape of choice?" I began to wonder about the huge number of troubled teenagers who were not getting the professional treatment they needed. I pondered about those adolescents who were fortunate enough to get psychological treatment but were illiterate. Finally, I began to question if there were ways to help them while also improving their literacy development.

My thinking generated two theories on which this series is based: (1) Being literate increases a person's chances of emotional health, and (2) Twenty-five percent of today's students are "unteachable." The first theory was generated by my pondering these two statistics: 80% of our prisoners are illiterate (Hodgkinson, 1991), and 80% of our prisoners have been sexually abused (Child Abuse Council, 1993). If a correlation actually exists between these two statistics, then it suggests a strong need for literacy skills in order for a person to be able to address emotional turmoil in healthy or constructive ways. The second theory came out of work I did for my book, *Adolescents at Risk: A Guide to Fiction and Nonfiction for Young Adults, Parents and Professionals* (Greenwood), and my involvement in working with teachers and students in middle and secondary schools. Some of the emotional baggage our youth bring to school is way too heavy for them to handle without help. These students simply cannot handle additional academic responsibilities when they are "not right" emotionally.

THEORY ONE: BEING LITERATE INCREASES A PERSON'S CHANCES OF EMOTIONAL HEALTH

Well-educated adults who experience intense emotional pain, whether it is from the loss of a loved one or from a traumatic event, have several options available for dealing with their feelings. Most will find comfort in talking with friends or family members, and some will resort to reading books to find the help they need. For example, reading Dr. Kubler-Ross's five stages for coping with death—denial, anger, bargaining, depression, and acceptance or growth—might help a person understand the various stages he or she is going through after the death of a friend or relative. Sometimes, however, additional help is needed when an individual is experiencing extreme emotions and is unable to handle them.

Consider a mother whose improper left-hand turn causes the death of her seven-year-old daughter and the injury of her four-year-old daughter. It is quite probable that the mother will need to seek additional help from a therapist who will help her deal with such a trauma. A psychologist or psychiatrist will, more than likely, get her to talk openly about her feelings, read some books written by others who have survived such a tragedy, and do regular journal writing. A psychiatrist may also prescribe some medication during this emotionally challenging time. This parent's literacy skills of talking, reading, and writing are essential to her getting through this difficult period of her life.

Now, consider her four-year-old daughter who is also experiencing extreme grief over the loss of her beloved older sister. If this child is taken to counseling, the therapist will probably get her to talk, role-play, and draw out her feelings. These are the literacy skills appropriate to the developmental level of a four-year-old child. Such a child, if not taken to a counselor when needed, will manifest her emotions in one of two ways— either by acting out or by withdrawing.

Lev Vygotsky, a well-respected learning theorist, suggests that without words there could be no thoughts and the more words a person has at his or her disposal, the bigger that person's world. If what Vygotsky suggests is true, then a person with a limited or no vocabulary is only capable of operating at an emotional level. *The Story of My Life* by Helen Keller adds credibility to that view. In the introduction to the novel, written by Robert Russell, he describes Helen Keller's frustration at not being able to communicate:

> Perhaps the main cause for her early tantrums was plain frustration at not being able to communicate.... Not being able to hear, Helen had nothing to imitate, so she had no language. This meant more than simply not being able to talk. It meant having nothing clear to talk about because for her things had no names. Without names, things have no distinctness or individuality. Without language, we could not describe the difference between an elephant and an egg. Without the words we would have no clear conception of either elephant or egg. The name of a thing confers identity upon it and makes it possible for us to think about it. Without names for love or sorrow, we do not know we are experiencing them. Without words, we could not say, "I love you," and human beings need to say this and much more. Helen had the need, too, but she had not the means. As she grew older and the need increased, no wonder her fits of anger and misery grew. (pp. 7–8)

Helen, herself, writes,

> .... the desire to express myself grew. The few signs I used became less and less adequate, and my failures to make myself understood were invariably followed by outbursts of passion. I felt as if invisible hands were holding me, and I made frantic efforts to free myself. I struggled—not that struggling helped matters, but the spirit of resistance was strong within me; I generally broke down in tears and physical exhaustion. If my mother happened to be near I crept into her arms, too miserable even to remember the cause of the tempest. After awhile the need of some means of communication became so urgent that these outbursts occurred daily, sometimes hourly. (p. 28)

If Vygotsky's theory reflected by the illuminating words of a deaf, blind, and mute child is true, then it is no wonder that 80% of our prisoners are illiterate victims of abuse.

THEORY TWO: 25% OF TODAY'S TEENAGERS ARE "UNTEACHABLE" BY TODAY'S STANDARDS

Teachers are finding it increasingly more difficult to teach their students, and I believe that 25% of teenagers are "unteachable" by today's standards. A small percentage of these troubled youth do choose academics as their escape of choice, and they are the overachievers to the nth degree. That is not to say that all overachievers are emotionally disturbed teenagers, but some of them are learning, not because of their teachers, but because their very survival depends upon it. I know. I was one of them. The other adolescents going through inordinately difficult times (beyond the difficulty inherent in adolescence itself) might not find the curriculum very relevant to their lives. Their escapes of choice include rampant sex, drug use, gang membership, and other self-destructive behaviors. Perhaps the violence permeating our schools is a direct result of the utter frustration of some of our youth.

Consider these data describing the modern teenage family. At any given time, 25% of American children live with one parent, usually a divorced or never-married mother (Edwards & Young, 1992). Fifty percent of America's youth will spend some school years being raised by a single parent, and almost four million school-age children are being reared by neither parent (Hodgkinson, 1991). In 1990, 20% of American children grew up in poverty, and it is probable that 25% will be raised in poverty by the year 2000 (Howe, 1991). Children in homeless families often experience developmental delays, severe depression, anxiety, and learning disorders (Bassuk & Rubin, 1987).

Between one-fourth and one-third of school-aged children are living in a family with one or more alcoholics (Gress, 1988). Fourteen percent of children between the ages of 3 and 17 experience some form of family violence (Craig, 1992). Approximately 27% of girls and 16% of boys are sexually abused before the age of 18 (Krueger, 1993), and experts believe that it is reasonable to say that 25% of children will be sexually abused before adulthood (Child Abuse Council, 1993). Remember to note that eight out of ten criminals in prison were abused when they were children (Child Abuse Council, 1993).

Consider these data describing the modern teenager. Approximately two out of ten school-aged youth are affected by anorexia nervosa and bulimia (Phelps & Bajorek, 1991) and between 14% to 23% have vomited to lose weight (National Centers for Disease Control, 1991). By the time students become high school seniors, 90% have experimented with alcohol use and nearly two-thirds have used drugs (National Institute on Drug Abuse, 1992). In 1987, 40% of seniors admitted they had used dangerous drugs and 60% had used marijuana (National Adolescent Student Health Survey). In 1974, the average age American high school students tried marijuana was 16; in 1984, the average age was 12 (Nowinski, 1990).

By the age of 15, a fourth of the girls and a third of the boys are sexually active (Gibbs, 1993), and three out of four teenagers have had sexual intercourse by their senior years (Males, 1993). Seventy-five percent of the mothers who gave birth between the ages of 15 to 17 are on welfare (Simkins, 1984). In 1989, AIDS was the sixth leading cause of death for 15- to 24-year-olds (Tonks, 1993), and many AIDS experts see adolescents as the third wave of individuals affected by HIV (Kaywell, 1993). Thirty-nine percent of sexually active teenagers said they preferred not to use any method of contraception (Harris Planned Parenthood Poll, 1986).

Ten percent of our students are gay (Williams, 1993), and the suicide rate for gay and lesbian teenagers is two to six times higher than that of heterosexual teens (Krueger, 1993). Suicide is the second leading cause of teenage deaths; "accidents" rated first (Centers for Disease Control, 1987). An adolescent commits suicide every one hour and 47 minutes (National Center for Health Statistics, 1987), and nine children die from gunshot wounds every day in America (Edelman, 1989). For those children growing up in poor, high crime neighborhoods, one in three has seen a homicide by the time they reach adolescence (Beck, 1992).

Consider these data describing the dropout problem. In 1988, the dropout rate among high school students was 28.9% (Monroe, Borzi, & Burrell, 1992). More than 80% of America's one million prisoners are high school dropouts (Hodgkinson, 1991). We spend more than $20,000 per year per prisoner (Hodgkinson, 1991) but spend less than $4,000 per year per student. Forty-five percent of special education students drop out of high school (Wagner, 1989).

Numbers and statistics such as these are often incomprehensible, but consider the data in light of a 12th grade classroom of 30 students. Eight to 15 are being raised by a single parent, 6 are in poverty, 8 to 10 are being raised in families with alcoholics, 4 have experienced some form of family violence, and 8 of the female and 5 of the male students have been sexually violated. Six are anorectic or bulimic, 27 have used alcohol, 18 have used marijuana, and 12 have used dangerous drugs. Twenty-two have had sexual intercourse and 12 of them use no protection. Three students are gay. Eight will drop out of school, and 6 of those 8 will become criminals. Everyday in our country, 2 adolescents commit suicide by lunchtime.

These are the students that our teachers must teach everyday, and these are the students who need help beyond what schools are currently able to provide. Think about the young adults who are both illiterate and in pain! Is there anything that can be done to not only help these young people with their problems while increasing their literacy skills? Since most of our nation's prisoners are illiterate—the acting out side—and most homeless people are not connected to society—the withdrawal side—it seems logical to try to help these adolescents while they are still within the educational system.

Perhaps this series that actually pairs literacy experts with therapists can help the caretakers of our nation's distraught youth—teachers, counselors, parents, clergy, and librarians—acquire understanding and knowledge on how to better help these troubled teenagers. The series provides a unique approach to guide these caretakers working with troubled teenagers. Experts discuss young adult literature, while therapists provide analysis and advice for protagonists in these novels. Annotated bibliographies provide the reader with similar sources that can be used to help teenagers discuss these issues while increasing their literacy skills.

Joan F. Kaywell

REFERENCES

Bassuk, E.L. & Rubin, L. (1987). Homeless children: A neglected population. *American Journal of Orthopsychiatry, 57* (2), p. 279 ff.

Beck, J. (1992, May 19). Inner-city kids beat the odds to survive. *The Tampa Tribune.*

Craig, S.E. (1992, September). The educational needs of children living with violence. *Phi Delta Kappan, 74* (1), p. 67 ff.

Edelman, M.W. (1989, May). Defending America's children. *Educational Leadership, 46* (8), p. 77 ff.

Edwards, P.A. & Young, L.S.J. (1992, September). Beyond parents: Family, community, and school involvement. *Phi Delta Kappan, 74* (1), p. 72 ff.

Gibbs, N. (1993, May 24). How should we teach our children about sex? *Time, 140* (21), p. 60 ff.

Gress, J.R. (1988, March). Alcoholism's hidden curriculum. *Educational Leadership, 45* (6), p. 18 ff.

Hodgkinson, H. (1991, September). Reform versus reality. *Phi Delta Kappan, 73* (1), p. 9 ff.

Howe II, H. (1991, November). America 2000: A bumpy ride on four trains. *Phi Delta Kappan, 73* (3), p. 192 ff.

Kaywell, J.F. (1993). *Adolescents at risk: A guide to fiction and nonfiction for young adults, parents and professionals.* Westport, CT: Greenwood Publishing Group.

Keller, H. (1967). *The story of my life.* New York: Scholastic.

Krueger, M.M. (1993, March). Everyone is an exception: Assumptions to avoid in the sex education classroom. *Phi Delta Kappan, 74* (7), p. 569 ff.

Males, M. (1993, March). Schools, society, and "teen" pregnancy. *Phi Delta Kappan, 74* (7), p. 566 ff.

Monroe, C., Borzi, M.G., & Burrell, R.D. (1992, January). Communication apprehension among high school dropouts. *The School Counselor, 39* (4), p. 273 ff.

Nowinski, J. (1990). *Substance abuse in adolescents and young adults.* New York: Norton.

Phelps, L. & Bajorek, E. (1991). Eating disorders of the adolescent: Current issues in etiology, assessment, and treatment. *School Psychology Review, 20* (1), p. 9 ff.

Simkins, L. (1984, Spring). Consequences of teenage pregnancy and motherhood. *Adolescence, 19* (73), p. 39 ff.

Tonks, D. (1992–1993, December–January). Can you save your students' lives? Educating to prevent AIDS. *Educational Leadership, 50* (4), p. 48 ff.

Wagner, M. (1989). *Youth with disabilities during transition: An overview of descriptive findings from the national longitudinal transition study.* Stanford, CA: SRI International.

Williams, R.F. (1993, Spring). Gay and lesbian teenagers: A reading ladder for students, media specialists, and parents. *The ALAN Review, 20* (3), p. 12 ff.

Acknowledgments

I would like to acknowledge and thank all the students who took my distance-learning class on "Young Adult Literature and Abuse Issues" during Fall 2001. Without this class, this book would not have materialized. Hugs to Teresa Agosta, Courtney Canady, Shelley DeBlasis, Jennifer Dobbs, Shannon Dosh, Mary Ferguson, Leslie Hibbs, Danielle Lyons, Laura Marshall, Chris Munoz, Jessica Pawelkop, Terry Plaia, Diane Ressler, Nicole Schaefer-Farrell, and Mike Tullio.

Blessings to all the givers of this world, including Father Ed Rich, Father Jerry Kaywell, the Renew Family—Debbie Brown, Monica Dousdebes, Marie Fischer, John and Anne Laffan, Terrie and Larry Gil, Lynne Grigelevich, and Julianne Maranda—and to the many teachers and counselors who care and give so much of themselves to help others.

I would also like to extend my gratitude to Emily Birch for launching the *Using Literature to Help Troubled Teenagers Cope with...Issues* series and to Lynn Araujo for seeing that all six books—*Family, Societal, Alienation and Identity, Health, End-of Life,* and *Abuse* were completed. Thanks to Greenwood Publishing Group for making the series available.

Introduction

This volume—focusing on abuse issues—was written in hope that the caretakers of our nation's distraught youth can acquire understanding and new knowledge on how to better help troubled teenagers cope with various abuse problems in healthier and more constructive ways. By combining the expertise of literacy experts with psychologists, psychiatrists, or counselors, this resource provides therapists and educators with ideas for bibliotherapy. The primary hope is to increase these adolescents' literacy while offering them the special help they need. It is important to note that this is a reference book and not a medical advice book, nor should it be viewed as a diagnostic text; trained therapists—not educators—are the ones who diagnose abuse. Educators, however, can objectively report what they observe to the proper authorities when suspicions arise.

The organization of this sixth and final volume departs slightly from the other five books in this series in that each part is organized around the four types of abuse: neglect, emotional, physical, and sexual. The chapters included in each part are preceded with reference information about each type of abuse in the following order: a definition of the type of abuse, the extent of the problem, recognizing the particular type of abused child, and the results of the particular kind of abuse. These four headings are explained by independent paragraphs as a webography, where a credible site is summarized followed by the complete URL so that a reader may visit the entire site if interested.

Following the four aforementioned headings, two additional reference sections are included: young adult (YA) novels that include that particular type of abuse as part of their content, and nonfiction texts that explain the problems incurred by that type of abuse. For these texts, standard bibliographic format is followed, with the citation preceding the annotations or summaries. These independent reference sections were included because of the controversy that exists in the literature, which sometimes appears as conflicting data if one doesn't understand what kind of abuse is being described.

Finally, the heart of this volume follows the format of the five other books in the series. For each chapter included in one of the four abuse parts (neglect, emotional, physical, and sexual), a therapist read a specific YA novel and provided therapy to the young adult protagonist, using appropriate terminology wherever possible. In some cases, therapists also respond to teachers' reader responses to the text. Because the protagonists and families are all fictional characters, helping professionals may discuss each case without fear of libel.

As mentioned in the "Series Foreword," my escape and my salvation during my teenage years came from books—not drugs, alcohol, sex, food, gangs, or guns. Many of our young people truly are both illiterate and in pain. Not too long ago—after experiencing extensive therapy for being a "severe trauma survivor"—I asked myself, "Is there anything we can do to help unfortunate teenagers with their problems while increasing their literacy skills?" As I stated previously, most of our nation's prisoners are illiterate—the acting-out side—and most homeless people are not connected to society—the withdrawal side. With this in mind, it makes sense to try to help these adolescents while they are still within our educational system. Like education, psychology as a profession has become research based. Educators and parents, by and large, have not been exposed to various terms frequently used by counselors. I did not even know, for example, what a "severe trauma survivor" was, much less realize that I was one. I believe we can better help our abused youth, but all involved parties must learn how to communicate better. Much can be learned by combining the expertise of different helping professionals.

We all know what it's like to find the perfect card or song that expresses our feelings exactly right. Because it is much easier to talk about someone else's problems using words artistically conveyed by masterful writers, therapists might consider using young adult literature to offer their patients words, ideas, situations, and feelings.

Part I

Neglect

According to the following professional sources identified at the end of each paragraph, the following are signs of neglect.

DEFINITION OF NEGLECT

An action-based definition of child neglect includes rejecting the legitimacy of the child's needs, isolating the child from social experience, terrorizing the child and making him believe in a hostile world, ignoring the child, corrupting the child by reinforcing deviant behavior, verbally assaulting him with demeaning names, and pressuring the child to grow up quickly. http://www.childresearch.net/CYBRARY/NEWS/200012.HTM#1

Unlike physical and sexual abuse, neglect is usually typified by an ongoing pattern of inadequate care and is readily observed by individuals in close contact with the child. Physicians, nurses, day-care personnel, relatives, and neighbors are frequently the ones to suspect and report neglected infants, toddlers, and preschool-aged children. Once children are in school, school personnel often notice indicators of child neglect such as poor hygiene, poor weight gain, inadequate medical care, or frequent absences from school. Professionals have defined four types of neglect: physical, emotional, educational, and medical. http://www.amer humane.org (American Humane Association. Information from the National Child Abuse and Neglect Data System [NCANDS])

Physical Neglect

Physical neglect may include, but is not limited to, the following: abandonment; lack of supervision; life-endangering hygiene; lack of adequate nutrition that places the child below the normal growth curve; lack of shelter; or lack of medical or dental care that results in health-compromising conditions. http://www.gangfreekids.org/childAbuse2.html (National Foun-ation for Abused and Neglected Children, 1997)

Emotional Neglect

Emotional neglect is failure to provide an environment in which a child can thrive, learn, and develop. http://www.parentanon.org/Neglect.htm

EXTENT OF THE PROBLEM

Child neglect is the most frequent cause of child death. http://www.safe child.org/childabuse4.htm (Safe Child; Coalition for Children, 2001)

Child neglect is the most common form of child maltreatment reported to public child-protective services. In 1995, the National Child Abuse and Neglect Data System (NCANDS) reported that an estimated three million children suffered maltreatment, and over one million of those cases were substantiated; more than half were cases of neglect. http://www.amer humane.org/children/factsheets/neg_abuse.htm (American Humane Association, 2001)

More children suffer neglect than any other form of maltreatment. In 1998, investigations determined that about 53% of victims suffered neglect, 22% physical abuse, 12% sexual abuse, 6% emotional maltreatment, 2% medical neglect, and 25% other forms of maltreatment. Some children suffer more than one type of maltreatment. http://www.acf.dhhs. gov/programs/cb/publications/ncanprob.htm (U.S. Department of Health and Human Services, Administration for Children and Families, National Child Abuse and Neglect Data System, 1998)

Approximately 8 out of every 1,000 children experience physical neglect—the refusal of or extreme delay of health care, child abandonment, and/or inadequate supervision. http://www.americanhumane.org/ children/factsheets/neg_abuse.htm

In 1998, a study conducted in Florida showed a 3.8% increase in child abuse and neglect since 1990; 35.5% of these 82,119 victims suffered neglect. http://www.childadvocacy.org/implinks.html (National Association of Child Advocates, Children's Defense Fund, "State of Florida's Children–2000")

Child neglect, the most commonly reported form of child maltreatment, has remained relatively understudied. Conducting research with maltreated youth is a difficult process because of troubles in recruiting samples and in navigating the ethical and legal reporting requirements in collecting information from families where abuse has occurred. http://www.nimh.nih.gov/childhp/nihabuse.htm (National Institute of Mental Health, May 18, 1999)

RECOGNIZING NEGLECTED CHILDREN

According to the National Network for Child Care (NNCC), possible neglect can be recognized in children who exhibit the following behaviors: consistent hunger; poor hygiene; inappropriate dress; consistent lack of supervision (especially in dangerous activities or for long periods); unattended physical problems or medical needs; abandonment in parked cars, buses, on field trips, at home, or at the child-care facility; underweight appearance or poor growth pattern (small in stature, failure to thrive). http://www.nncc.org/Abuse/abuse.neglect.html (National Network for Child Care, 2001)

Parental indicators of neglected children include those parents who misuse alcohol or drugs; have disorganized, upsetting home lives; are apathetic and feel that nothing will change; are isolated from friends, relatives, and neighbors; have long-term, chronic illnesses; have a history of neglect as children themselves; expose children to unsafe living conditions; or display limited intellectual capacities. http://www.kidsafe-caps.org/neglect.html (Child Abuse Prevention Services—The Child Safety Institute, 1999)

Parents and family of neglected children tend to promise but not follow up on recommendations; fail to keep appointments or accept help; have a lifestyle of isolation; have their own histories of abuse or neglect as children; have disorganized, chaotic home lives; be chronically ill; act indifferent; and fail to provide adequate supervision. http://www.safechild.org/childabuse4.htm

The assessment of child neglect requires recognition that the failure to provide the necessities of life may be related to poverty as well as the consideration of cultural values and standards of care. http://www.calib.com/nccanch/pubs/factsheets/childmal.cfm (National Clearinghouse on Neglect and Child Abuse Information, Web Site updated on April 6, 2001)

RESULTS OF NEGLECT

Emotional neglect is a hidden danger in our society, leading to severely damaged intellectual and social development of children. http://www.theledger.com/life/health/18kid.htm (newspaper article describing reasons for more research studies on the effects of childhood neglect, March 18, 1999).

Children who are neglected or emotionally abused may have difficulty learning to talk, find it hard to develop close relationships, be overly friendly with strangers, be unable to play imaginatively, have poor self-images, and underachieve at school. http://www.preventchildabuse.org/family_community/index.html (Prevent Child Abuse America, 2001)

The accumulated evidence indicates that children who are maltreated often experience disrupted growth and development. Adverse effects have been identified in children's physical, cognitive, emotional, and social development, and these adverse effects accumulate over time. http://www.futureofchildren.org/ ("The Extent and Consequences of Child Maltreatment" by Diana J. English, in the *The Future of Children,* Spring 1998)

YOUNG ADULT NOVELS INVOLVING NEGLECT

Throughout the following sources, RL: MS = Reading Level: Middle School and RL: HS = Reading Level: High School.

Nolan, Han. (2001). *Born Blue.* New York: Harcourt. 277 pp. (ISBN: 0–15–201916–2)

Janie is placed in a foster home after her mother suffers from a spell of amnesia—actually a heroin high—and leaves her to drown in the Gulf of Mexico. Janie refers to her foster home as the "stink house" because it smells of baby vomit and dirty diapers. The only positive thing about the stink house is Harmon, her foster brother. Harmon shares his most valuable possessions with Janie, including his music collection. Together, they spend hours after school listening to Aretha Franklin, Billie Holiday, and Etta James. As it turns out, Janie is a natural-born blues singer. After a wealthy family adopts Harmon, Janie copes with her loss through her own singing and through dreaming about singing with Etta James. Things get worse when Janie's mother kidnaps her and trades her to a drug-dealing couple for heroin. Janie's music helps her, but in striving to become a professional singer, Janie still adopts some of her mother's bad habits. Readers learn about how cycles of abuse and neglect occur when professionals are not there to intervene. RL: MS (neglect and emotional abuse)

Pelzer, David. (1997). *The Lost Boy.* Deerfield Beach, FL: Health Communications, Inc. 340 pp. (ISBN: 1–55874–515–7)

This autobiography and sequel to his first novel, *A Child Called "It,"* is Pelzer's account of his life from age 9 to 18. While revealing accounts of his highly dysfunctional childhood—living in the garage with no heat; wearing old, discarded, and torn clothing; and eating leftover scraps for meals—he shares his personal feelings in regard to being alone, neglected, and abandoned by his family. Eventually, David runs away to find a new life for himself and winds up in foster care. During the six years he spends in foster care, this child formerly called "It" learns about life and develops hope for himself. RL: HS (neglect and emotional abuse)

Quarles, Heather. (2000). *A Door Near Here.* New York: Dell Laurel-Leaf. 231 pp. (ISBN: 0–440–22761–5)

At 15 years of age, Katherine struggles to hold the family together while her mother slips further and further into the grip of alcoholism. While Katherine's mother neglects her children, living in her bedroom for months at a time, Katherine does her best to keep her sisters and brothers fed. As the weeks go on, however, Katherine finds it increasingly difficult to make ends meet and care for her siblings. As a frightened and stressed adolescent, Katherine does not dare tell anyone about their situation for fear that they will all be split up by the social services agency if they are discovered. Katherine needs to stop denying her mother's serious problem and admit to herself that drinking too much and not feeding your kids is child abuse. (An ALA Best Book for Young Adults, New York Public Library Book for the Teen Age, and the Delacorte Press Prize for a First Young Adult Novel.) RL: MS (neglect)

Rottman, S.L. (1997). *Hero.* Atlanta: Peachtree Publishers. 134 pp. (ISBN: 1–56145–159)

Sean Parker is the epitome of resiliency. Readers are initially introduced to an angry, troubled teen hardened by years of abuse and neglect from his alcoholic mother and his estranged father. Unloved by the adults who should love him the most, Sean lashes out when his mother steals his money from a secret hiding place (something essential to a neglected child's survival); angry outbursts at school compound his problems. The reader is not surprised when Sean ends up in the juvenile justice system. Thankfully, the arrest leads to the most compassionate relationship this teen has ever known. When Sean is placed in the partial custody of Mr. Hassler, an old man who takes in juveniles to work on his horse farm, Sean receives his first real lessons in unconditional love. The author draws a clever parallel between a foal Sean helps to deliver and the boy, both of whom need to be removed from their mothers for their own safety. The novel's climax is a huge surprise, providing those who enjoy it perhaps the best definition of a hero ever. (Winner of the 1998 Oklahoma Book Award.) RL: MS (neglect and emotional abuse)

NONFICTION TEXTS EXPLAINING THE PROBLEM OF NEGLECT

Ackard, Diann M., Neumark-Sztainer, Dianne, Hannan, Peter J., French, Simone, Story, Mary. (2001, June). Binge and Purge Behavior among Adolescents: Associations with Sexual and Physical Abuse in a Nationally Representative Sample (The Commonwealth Fund Survey). *Child Abuse & Neglect, 25* (6), pp. 771–785.

In a study of a nationally representative sample of 6,728 adolescents in fifth through twelfth grades, binge-purge behavior was significantly associated with all abuse types (sexual, physical, emotional, neglect). Gender differences were found, with 13% of girls exhibiting binge-purge behavior related to abuse compared with 7% of boys. Discussing the abuse with another person may help reduce binge-purge behavior, as abused adolescents who did not discuss the abuse were more likely to continue binge-purge behavior.

Baron, Mary. (2000, Spring). Why I Choose to Teach Sapphire's *Push. The ALAN Review, 27* (3), p. 50.

In an adolescent literature class offered at the University of North Florida, Mary Baron requires *Push* as one of the novels addressed in her course. Her rationale for including this controversial novel stems from her belief that future teachers need to be aware of "the terrible truths of their students' lives." Like Precious Jones, the novel's protagonist, they will have students who have been and are beaten, abused, neglected, hungry, or homeless.

Child Maltreatment Division. (1999). *A Selected, Annotated Bibliography of Child Maltreatment Reporting by Education Professionals.* Canada: Health Canada. Bibliography found at http://www.hc-sc.gc.ca/hppb/familyviolence/pdfs/anno_e.pdf may be printed out in its original booklet format.

This collection of articles from Canada, the United States, Israel, Sweden, Ireland, and Australia reveals barriers to reporting child abuse within school environments, the most common being "lack of evidence, fear of legal ramification, and fear of parental retaliations on the child." For teachers willing to make reports, there "seems to be a significant lack of knowledge regarding both the identification of abuse and reporting procedures." In one article, only one respondent of 46 had received any kind of formal training in child abuse and neglect whereas, in other articles, teachers who received training on abuse were more confident in their abilities to observe signs of abuse but felt that their training was inadequate. The editors conclude that "more training in the identification of symptoms of abuse and neglect, especially sexual and emotional abuse, as well as training regarding reporting procedures is necessary to insure that this group of mandated reporters continues its role as one of the most important stakeholders in child abuse and neglect prevention."

Cowen, Perle Slavik. (1999, July/August). Child Neglect: Injuries of Omission. *Pediatric Nursing, 25* (4), pp. 401–416.

Although 52% of substantiated cases of abuse fall in the category of emotional abuse and neglect, there is more social outrage and indignation for physical or sexual abuse than there is for these serious forms of abuse. The author points to limited public awareness of neglect as a serious and prevalent danger to children as a possible explanation for this lack of social outcry. Neglect is generally defined as the failure of the child's parents or caretakers to provide the child with the basic necessities of life when financially able to do so or when offered reasonable means to do so. The basic necessities include minimally adequate care in the areas of shelter, nutrition, health, supervision, education, affection, and protection. Researchers have indicated that child neglect is strongly correlated with poverty, single-parent caretakers, unemployment, and multifaceted family problems.

Cruise, T. & Horton, C. (1997, Winter). Clinical Assessment of Child Victims and Adult Survivors of Child Maltreatment. *Journal of Counseling and Development, 76* (1), pp. 94–104.

According to a national study conducted in 1996 of abuse cases reported to state agencies, 53% of the children in these cases experienced neglect, and 4% suffered some form of psychological maltreatment. Neglect is normally considered as a failure to adequately furnish a child with his or her fundamental educational, medical, physical, mental health, and emotional needs. Psychological maltreatment includes extreme verbal attacks—screaming, belittling, and threatening—as well as neglect. Neglected children may appear helpless in high-stress environments or seem passive and withdrawn. They tend to repress thoughts and feelings because they have no one who responds to them. Individuals who have been psychologically mistreated may form maladaptive peer relationships because of negative self-images.

deMause, Lloyd. (1998, Winter). The History of Child Abuse. *The Journal of Psychohistory, 25* (3), pp. 216–236. Article also found at http://www.psychohistory.com/htm/05_history.html

After years of studying the history of humanity, deMause presents the evolution of childhood abuse in six child-rearing modes: (1) the infanticidal mode, where children were killed and abused, (2) the abandoning mode, where children were "dumped" elsewhere to be abused there, (3) the ambivalent mode, where the parents' role was to mold and beat the child into shape, (4) the intrusive mode, where the mother used "steady pressure on the child to 'break its will' and discipline it properly," (5) the socializing mode, where parents used more gentle psychological means to "socialize" the child, and (6) the helping mode in our present day, where a minority of parents are trying to help children reach their own goals at their own rate. In the midst of a myriad of examples of the continued exploitation of children in the United States and around the world, deMause gives hope that with the teaching of parenting skills, a nonviolent society where children are not abused can emerge.

English, Diana J. (1998, Spring). The Extent and Consequences of Child Maltreatment. *Protecting Children from Abuse and Neglect, 8* (1), pp. 39–53.

"For some children the maltreatment experience is fatal. From 1990 to 1994, a total of 5,400 children are known to have died from an act of abuse or neglect. A survey of 26 states that could report the type of maltreatment that caused fatalities between 1993 and 1995 revealed that 37% of the children died from neglect, 48% died from abuse, and 15% died as a result of both types of maltreatment."

Gardner, Richard A. (1999, April–June). Differentiating between Parental Alienation Syndrome and Bona Fide Abuse-Neglect. *The American Journal of Family Therapy, 27* (2), pp. 97–107.

In the context of child custody suits, it has become increasingly important to differentiate between bona fide child abuse/neglect and parental alienation syndrome (PAS). PAS occurs when one parent tries to make the other look like an abuser and uses the child to falsely support that claim. This in itself is a form of child abuse, because it requires the accusing parent to "program" the child's beliefs in a false pattern. Frequently, court-appointed psychiatrists and social workers are called upon to determine which parent is telling the truth and which is the abuser. The article describes specific criteria that can be used to detect the true abuser.

Jaswant, Guzder, Paris, Joel, Zelkowitz, Phyllis, & Feldman, Ronald. (1999, February). Psychological Risk Factors for Borderline Pathology in School Age Children. *Journal of the American Academy of Child and Adolescent Psychiatry, 38* (7), pp. 206–217.

Children who were diagnosed with borderline pathology had histories containing significantly higher numbers of severe neglect, physical abuse, sexual abuse, frequent separations, parental divorce, and parental criminality. Additionally, community studies of child abuse have shown that chronically neglected children are more likely to experience sexual molestation.

Kaplan, Sandra J., Pelcovitz, David, & Labruna, Victor. (1999, October). Child and Adolescent Abuse and Neglect Research: A Review of the Past 10 Years. Part I: Physical and Emotional Abuse and Neglect. *Journal of the American Academy of Child and Adolescent Psychiatry, 38* (10), pp. 1214–1222. http://newfirstsearch.altip.oclc.org/

A differentiation is made in this research among four forms of child abuse: physical neglect, emotional neglect, emotional abuse, and physical abuse. Physical neglect refers to harm or endangerment of a child as a result of inadequate nutrition, clothing, hygiene, and supervision. Emotional neglect entails failure to provide adequate affection and emotional support or permitting a child to be exposed to domestic violence. Emotional abuse includes verbal abuse, harsh nonphysical punishments (e.g., being tied up), or threats of maltreatment. Physical abuse is present when a minor has experienced injury (harm standard) or risk of injury (endangerment standard) as a result of having been hit with a hand or other object or having been kicked, shaken, thrown, burned, stabbed, or choked by a parent or parent substitute. Although most physically abused children also suffer from emotional abuse and/or neglect, emotional abuse can occur with or without physical abuse. Emotional abuse and neglect are the most frequent form of abuse experienced by children.

Traditionally, research has looked past exploring the nature of emotional abuse because it was mistakenly regarded as less damaging than physical abuse. Current research finds that the lasting effects of emotional abuse may have a stronger link to long-term psychological functioning than other forms of abuse. These lasting effects may include, but are not limited to, low self-esteem, depression, and suicidal tendencies. Emotionally abused children display insecure patterns of attachment, which affect social skills, prompt aggression toward peers, and sometimes lead to the victimization of others. Prevention measures include targeting teen parents, impoverished parents, substance-abusing parents, and first-time parents with home-visit counseling comprised of social support and educational measures concerning parenting strategies.

Kenny, Maureen C. (2001, January). Child Abuse Reporting: Teachers' Perceived Deterrents. *Child Abuse & Neglect, 25* (1), pp. 81–92.

Kenny investigated the tremendous need to educate teachers in order to make them confident in evaluating and reporting abuse. A questionnaire survey of 197 teachers had three general objectives: (1) to determine the number of reports of abuse made by teachers, their knowledge of child abuse laws and reporting procedures, and their perceived deterrents in reporting abuse; (2) to determine whether gender or ethnic differences affected reporting; and (3) to evaluate teachers' responses to case scenarios. The results of the study showed the following: The majority of the sample (73%) had never made a child-abuse report, with 11% of teachers reporting that they had suspected instances of child abuse but did not report because of fear of submitting an inadequate report. These teachers believed that their pre- and post-service training inadequately prepared them for reporting. Teachers also said they feared reporting child abuse because they felt child protective services could not adequately assist families. There were no differences by gender in reporting. When presented with legally reportable case scenarios, many teachers failed to report abuse.

Miller, Susanne M. (1999, Fall). Why Sue Ellen Bridgers' *All We Know of Heaven* Should Be Taught in Our High Schools. *The ALAN Review, 27* (1), pp. 5–8.

By comparing *All We Know of Heaven* to the classics *The Scarlet Letter* and *Romeo and Juliet* in regard to the topics of adultery and suicide, Miller makes some valid points about the need to discuss domestic violence and abuse among teenagers. Understanding the warning signs and being able to recognize them are vital in today's society. Knowledge is power, and getting the strength to get out of an abusive relationship is key.

Reid, Suzanne & Stringer, Sharon. (1997, Winter). Ethical Dilemmas in Teaching Problem Novels: The Psychological Impact of Troubling YA Literature on Adolescent Readers in the Classroom. *The ALAN Review, 24* (2), pp. 16–18.

According to Reid and Stringer, three major ethical dilemmas complicate teachers' choices about what to teach in the classroom. First, "knowledge is power" versus "the right to innocence" is the conflict between teachers' responsibility as educators to inform students about the "real world" and the realization that they may desensitize students by exposing them to the "real world." Next, "I feel so alone" versus "this happens to everyone" is the conflict between letting some adolescents know that they are not alone and isolated in what is happening to them while making others feel through constant exposure that violence, substance abuse, and other types of abuse are normal behaviors. Third, "a teacher is not a counselor" versus "any discussion is helpful" is the conflict between a teacher's training not as counselor but as educator and the need for students to disclose their reactions to the stories they read. The authors suggest that teachers use young adult literature that they have read and evaluated, balance awareness of problems with vision of breadth of life and human strength, and provide a variety of resources and options appropriate for individual students.

CHAPTER 1

Understanding the Parentified Child by Reading Margaret Haddix's *Don't You Dare Read This, Mrs. Dunphrey*

Sue Street and Joan F. Kaywell

INTRODUCTION

Don't You Dare Read This, Mrs. Dunphrey is the story of a family we could call dysfunctional by today's definition. The father is largely disengaged from his role as a parent and only occasionally engages in his role as husband. The mother is also largely disengaged from her parenting role, primarily because she invests the majority of her energy in maintaining her marriage at any cost. The result is that their two children are severely neglected, not because their mother necessarily dislikes her children, but because she is completely obsessed with her husband as the source of her own sense of worth and value. Both parents are immature and evidence little sense of ownership of the responsibilities that are consequences of the choices they have made in their lives.

SYNOPSIS OF *DON'T YOU DARE READ THIS, MRS. DUNPHREY* BY MARGARET PETERSON HADDIX

Two children, Tish and Matt Bonner, are neglected by their two parents whose lives are out of control. The novel is told from the point of view of Tish Bonner, the older child, through a series of journal entries that her English teacher, Mrs. Dunphrey, has assigned. Ordinarily, Tish would ignore such an assignment, but she desperately needs an outlet for her thoughts on what's happening at home. She begins to open up in the journal as she learns that Mrs. Dunphrey keeps her word and doesn't read entries marked, "Do Not Read!" As things become increasingly more complex and critical, especially in regard to Tish's younger brother, Tish must decide whether or not she should let Mrs. Dunphrey read her journal. In desperation, she caves in, knowing full well that no one would believe her story if she hadn't written it all down.

ORGANIZATION

After providing factual information about neglect, we will pick up where the book leaves off. At the end of the novel, Tish writes a final letter to Mrs. Dunphrey saying that her family is in family counseling. Information will be provided about possible family counseling approaches that might best be used with the Bonner family. First, we will provide a mock counseling session with Mom Bonner and her two children. Then we will provide an evaluation of Mom Bonner, Tish Bonner (including a mock session singly with Tish), and finally an evaluation of Matt Bonner.

FACTS ABOUT NEGLECT AND HOW THEY RELATE TO THE BONNER FAMILY

At the close of *Don't You Dare Read This, Mrs. Dunphrey,* chapters of life are also closing for Tish and Matt Bonner and their mother. The opportunity for a fresh start and new beginning has presented itself. In Tish's final letter to Mrs. Dunphrey, she mentions that the three of them have started counseling. The decision to begin counseling is often the signal that a person has started a new life chapter, even though he or she doesn't always know where it is going or even the name of the chapter. Sometimes a person goes through a period of intense tribulation, trying desperately to resolve things alone. If the situation isn't too demanding, a person may possess the resources to adapt. But often, life requires an adaptation that requires skills, competencies, and values beyond those that the individual yet possesses. When a person finally admits he or she needs outside help, as Tish eventually does when she asks Mrs. Dunphrey for help, then that person is ready to develop new skills and new levels of consciousness. Growth involves change; it entails doing things in new ways.

Kanel (2003) discusses the opportunities inherent in crises. She notes that the Chinese word for *crisis* is a combination of the two pictographs for *danger* and *opportunity.* Kanel and others believe that a crisis can precipitate meaningful growth. Daily life may include a number of minimal crises, which may be somewhat stressful, but we usually adapt and adjust. But, Kanel notes, for all of us, some developmental (normal transitional phases as one moves from one life stage to another) or situational (unanticipated events) tasks are more challenging than others. And, though we struggle, twist, and turn, we have no tricks to use for meeting these new challenges. Tensions build, and ultimately a crisis may ensue. While the danger of such a crisis is that one may, in fact, fall back to an earlier, more fundamental means of coping, the crisis also presents the opportunity to learn new adaptive strategies requiring a higher level of consciousness.

At the novel's end, Tish is at one such crisis point. The provision of counseling in Tish's life is a hopeful sign, one that may facilitate enhanced self-awareness and personal growth. Matt and Mom are also in counseling, and, as participants in the family crisis, also are facing the opportunity for growth. At the same time, while each of the three is a participant in a family system, each has her or his own individuation issues. It is possible that at some point, or even concurrently, family members might be participating in individual counseling for their own issues. Let's give some thought to what might be going on in each of these counseling settings.

It is important to understand that there are many ways to approach the problems experienced by these three individuals. A number of counseling theories, approaches, and strategies converge to address a host of human ailments. Problems that are more severe may be given a formal psychological diagnosis and may include medications for chemical and neurological imbalances, as appears to be the case with Mom Bonner. Most of the problems people experience may be conceptualized in many ways and may respond to a range of counseling approaches and strategies. The approaches suggested here are some possible ways to address the family and individual dynamics experienced by these individuals at the close of the book.

FAMILY COUNSELING

Family therapy, or family counseling, examines the problems of the individuals in the framework of their relationships to their family system. Family work is based on the assumption that problems exist and are maintained within the context of the systems in which an individual functions. One of the most significant of these systems is the family, which may be contributing to and supporting the existence of an individual family member's problems. Many times when counselors are working with a person's problems, their understanding is restricted to that provided by the individual. Particularly in a family situation that involves several children, family counseling may offer more information about the contributing dynamics. It allows the counselor to observe the communication dynamics in the family as well as the individual personality traits of family members, rather than relying solely on the perceptions and interpretations of a single client. The interactions and relationships of all family members can be examined in live situations. Gladding (1998) noted empirical findings supporting the effectiveness of and the client satisfaction with family counseling.

Possible Approaches for the Bonners

A family therapist would most likely be trained in one or more of the prominent therapeutic approaches to working with families, such as structural family counseling (Minuchin, 1974; Minuchin & Fishman, 1981) or strategic approaches (Haley, 1973; Madanes, 1981). Becvar and Becvar (1996) note that the structural approach has probably contributed most to the acceptance and popularization of family therapy. The effectiveness of this approach has been demonstrated through much empirical research, and it has proved effective in addressing a range of family issues. Problems are assumed to be an outcome of family transaction patterns (Gladding, 1998). A major goal of structural counseling is the restructuring of the family subsystems, of which three are defined in this novel: the spouse subsystem, the parenting subsystem, and the siblings subsystem. The boundaries between these subsystems, or family members, may be clear, rigid, or diffuse.

In healthily functioning families, the parents form a parenting subsystem with clear boundaries. When the boundaries between the parent subsystem and the children's subsystem are diffuse, one parent may bond more with a child against the other parent. If boundaries are too rigid, one or both parents may become disengaged or move away from healthy family relationships. In the Bonner family, the father and mother formed a parent subsystem that disengaged from healthy involvement with their children to the point that both parents neglected, and eventually deserted, the child subsystem.

The assumption of the counselor working with the Bonner family is that if the mother can assume her role as a single parent within a healthy parenting subsystem, then Tish, who has functioned as the parenting subsystem for herself and Matt, can go back to being a member of the sibling subsystem with age-appropriate developmental tasks and responsibilities. At the same time, as Mother assumes her appropriate parenting role, she can begin to develop the responsibilities and personal satisfaction that accompany the role of a parent. Given the fact that Mom Bonner may be some distance from assuming a healthy parenting role, the counselor may initially help the two children "join" in their role as a sibling subsystem, pulling Tish out of the parenting subsystem. At this time, the grandparents form the parenting subsystem.

A technique that has been found effective in much of counseling, both individual and in many schools of family therapy, is called reframing. Reframing is a technique a therapist uses to create a different paradigm around a person's actions. It is a way of interpreting persons' previously perceived dysfunctional behavior into behavior that is more acceptable by the actor. Reframing would be particularly useful in this family's counseling. Thus a counseling session might go something like the one that follows.

A MOCK FAMILY COUNSELING SESSION WITH MOM, TISH, AND MATT

Counselor:	So, tell me about your family.
Tish (after a long, uncomfortable silence):	Well, we really don't have a family.
	(Mom cringes but says nothing. Tish looks down.)
Matt:	Well, we had a family once. When Dad was there. Sometimes he was there and we were like a family. He brought us presents and stuff.
Counselor:	I see. You have a family when you have presents?
Matt and Tish together:	Well, no, not really.
Counselor:	Hmm. I see. Maybe you mean you have a family when you have a dad?
Matt:	Yeah!
	(Tish looks wryly at her brother.)
Counselor (observing Tish's look):	Tish, what do you say? Does having a dad make a family?
Tish:	Not our dad!!
Mom (after another long uncomfortable silence):	I'm really the reason we don't have a family. If I had been a better wife, then their father would still be here, and we would have a family. It's all my fault.
	(Tish looks at her mother in disbelief and disdain.)

Counselor:	What would you like to say to your mother, Tish?
Tish (after a moment of hesitation):	Mom, we didn't have a family because Dad was not a good father, not because you weren't a good wife. He wasn't a good husband either. (She stops herself abruptly. More silence.)
Counselor:	Mom, what do you think about what Tish just said?
Mom:	It was all my fault. I didn't do a good job at anything. (Silence.)
Counselor:	Let's think about this. What does it take to make a good family?
Matt:	A mom, a dad, kids, money, and fun.
Tish:	Love and caring. The parents care about the kids. And take care of them. (She elbows Matt.)
Matt:	Yeah. They take care of us and make sure there is enough food.
Tish (dryly):	And provide us with clothes that are warm and nice, clothes that the other kids don't make fun of.
Counselor:	I wonder. Can you have a good family without a dad?
	(Mom sits numbly, eyes downcast.)
Tish (somewhat defiantly):	Of course! Our family would be much better without a dad like ours. We could do it. I did it. I took care of us for a while. I just ran out of money. But Mom could take care of us without Dad. We are a better family without him. Lots of kids don't have dads and their families are fine. Their moms take care of them.
Mom:	I'm not sure I could do that. I wasn't so good at it before.

EVALUATING MOM

Mom is continuing her position of disengagement, and she may continue this for some time. She is operating out of the same behavioral paradigms she has used most of her life. Change will not come easily for her, and the novel does not let us know how motivated Mom is to change. In one of her last letters, Tish reports several of the diagnoses that the counselor has suggested for her mother: a borderline personality, obsessive, and delusional. The counselor notes that Mom Bonner is also a victim of battered wife syndrome. Tish's and Matt's mother may be taking a prescription, or maybe more than one, to help regulate the chemical and neurological imbalances that contribute to her dysfunctional behaviors.

The medications may allow Mom to enter individual counseling to address her own personal and relationship issues. Often, with the moderating effects of the medication, people can address their challenges with reasonable attitudes and can make positive changes. Later, the family counselor may be able to facilitate the movement of the mother into a healthy assumption of the parenting subsystem. The family counselor might also reframe Mom's previous behavior as a valiant attempt to save the spouse subsystem because she thought it was integral to a happy and healthy family and thus to the well-being of the children. Eventually the family may reframe its previous experience with Dad by trying to help him assume his appropriate role as a husband and father. Both these reframings will empower the three family members to be in control of their own roles and values in the family whether Dad is present or not.

Several other counseling goals can be identified for Mom. She would need to develop an awareness of herself as an individual, a more introspective awareness than she has previously demonstrated. With this awareness would come a second goal: for her to accept herself as a valuable and worthwhile person, in light of who she is, what she has done, and where she has been in her life. A third goal would be for her to work toward personal autonomy, particularly in terms of holding a job, paying bills, and meeting financial responsibilities. From here, a fourth goal would be to begin to be a responsible parent, supervising the children appropriately and providing for their physical and emotional needs.

Finally, Mom would want to apply her "I Am," or her perception of herself as a strong individual who is worthy of love and respect. In particular, Mom will have to reframe herself and her relationships with men. She, who has estimated her value in terms of a man's presence, will need to learn to place her own worth prominently in the relationship. Mom has previously allowed herself to be invisible by choosing to see herself that way. With counseling, Mom could develop her own self-awareness, her own respect and value of self, which would be major variables in her relationships. This will be the biggest test of her own personal growth work. Fulfilling the goal of being a healthy partner in a healthy relationship will be a major step for Mom. Being able to tell Dad she isn't interested in his being around anymore will also be an important step. These counseling goals will require a lot of hard work. Mom will have to be motivated to spend several years of consistent effort to reshape her life. It is certainly possible for her to do this.

EVALUATING TISH

Tish probably needs to spend some time in counseling learning some of the same values Mom is learning. Tish has observed little in the way of healthy self-esteem from her mother and little about healthy romantic relationships. Up to this point, Tish has held onto her independence fiercely, almost too much so. She has built a thick wall of defenses against emotional vulnerability. These walls have helped her get through life to this point. She has managed to stay in school and to take care of herself and her little brother. She has developed excellent survival skills. Tish developed these skills, as do many other girls and young women, because she had to assume many of the responsibilities that rightfully belonged in the parenting subsystem. Helping professionals refer to these children as *parentified*. Tish has developed some parenting skills that would not usually be required or expected of girls her age.

Professionals might also describe Tish as *resilient* at this point. By definition, Tish has grown up in a family environment that would classify her as an at-risk child, but she has developed the survival skills she needed to get by up to this point. Will this same set of skills pull her through life's next challenges? Maybe. But there will come a point where she will need to develop a new level of conscious awareness. Clearly one area in which Tish will need to develop new values and new behaviors is that of emotional closeness in relationships.

We have not yet seen Tish in a romantic emotional relationship, and that will be another story. But as Tish is able to assume her role as part of the sibling subsystem, with grandparents being a clear parent subsystem with clear boundaries, Tish will return to the developmental tasks of adolescence, one of which is to begin the process of developing the capacity for intimacy. Tish will likely experience some real problems here. Despite her laudable efforts at creating a strong self, she may find herself at a real disadvantage in relationships. Her strong self persona is a façade; it is a strong defense around a self that is not yet really strong. A strong self, an "I Am," comes from within and is built on an individual's conscious decision that she or he is a valuable human being, worthy of love and respect.

Tish is simply very effective at erecting external defenses, but once she relinquishes those defenses, Tish is likely to be extremely vulnerable. It is probable that she will revert to much of the dependent behavior exhibited by her mother, since this is all she knows about how women relate to men. There is still much work to do before a truly resilient and healthy Tish stands before us.

Counseling goals for Tish might first include helping her realistically assess all she has experienced in recent years, particularly emphasizing her strengths. The counselor would help Tish see that whatever did or did not happen was not her fault. She was a child, and it was not her responsibility to be the adult. Nonetheless, Tish did assume many of those responsibilities for herself and Matt and did so successfully. She protected her brother well. Those experiences should be reframed so that Tish sees herself as having performed barely short of heroic acts to take care of herself and her brother. This work will minimize the trauma Tish is experiencing and will affirm her own strengths. This sets the groundwork for much of what follows, which will include more work on her self-perceptions, self-awareness, and self-acceptance.

The second goal will be for Tish to learn to know, to be comfortable with, and to accept herself. Achieving this goal will require much effort and a major change in Tish's focus. In her closing letter, Tish tells Mrs. Dunphrey that her counselor wants her to focus more on her own thoughts and feelings and is encouraging her to write about herself. Tish has developed a very external focus to survive in her life circumstances. She has had to be vigilant, protecting herself and her younger brother against random, unpredictable challenges precipitated by her mother's emotional upheavals. Tish has focused most of her energies on responding to and protecting against external events. She will need to develop an internal focus to do her "I Am" work. As Tish learns to focus within, she can begin to see herself as a person with talents, needs, and intrinsic value. From here, she may begin to build a strong sense of self, a sense that "I Am" a valuable human being, worthy of love and respect. This will be hard work. Tish's mother did not exhibit this behavior, so Tish has seen little of it modeled for her.

Tish does, however, have a set of positive experiences to draw on: the unconditional positive regard she experienced from her mother's mother, Granma. Carl Rogers (1965), widely considered to be the father of counseling, explained that the process of socializing children demands that parents approve of certain behaviors and disapprove of other behaviors exhibited by the child. Parenting responsibility means extending conditional regard to your child—children experience themselves being loved for some behaviors and not so loved for others. Rogers suggested that the counselor is the purveyor of unconditional positive regard, loving the client unconditionally. Grandparents are often also a source of unconditional positive regard for children, and it seems Tish experienced this level of caring from Granma. Granma accepted and loved Tish for who she was. Tish frequently refers to her wish to be with Granma again so things could be better. She obviously felt loved and cared for while in Granma's care. The counselor can encourage Tish to draw on this feeling of being loved unconditionally, for who she is, and this will help her develop and strengthen her own feeling of unconditional positive regard for herself.

A Mock Counseling Session with Tish

Counselor:	Hi Tish. How's it going today?
Tish:	Good. Fine.
Counselor:	Is school going okay? Are you getting settled in? Are you making friends?
Tish (with a shrug):	I guess so.
	(Silence. Counselor knows the school adjustment process will take a while, as will making friends. This will happen as Tish becomes comfortable in her new surroundings and increasingly more comfortable within herself.)
Counselor:	Well, where shall we go today? Is there anything special on your mind?
Tish (slowly):	No, not really. I did get sort of mad at Poppy because he wouldn't let me go to the mall last night.
Counselor:	Sort of mad?
Tish:	Well, I threw some things. I have a new friend, and she was going to the mall with some other friends, and I wanted to meet them there.
Counselor:	But Poppy said no?
	(Tish nods.)
Counselor:	Was his decision reasonable? Was it late?
Tish (after a long silence):	Well, I was going to walk there and then walk home. They said they would take me, but I

	didn't want to be dropped off by my grandparents. So I said no, and then they said no, and then I walked off.
Counselor:	Hmm. It sounds to me like they were concerned about your safety. (Brief silence) Sounds like they wanted to make sure you were not walking the streets at night where someone might harm you. (More silence) Sounds like they really care about you and care about what happens to you. (Silence)
Tish (wearily):	Yes, I know. You're right. This business of being cared about is kind of a nuisance sometimes. Like I'm used to being my own boss and coming and going when I want to. Mom never paid any attention to how I got to work, or got to the mall, or anything. I have good judgment. I wouldn't do anything stupid.
	(Counselor smiles, allowing for more silence so that Tish can assess her thinking.)
Counselor:	Yes, being loved is a kind of a burden sometimes. But it may be the most important thing we experience in life.
Tish (snorts):	I don't know what love is! (She stops short, realizing she has revealed something about some part of herself she did not want out in the open.)
Counselor (mildly and calmly):	Love is very difficult to understand. Yet the most important thing we can do for ourselves in life is to learn to love ourselves.
Tish (thinking she can get the counselor off the subject of herself when she has just revealed a bit more than she intended):	What are you talking about?
Counselor:	Loving ourselves means we see ourselves as special people, as valuable, as important and worthy of respect. Do you know anyone who you think is like that?

Tish (shrugging her right shoulder):	I guess the popular kids in school are like that.
Counselor:	Hmm. I see. (After a pause) Tell me, has anyone ever made you feel that way?
Tish:	How? What way?
Counselor:	Has anyone ever made you feel like you were special and important? Has anyone ever made you feel you were a really good person, even though you weren't perfect? Has anyone ever made you feel you were lovable and loved?
Tish (after a deep breath):	Nobody really, unless you count my granma.
Counselor:	Aha. Does Granma count? Isn't she a person?
Tish:	Well yes, but she was my granma. I mean she was supposed to love me. I mean, that doesn't really count.
Counselor:	Hmm. I think your mother and father are supposed to love you. And I think they do, or at least I believe that your mother does. But did they make you feel this way? Did you feel loved by them?
Tish (dryly):	No.
Counselor:	Can you remember what it felt like when you were with your granma? You have told me about a few times when you were with her and it felt really good. You told me if you could have your wish, she would be alive again and you and your brother could live with her and only her.
Tish:	Yeah. It felt really good to be with Granma. She cared about us.
Counselor:	Now. I want you to think very carefully. See if you can capture that same way she made you feel. See if you can feel what that felt like. See if you can feel what Granma's love for you felt like. (Tish squirms, partly out of discomfort with the whole exercise, and partly because it is somewhat difficult to capture the feeling.) Can you feel that feeling?
Tish:	Yeah (pause), sorta.

Counselor:	If you can practice that feeling every day, you can start to feel it for yourself—without Granma. But still with Granma. She showed you how. It was her most important gift to you. She showed you how special you are and how good you are. Now you need to learn to feel those feelings for yourself, from yourself. You can feel the same way about you that Granma felt. That is who you really are.
Tish:	But it's not real.
Counselor:	Why not?
Tish:	That's not really me. I mean, I'm not really like that.
Counselor (humorously mocking):	No? You're not a good person, a kind person? You're not a very special and unique person who took care of herself and her little brother for years?
Tish (after a thoughtful silence):	Well, just because Granma thought I was good doesn't make it real.
Counselor:	No, I suppose not. But you tell me. Are you a good person? Do you deserve to be loved? Are you a strong person? Are you a person who can do pretty much anything she puts her mind to?
Tish:	I've been thinking about this since we have been talking about it. I think I am a strong person, but I don't know how to love myself and I don't know if I even want to (at this point Tish is almost ruminating), or if I should. I mean, yes, I really did like the feeling when Granma was here, but I don't think I could feel that way about myself without her. I don't know.
Counselor:	Would you like to have that feeling all the time?
Tish (emphatically):	Yes, of course! I like that feeling. I can feel it sometimes when I am doing that quiet thinking time in the evening like you told me to, but I've had this planned. I will wait for the right man to come along. And I have always known I will

find a man who will love me like that. Who would love me so totally, so completely, that he would not be at all like my dad. I won't marry a man like my mom did. I'll make sure he really loves me. And that's when my life will really be better.

Counselor: I see. And how will that work? Don't you think your mom thought your dad really loved her?

Tish: Well, maybe, but she was wrong. I won't be wrong.

Counselor: I see. What will you do different?

Tish: Well, I know what Dad was like, so I'll be sure he won't be like Dad.

Counselor: Hmm. Well, I'll tell you something that may come as a surprise to you. If your mom had just had a strong "I Am" and if she had just had that same feeling of love for herself that we have been talking about, then I am pretty sure she would never have married your dad anyway. She would have found someone who felt the same way about her that she does, with that feeling of love and respect. That was what would have made the difference.

Tish (looking incredulous): Are you sure? I mean, my mom definitely doesn't feel that way about herself. In fact, she feels just the opposite. But how can that be?

Counselor: Because if we want someone else to love us, we have to love ourselves first. That's the way it works. Love begins at home! Other people buy our opinion of ourselves. If we love ourselves, other people also love us. (Silence while Tish absorbs this.) Besides, Tish, I wonder when I hear you say that when you find this one man who loves you totally if that will make your life better. Isn't that the way your mother lived? Didn't she depend totally on your dad to make her life better? She didn't do anything on her own to make her own life better, did she? Don't you see that you are saying the same thing? That you are depending on a man to make everything in your life better with his everlasting love? (Silence, while Tish looks stunned.) It seems to me that you might be better off to make yourself strong enough and love yourself enough so that you don't depend on one man, or on any other person for that matter, to make you happy. You make you happy. Of course, I am sure there will be special men in your life, but you don't want to make the same mistake your mother did and put them at the center of your world. (Tish looks thoughtful but remains silent.) You certainly have some things to think about this week. I like that you are doing your evening quiet thinking time. Maybe when you are doing it this week, you can think about what we said about depending on one man to make you happy. Maybe you could think about how that is just like what Mom did. (Tish smiles warmly and is relieved to end.)

Tish: Thanks. You've given me a lot to think about.

EVALUATING MATT

Matt may benefit from the family counseling. He has always been a member of the sibling subsystem, but the changes in family structure will require some adaptation from him. Tish, who used to be a major figure in his parenting subsystem, will adapt to being his sister again. He will need to join with her in this subsystem in roles differing from before. This may create some initial confusion. At the time of the family transition at the end of the book, Matt has exhibited no major adjustment problems, but certainly some can be anticipated. In his previous school, Matt's poverty and family instability contributed to social adjustment difficulties. In Tish's last letter it sounds as if he is adjusting more happily in his grandparents' environment. A weight gain of 20 pounds is considerable for a seven-year-old child, attesting to his previous malnourishment and newfound nurturing. Matt is probably behind academically, requiring tutoring and remedial help. He ought to be tested for learning difficulties.

Matt could probably benefit from individual counseling as well. At his age, verbal or talk therapy may be of limited effectiveness. Matt likely would do very well in a play therapy situation. Sand tray in particular would offer Matt the opportunity to express his anger and abandonment issues related to his father. Sand tray will allow him to create his own world where he is in control. He can manipulate the people in his sand tray and reconstruct this world to a place where he is comfortable. Over time, the earlier scenes of war and conflict, reflecting his own internal state, will evolve into more harmonious scenes with indications of more positive interpersonal relationships. As well, play therapy with a registered play therapist could contribute much to Matt's ability to sort out his life. Art therapy may also be a useful adjunct. Matt has yet to demonstrate many problems, but it would be very helpful to address and perhaps facilitate resolution of his trauma, conflict, and feelings of abandonment at this point.

CONCLUSION

The future is hopeful for Tish, Matt, and Mom Bonner. Structure and supervision have been provided for the two children, allowing them to address cognitive, social, and emotional developmental issues appropriate to their age groups. They are in a home of caring parent figures. We would fervently hope that the previous trauma was not such that the children cannot resume a fairly normal developmental trajectory. While there was some physical abuse, it apparently was not chronic or severely debilitating. There is much hope for their future. Tish will likely respond to counseling if she remains in it. She is bright, capable, and seems to possess an internal source of strength and resilience.

REFERENCES

Becvar, D., & Becvar, R. (1996). *Family therapy: A systemic integration.* Boston: Allyn & Bacon.

Gladding, S. (1998). *Family therapy: History, theory and practice* (second edition). Upper Saddle River, NJ: Prentice Hall.

Haddix, M.P. (1996). *Don't you dare read this, Mrs. Dunphrey.* New York: Aladdin Paperbacks.

Haley, J. (1973). *Uncommon therapy.* New York: W.W Norton.

Kanel, K. (2003). *A guide to crisis intervention.* Pacific Grove, CA: Brooks-Cole.

Madanes, C. (1981). *Strategic family therapy.* San Francisco: Jossey-Bass.

Minuchin, S. (1974). *Families and family therapy.* Cambridge, MA: Harvard University Press.

Minuchin, S., & Fishman, H. (1981). *Family therapy techniques.* Cambridge, MA: Harvard University Press.

Rogers, C. (1965). *Client-centered therapy: Its practice, implications and theory.* Boston: Houghton Mifflin.

CHAPTER 2

A Reader's and Counselor's Response to Heather Quarles's *A Door Near Here*

Jessica Pawelkop-Muroff and Leah Armstrong

INTRODUCTION

Neglect is one of the most prevalent forms of child maltreatment. This type of abuse may not leave obvious physically destructive wounds, but neglect can leave profound psychological wounds as well as cause problems related to malnutrition. According to statistics, nearly half of all child fatalities involve neglect. Often, neglect is an indicator that the abusive situation may escalate into a more serious case of child maltreatment (Waldfogel, 1998, p. 4). There are three categories of neglect: physical, educational, and emotional (Lowenthal, 2001, p. 13). Heather Quarles's book, *A Door Near Here,* tells the story of neglect that involves all three of these categories.

Heather Quarles's award-winning novel offers a picture of siblings trying to keep themselves alive while their constantly drunk mother neglects them. This book can be a benefit to both teachers and students facing these sensitive and destructive situations. "Because of their daily contact with the students in the classroom and their knowledge of child development, teachers are in a unique position to help children who are maltreated feel valued, respected, cared for, and safe at school" (Lowenthal, 2001, p. 1). Teachers have the responsibility to be careful observers of their students and must know the signs of all forms of maltreatment. *A Door Near Here* also offers students an outlet to read about something that may be similar in their own family situation.

ORGANIZATION

I kept a reader-response journal as I was reading the book and posed many questions for which I wanted to find answers about the situation described in the book. In writing this chapter, I contacted a school psychologist, Leah Armstrong, who also read the book and responded to my reader-response entries. It is my hope that teachers and students can benefit from reading the dialogue we share and having my concerns responded to by a professional. In my reader responses I have outlined the events that are taking place in the book.

SYNOPSIS OF *A DOOR NEAR HERE* BY HEATHER QUARLES

The story opens with Katherine, the main character, making lunches for all her siblings and getting them ready for school in the morning. Immediately, the reader gets the notion that Katherine takes care of everything around the house. A chaotic picture is described: bursting pipes in the kitchen, the kids wearing dirty clothes, and Katherine trying to put together a healthy lunch with what little food they have in the house. Katherine is under an intense amount of stress and is having a hard time keeping her patience. The reader discovers that their mother has been in a constant state of intoxication, sleeps all of the time, and never leaves her room except to get more alcohol. This behavior has been going on for weeks, ever since she was fired from her job. The food supply in the house is starting to dwindle, and Katherine realizes that she needs to do something.

Katherine desperately tries to keep her family together and keeps telling herself that her mom will snap out of this soon; she has to! Katherine makes a "to do" list of things to be taken care of around the house and prepares an action plan of what she is going to do about her family. Unfortunately, Katherine has another issue that comes up—her little half-sister, Alisa, has been writing letters to C.S. Lewis. Alisa believes that one of the main characters in his book, Aslan the lion, is the only one in the world who will help save their mother. Alisa wants to find the door to Narnia, the imaginary land in C.S. Lewis's books, so that she can find Aslan.

Reader Response #1

The opening section of the book reminded me of my childhood when my parents went through a divorce. My mom was forced to go back to work and she became depressed. I immediately had to begin taking care of the house and caring for my brother and sister. I had to grow up fast. I could no longer have my afternoons free to play outside with friends. I cannot even imagine the amount of stress that Katherine is experiencing because although I was forced to have a lot of responsibility at a young age, my needs were still being met. I was not neglected as Katherine and her siblings are. I wonder whether making a "to do" list is a way for Katherine to put her thoughts and frustrations on paper and to have a sense of security that things are going to be taken care of. Unlike my behavior, Katherine smokes cigarettes to calm her nerves. Is this a reaction to her environment or simply something that all teens seem to experiment with? Alisa's preoccupation with the lion being her mom's only savior also makes me wonder whether this is her reaction to the neglect that Alisa is experiencing or whether she is just desperately trying to help her mother.

Therapist's Response to #1

Katherine is under extreme pressure to maintain order within her chaotic home life. A natural response to this chaos and her feelings of being out of control is to find a way to create order. Her chore lists are a way for her to regain a sense of order and control. Smoking cigarettes could be Katherine's form of adolescent rebellion; however, smoking could have more pathological causes. Katherine has had to grow up too quickly to become the caregiver of her siblings. Smoking is one way the reader is witness to her inappropriate maturity. Also, it could be a way to illustrate the dysfunctional and addictive patterns in her family. Alisa's search for Narnia's door is both a reaction to her neglect and a way in which she believes she can aid her mother. If Alisa's mother did not need help, Alisa would see no need to find the door. She is intuitive to the purpose and character of Lewis's Aslan. Within the *Chronicles of Narnia,* Aslan is the Christ figure sent to be savior of Narnia. Alisa recognizes this and with her childlike faith believes that he is the savior for her mother's disease.

Reader Response #2

Later in the novel, Katherine and two of her siblings (Douglas and Tracey) meet their father for dinner. He has come into town for a conference and has his second wife with him, the woman he left their mother for. Katherine tells her brother and sister that they may absolutely *not* tell their father about their mother's condition. Evidently, Katherine does not want him to find out about the situation at home because she really does not want him in their lives. During this very awkward and uncomfortable dinner, it is obvious that their father is not very interested in them and what is happening in their lives. He only sends checks to support them and feels obligated to come and visit them occasionally during the year. He is a dentist and has the means to support them better, but he is too caught up in his new family.

Does this strained relationship with their father and his lack of interest in them compound the effects of the neglect they are experiencing at home? Katherine seems to resent her dad for his lack of involvement and wants to make it on her own. When the three return home, they get together to discuss their situation and, as a group, they compose a "to do" list to chart an action plan of taking care of themselves. They realize that their mother has a problem, but they do not want to tell anyone for fear that they will be separated. Do many children feel like they have to defend the actions of their parents? The children love their mother and realize that what she is doing is wrong, yet they do not display much anger.

Therapist's Response to #2

Katherine's relationship with her father compounds the neglect in that it delays the children's removal from the harmful environment. At this point in the story, her father—like all adults in her life—is viewed as one who could destroy her structure of functioning. No matter how dysfunctional Katherine's life may appear to the outsider, she has established a workable structure. As Katherine views the situation, any interference to her structure would result in chaos—even if it would mean deliverance from neglect. In this way, most children, and adults as well, involved in any form of abuse or dysfunction will defend to great lengths the troubled family member. This is in part caused by feelings of loyalty and love and a part ownership of guilt for the family's dysfunction. Katherine loves her mother and wishes to remain loyal to her. Any assistance from the outside world would be seen as a breech of Katherine's loyalty. Katherine views her mother's alcoholism as a family problem, requiring no assistance from anyone outside her immediate family structure.

Reader Response #3

Katherine begins to think that Alisa is going crazy, resulting from a note from Alisa's teacher that says Alisa has been running away from class. Alisa will not be admitted back into school unless she has a psychological evaluation and her mother comes into school for a meeting. Katherine does not know what to do. Katherine is also getting pressure from one of her teachers at school for her repeated absences. She has been absent on more than one occasion because of all of her responsibilities at home. Though she is absent many times from school, she is still one of the better students. I wonder how she can do this. Wouldn't the amount of stress she is experiencing at home affect her schoolwork? Or is this just her way of maintaining control over some aspect of her life?

Therapist's Response to #3

Abused children are at risk for many difficulties, one of which is poor academic achievement. In fact, when a student's performance drops for no apparent reason, teachers often look to the student's home life as a possible cause. Katherine, however, continues to do well in school with no mention of having to study. While her performance could be a way to instill control in her life, this is not the most plausible scenario. Katherine is a bright girl who is not having to work hard to comprehend and master her schoolwork. Despite her family life, she continues to succeed in the classroom. She is astutely aware that any disturbance in status quo, including her classwork, might trigger further investigation into her home life. This is something she will go to great lengths to avoid.

Reader Response #4

Katherine gets placed in detention for her absences. When Katherine finally reaches her house, she notices that her mother's car is gone. Dozens of horrific thoughts run through her mind as she is imagining what might have happened. When she gets in the door, she yells for everyone, hoping that everything is all right. Douglas tells her that their mother had to pick up Alisa from school because she got very sick and now she has gone to the store to get her some medicine. Katherine screams at her brother for letting her mother leave and for giving her part of the little bit of money that they have. Their mother finally returns home around midnight. She is obviously drunk, and Katherine helps her carry in the bags. There are two bags of food and four bags filled with alcohol. The food is not adequate, and the children have to come up with ways of rationing the food so that they can make it last. Mother tells Katherine about Alisa and asks her to stay home from school for nearly two weeks until Alisa's psychological evaluation. Katherine agrees, but how can she not? Katherine's the one who feels like she is responsible because her mother is incapable of taking care of even herself. How can a mother do this to her children?

Therapist's Response to #4

Alcoholism is viewed by many as a disease that consumes a person's focus. Alcoholics can be consumed to the point of neglecting those they love. Many fight the addiction for their lifetime. Ironically, what can cause a relapse is for the addict to see the damage she or he has done to those she or he loves. The sober reality of one's neglect and destruction can be too much to bear, causing a relapse.

Reader Response #5

By now in my reading, I am wondering when the teachers of these children will notice the signs of neglect being exhibited by Katherine and her siblings. Because Katherine has to watch Alisa for so long and it will bring attention to Katherine's own absenteeism, she and Tracey decide to take Alisa to school with them and hide her while they are in class. I am amazed that they think this idea will work. As expected, Alisa wanders out of her hiding spot to find a bathroom and is discovered by one of Katherine's teachers, Mr. Dodgson. When Katherine and Tracey learn that Alisa is with Mr. Dodgson, they fear that the worst is going to happen. They immediately think that this will be the end of their family as they know it and that they will all be separated by social services if they don't come up with a good lie. Mr. Dodgson tells Katherine everything that Alisa has told him about their mother. I believe that Alisa felt relief and comfort in being able to tell someone who would truly listen. Mr. Dodgson questions Katherine about her situation at home and asks why she had to bring her young sister with her to school. Unlike Alisa, Katherine lies to Mr. Dodgson about everything in a desperate attempt to cover up their situation at home. In chapter 12, Katherine sums up her feelings and her thoughts in dealing with the neglect she is experiencing:

> The whole thing was like a war, really. Douglas and Tracey and I were the soldiers defending my mom. Mr. Dodgson, the rest of the teachers, and the government were the enemy, and Alisa had been the captured prisoner we'd brought back safely. When I thought about it that way, things didn't seem so bad. For the time being all of us, including my mom, were safe. Maybe we'd lost a little ground, but as far as the major battle was concerned, we'd won. And if we could come out on top after a day like this, then we might even win the whole war. (Quarles, 2000, p. 126)

Katherine is determined to keep her family together and defend her mother's actions. Is this normal for teens dealing with abuse issues? Mr.

Dodgson gives Katherine and Tracey only an after-school detention for this situation. Why did he not do anything else at this point? Aren't there enough signs of neglect for him to have the responsibility to have their situation investigated?

Therapist's Response to #5

While reporting suspected abuse is never easy, it is essential to ensure children's safety. Mr. Dodgson knows that something is not right with this family and, consequently, should have followed through in an investigation of his suspicions. As a teacher, he is obligated to try and find the truth or seek the assistance of a trained professional to do so. Even insisting on personal contact with Katherine's mother or father would have been a start to either confirm or deny his suspicions. In addition, he should have consulted the appropriate school personnel of his concern so that they would have had the opportunity to get involved with this family much earlier.

Reader Response # 6

Things around the house are getting very tense. The lack of nutrition, food, love, and security is taking its toll on all the children. Katherine especially is reaching her limit of stress, feeling like she has to be the one in charge. They are starting to fight with one another about how much to eat or not to eat and about what to do with the little bit of money they have, and now Mr. Dodgson has been calling the house to inquire how they are. How much longer are they going to be able to hold it together? Katherine is determined to keep the family together on her own and to get no one else involved. Douglas and Tracey, on the other hand, are starting to see the reality and seriousness of their situation, and they are ready to seek help elsewhere; this infuriates Katherine. When they are at the brink, Tracey and Douglas find a child-support check from their father while going through the mail. They come up with a plan to cash the check so that they can have money to buy food. Their food supply is vanishing, and they ate only bread rolls for dinner that night.

In my opinion, all the adults in this story are neglecting the needs of these children; the signs are ignored. Why hasn't their father inquired as to why his child-support checks have not been deposited? How can a father not call to be sure that his children are being taken care of? How can a mother drink herself into a constant state of intoxication and neglect the needs of her precious children? How can a teacher neglect the signs of abuse with his students? I can see why Katherine so desperately wants to keep her family together on her own, but how long can she keep up the charade? Is the way she is reacting to the situation normal?

Therapist's Response to #6

All families have patterns of functioning. Each member in a family has a specific role and responsibility. It is Katherine's role to take care of her mother and her siblings. It is her responsibility to hide her mother's addiction from the outside world. She feels in control of her situation because she has no other choice. To feel any other thing would be to admit how serious the problem is. Few children are capable of understanding the severity of a situation like Katherine's. Therefore, as a way to protect her family and as a form of denial and inability to fully comprehend the situation, her response is neither atypical nor abnormal.

Reader Response #7

It occurs to me that Katherine, Douglas, and Tracey have probably been acting different toward their friends. Katherine does not have many friends because she mostly keeps to herself. I believe that this is in part because of what she is dealing with in her life and her lack of self-esteem. Tracey, on the other hand, is a social butterfly. She is very pretty, has many friends, and is the most popular girl in school. For a while, she is trying to cover up the situation at home and is trying to act normal in front of her friends. Eventually, she has to pay more attention to her family, and the stress she is under starts to affect her relationship with her friends. Wouldn't a person as open as Tracey confide in one of her friends? It seems as though at least one of her friends would notice that she is acting differently and would ask what was wrong with her. Do teens ever go to other adults if they notice that one of their friends is in trouble? I was wondering why none of Tracey's friends reached out to help her.

Therapist's Response to #7

Many children do not share their family difficulties with others. They are often embarrassed by their families and try to conceal their home life from their friends. Being with friends can help the adolescent forget the problems at home. While some teens may go to an adult for help when they are concerned about a friend, not all do. Since the highly publicized school shootings, many schools are trying to encourage teens to speak out when they are concerned about their peers. Unfortunately, many do not seek the help of adults, and even those that do will find that some adults, like Mr. Dodgson, are inadequately prepared about what to do or how to respond.

Reader Response #8

The situation is getting very desperate. They are running out of food and out of options. Douglas and Tracey decide to deposit the child-support check from their dad and are going to take 100 dollars of that to buy groceries. Katherine argues with them that this is wrong because she believes that they are stealing from their mother! Katherine goes to great lengths, making sure that she is doing everything right and protecting her mother. Douglas and Tracey both make the argument that the money was from their dad to their mom to take care of them. Katherine still feels uneasy about the situation but gives in because the two cups of rice that she cooked for dinner is just about all the food that they have left. Their emotional health and physical well-being is being damaged by the lack of nutrition and pressure that they are under. They have all lost weight, especially Alisa. Why don't they attempt to wake up their mom from her drunken state?

Therapist's Response to #8

Even if the children developed a plan to "wake up their mom from her drunken state," they would not be able to accomplish this. Their mother is sick, and they do not have the cure for her. The children do not see the severity of the problem like adults or outsiders would.

Reader Response #9

Douglas uses their mom's ATM card and withdraws money from the bank. On his way home, he stops to buy a huge bag of M & Ms and a gallon of milk. All four of them feast on the milk and candy, relieved to be able to have something to eat. This victory gives them spontaneous energy and hope that they can continue on their own without their mother's help. Late one night, they take their mother's car in order to go grocery shopping at a time when no one will see them. They are able to get enough groceries to last them some time, but Mrs. Haley, Alisa's school principal, is at the store as well. They see her and try to hide. They are not sure whether she saw them, but they are relieved that they finally have food in the house to take care of themselves.

The children go to great lengths to defend their mother and her neglect of them, but they do nothing to try to help her, too? Their mother comes out of her bedroom for something to drink and Katherine describes her being bloated, pale, and smelling like rot. Is the stress just too much for them that they can't handle trying to take care of her as well? Or are they still in extreme denial of the seriousness of their mother's condition? Even though they are in survival mode in trying to make it on their own, I would think that they would try to do something with their mother.

Therapist's Response to #9

Continuing life as if it were normal is the only way these children know how to help their mother. If they were to seek help from another adult, they think they would be betraying her, not helping her. These are children who are going through severe circumstances. They are not able to look at their mother's problem rationally, as an objective adult would. To them, they are helping her.

Reader Response #10

As it turns out, Mrs. Haley did see them and informs Mr. Dodgson, who approaches Katherine about the situation. I almost thought that he might actually do something about it this time, considering the fact that they were caught grocery shopping at 2 o'clock in the morning. Katherine tries lying at first, but Mr. Dodgson isn't falling for her story and decides to tell someone about their situation. In a desperate attempt to ruin his credibility, Katherine writes an anonymous letter to the dean of students about Mr. Dodgson, saying that he has been making harassing phone calls to her house. Katherine seriously believes that she and her siblings will be split apart by social services and it will be all her fault. I am amazed at the lengths Katherine goes to in taking full responsibility of the situation and protecting her mother. Katherine constantly refers to herself as a soldier on a battlefield, defending her mother.

Things get even worse. Their mother falls and cuts her head open, right when they discover that the electricity in the house has been shut off. They call an ambulance and get their mother to a hospital to take care of her gash. Katherine goes with her and again lies to protect her mother. The doctors question her mother's alcoholism and recommend that she be admitted to a detox facility. Katherine again lies to get out of the situation and gets her mom home by taxi. What else can Katherine endure? I do not think that I would be able to keep my composure under that much stress. I am totally amazed that this 15-year-old girl, who's holding up all the responsibility of her house, still has the wits about her to lie her way out of these situations.

Therapist's Response to #10

Katherine's life is a lie. For her to lie has become second nature; she does so effortlessly. In many ways, she and her siblings believe the lies they tell. This enables their survival.

Reader Response #11

When Katherine returns home with their mother, Douglas informs her that Alisa has run away. At first, Katherine tries to find Alisa on her own, but she can't. Finally, Katherine breaks down and calls the only adult she knows who will help, Mr. Dodgson. Together, they find Alisa in the woods behind her school on a quest to find the door to Narnia so that she can help her mother. For Alisa, things got so bad that she had to find Aslan, a fictional character, to help. Mr. Dodgson and Katherine take Alisa home, and Mrs. Haley comes over to be sure that Alisa's safe; she gets their electricity turned back on, too. At this point, readers know the children will finally get the help they need. Personally, I think Katherine is relieved, knowing there was nothing else she could do but reach out for help.

Therapist's Response to #11

For adults and children in crisis, a breaking point often has to occur before any change is made. For Katherine, Alisa's disappearance was the turning point that made her break all her previously established rules of silence. Her situation finally reached a point of extreme severity, requiring the assistance of an outsider.

Reader Response #12

Katherine, Tracey, Douglas, and Alisa have all gone to live with their father. Although he feels a little uncomfortable taking in Alisa, who is not his biological daughter, he sees how important it is not to separate them. Mrs. Haley takes their mother for admission into a detox facility. The children are a little uncomfortable in their new home. Their father had never really ever been there for them, but he was reaching out now. What will become of their future? Their needs are being met now, but the scars from what they endured to survive I am sure will last a lifetime. What are going to be some of the effects of the neglect they experienced? I wonder whether they harbor any negative feelings for their mother or whether they will continue to defend her actions. I am relieved that they are safe and in a nourishing home. They were lucky that things did not go too far. Or did they? Did the few months of neglect do irreparable damage?

Therapist's Response to #12

There is no way to know what these children's lives will be like years from now. Resiliency is a topic of interest to many researchers as they try to understand why some children can better overcome similar circumstances than others. The children are by no means doomed to have dysfunctional lives, especially if they remain in a nurturing environment and seek continual help in the form of counseling. The children are at risk, however, because of their difficult past, including the divorce of their parents. Possible areas of concern are academic failure, emotional deficits, social difficulties, relational difficulties, behavioral problems, and substance abuse. Throughout their development, the children will most likely go through many stages of relational development with their mother. Possible feelings to emerge would be denial, anger, regret, guilt, hurt, forgiveness, and acceptance.

CONCLUSION

"According to the U.S. Advisory Board on Child Abuse and Neglect (1991), child maltreatment is now designated a 'national emergency.' This designation is based on these findings: (1) Every year thousands of children are starved, abandoned, beaten, burned, raped, berated, and belittled in the United States; (2) the system that the United States has created to prevent this maltreatment is not successful; and (3) the government spends millions of dollars every year on programs to deal with the results of society's failure to identify and prevent child maltreatment" (Lowenthal, 2001, p. 5). Adolescent literature and the knowledge of identifying abuse can be valuable resources for teachers and families for helping abused children. It is our hope that *A Door Near Here* and the psychologist's responses to the reader responses will give insight into the issue of neglect.

REFERENCES

Lowenthal, Barbara. (2001). *Abuse and neglect.* Baltimore: Paul H. Brookes.
Quarles, Heather. (2000). *A door near here.* New York: Dell Laurel-Leaf.
Waldfogel, Jane. (1998). *The future of child protection.* Cambridge, MA: Harvard
        University Press.

Part II

Emotional Abuse

These are experts' views on defining and identifying emotional abuse according to the following sources, identified after the summary.

DEFINITION OF EMOTIONAL ABUSE

Emotional abuse is commonly defined as the systematic tearing down of another human being. http://www.preventchildabuse.com/emotion.htm (National Exchange Club Foundation, 2000)

Emotional abuse is patterns of behavior that attack a child's sense of self-worth and that can seriously interfere with a child's positive emotional development. Those patterns of behavior can include constant rejection of the child; terrorizing; refusal to provide basic nurturance; refusal to get help for a child's psychological problems; failure to provide the physical or mental stimulation that a child needs to be able to grow; and exposing a child to corruption, including drug abuse, criminal behavior, and so on. http://www.americanhumane.org/children/factsheets/emot_abuse.htm (American Humane Association, 2001)

The most common form of emotional abuse is terrorizing, which includes threats to harm a child or do something to him that he finds very frightening to him. http://www.nspcc.org.uk/search/

EXTENT OF THE PROBLEM

An infant who is deprived of emotional nurturance, even though physically cared for, may eventually die. http:www.amerihumane.org/children/factsheet/emotabuse.htm (American Humane Association, 2001)

In 1999, a public awareness survey revealed that two-thirds of all Americans have witnessed an adult emotionally abuse a child. http://www.child advocacy.org/implinks.html (National Association of Child Advocates, American Academy of Pediatrics Report, 2001)

Many researchers conclude that psychopathologic symptoms are more likely to occur in emotionally abused children. http://www.preventchild abuse.org.research_ctr

Women with irritable bowel syndrome scored higher on tests of having been emotionally abused, defined as being threatened verbally, being personally insulted or put down, being denied personal or economic independence, or being deliberately humiliated or degraded in public. http://mentalhelp.net/articles/abuse6.htm (Reuters Health: Psychosomatic Medicine 2000, 2001)

RECOGNIZING EMOTIONALLY ABUSED CHILDREN

Although emotional abuse can hurt as much as physical abuse, it can be harder to identify because the marks are left on the inside instead of the outside. Not surprisingly, there exist few well-validated measures of childhood emotional abuse. Clinicians can use a revised version of the Child Abuse and Trauma Scale (CATS), which targets measures for emotional abuse. Caregivers can also closely observe children's behaviors and personalities. Children suffering from emotional abuse are often extremely loyal to the parent, afraid of being punished if they report abuse, or think that this type of abuse is a normal way of life. http://www.preventchild abuse.org/research_ctr/fact_sheets/emotional_child_abuse.html (Dr. John K. Holton, director for the National Center for Child Abuse and Neglect Prevention Research, a program of Prevent Child Abuse America, 2001).

An emotionally abused child may exhibit the following tendencies: difficulty in making friends; avoiding doing things with other children and being places where he or she is expected to be loving; being pushy and hostile; having a hard time learning; being overly active; experiencing problems such as bed-wetting or soiling; acting falsely grown up; and being the caretaker for adults or others far beyond what should be expected for the child's age. http://www.aap.org/advocacy/childhealth month/abuse2.html (American Academy of Pediatrics, 2001)

The behavioral indicators of an emotionally abusive parent include the following: acts cold and rejecting, blames or belittles the child, treats children in the family unequally, does not seem to care much about the child's problems, withholds love, finds nothing good or attractive in the child, and demonstrates inconsistent behavior toward the child. http://www.kidsafe - caps.org (Child Abuse Prevention Services, 1999)

Most emotional abusers are adept at convincing the victim that the abuse is his or her fault, making the victim responsible for what happened. http:www.cyberparent.com/abuse/mentalemotionalabusers.htm   (Understanding Mental and Emotional or Psychological Abuse, 2000)

RESULTS OF EMOTIONAL ABUSE

Emotional abuse is harder to recognize than outright physical abuse but can be as damaging. Emotionally abused children need immediate expert attention because the abuse leaves children with scars that will get in their way for the rest of their lives. They may become rebellious, fearful, distrusting, lacking in confidence, or lacking in self-esteem. These bad feelings about themselves and others often lead to problems in school, with their friends, and in later life with their own spouses and children. http://www.nara-licensing.org/emotionalabuse.htm

Emotional abuse is destructive to a child's self-confidence and self-esteem, affecting his or her emotional development and often resulting in a sense of worthlessness and inadequacy. Some indicators include extreme patterned behavior such as lying, stealing, and/or fighting; over-aggressiveness and acting out inappropriately; being defensive, shy, or overly dependent; and verbal abusiveness to others, using the same language and demeaning terms she or he has experienced. http://www. nccafv.org/ (National Council on Child Abuse and Family Violence, Updated August 11, 2001)

Emotional abuse of children can result in serious emotional and/or behavioral problems, including depression, lack of attachment to or emotional bond with a parent or guardian, low cognitive ability and educational achievement, and poor social skills. One study that looked at emotionally abused children in infancy and then again during their preschool years consistently found them to be angry, uncooperative, and unattached to their primary caregiver. The children also lacked creativity, persistence, and enthusiasm. http://www.hc-sc.gc.ca/hppb/family violence/html/emotioneng.html (National Clearinghouse on Family Violence, 2001)

YOUNG ADULT NOVELS INVOLVING EMOTIONAL ABUSE

Throughout the following sources, RL: MS = Reading Level: Middle School and RL: HS = Reading Level: High School.

Draper, Sharon. (1997). *Forged by Fire*. New York: Aladdin. 156 pp. (ISBN: 0–689–81851–3)

From the moment he is left unattended at the age of three and burns down his house until the final confrontation with his abusive stepfather, Gerald is truly "forged by fire." When his loving aunt dies, Gerald is suddenly thrust back into a new home with his drug-addicted mother, a home filled with anger and abuse. He inherits a brutal stepfather with a flaming anger and taste for the perverse, but he also gets Angel, a wonderful young stepsister. As he battles to protect her from the evils of his stepfather, Jordan, Gerald shows all of us that even in the worst of circumstances, there is hope. Draper paints a fantastic picture of a young African-American protagonist who survives horrible experiences. The message rings out loudly: No matter what hand life deals you, you can be a victim or choose to overcome. (Ms. Draper is the winner of the Coretta Scott King Genesis Award). RL: MS (emotional abuse)

Fitch, Janet. (1999). *White Oleander.* Boston: Little, Brown & Company. 446 pp. (ISBN: 0–316–56932–1)

Astrid Magnussen struggles to both love and find release from her poetic but emotionally abusive mother, Ingrid. Forced to survive on her own in foster care after her mother is charged with the murder of an ex-boyfriend, Astrid moves from family to family, trying to recreate herself and escape from her mother's sinister emotional vise grip. Fitch creates characters so achingly beautiful and flawed that the reader is seductively absorbed into Astrid's coming-of-age struggle, set against Los Angeles trailer parks and the Santa Anas. Fitch writes without judgment, holding her artistic pen just far enough away to allow us to see the greater picture. That detachment offers a unique truth—that love and abuse are often tightly intertwined. This is a mature novel meant for adults and for youth who are dealing with similar issues. RL: HS (emotional abuse)

McCormick, Patricia. (2000). *Cut.* New York: Scholastic. 151 pp. (ISBN: 0–439–32459–9)

Fifteen-year-old Callie cuts herself as a way to feel a sense of control and success in her life. She recalls her first cutting this way: "... I felt awesome. Satisfied, finally. Then exhausted." Callie has stopped talking, and her therapist at Sea Pines (a.k.a. Sick Minds) is trying to guide Callie out of her darkness. Eventually, Callie begins to communicate and discloses the sadness and pain of her life. Callie lives with a severely asthmatic younger brother, a mother who is battling her own depression and fears, and a father who has detached himself from the chaos of their lives. When Callie is talking to her therapist, readers feel as though she is talking to them directly. During group therapy, readers learn about equally dysfunctional girls, some with eating disorders and some with emotional problems. RL: HS (emotional abuse)

Plum-Ucci, Carol. (2000). *The Body of Christopher Creed.* New York: Harcourt. 248 pp. (ISBN: 0–15–002388–7)

Christopher Creed's mother did not hit him or sexually abuse him. She merely walked into his room when he was changing, routinely rooted through his belongings when he wasn't home, and controlled every aspect of Chris's life. When Chris Creed disappears no one knows whether he has been murdered, committed suicide, or run away. Torey, the boy who has great parents, and Ali, whose mother's boyfriend often has loud, impossible-to-ignore sex with Ali's mother when Ali and her little brother are home, discuss Chris's weirdness. Ali and Torey agree that sometimes "it's more dangerous to have a slightly weird family than a totally weird family...a slightly weird family can have more lasting effects over a lifetime, effects that are harder to untangle because of their subtleties" (p. 37). In addition to subtle abuse from his mother, Chris was abused by his classmates, who one day hit him until he cried. Torey, who also hit Chris during sixth grade, wonders whether his and the others' abuse had left Chris wishing he were dead. For any adolescent who has hurt a peer or who has been a victim in school, this 2000 Printz Honor Book gives insight into long-term consequences of such actions. At the end of the day, the class punching bag might be gone from the abusers' lives, but the children who hit or stood by while other students were abused will have to deal with the results of their and others' actions as adults. RL: MS (emotional and physical abuse)

Snicket, Lemony. (1999). *The Bad Beginning: A Series of Unfortunate Events.* New York: Scholastic. 163 pp. (ISBN: 0–439–20647–2)

In this fantastical tale, we meet the Baudelaire siblings: Violet, Klauss, and Sunny. As they stroll on the beach, a stranger meets them with horrible news that their house has burned down and their parents have died. They must go and live with their distant uncle, Count Olaf, who is an insidious, abusive man who threatens the children into submission. Though luck is certainly not on their side and Olaf's main objective is stealing their inheritance, the children survive his abuse and evil schemes through courage and creativity. Although a bit on the light side, this book could be a helpful escape for many young adults who need to remove themselves from daily hurt and does provide a great model for dealing with life's tragedies. RL: MS (emotional abuse)

NONFICTION TEXTS EXPLAINING THE PROBLEM OF EMOTIONAL ABUSE

Beineke, Rachel. (1998, Spring). The Portrayal of Obese Adolescents. *The ALAN Review, 25* (3), 44–45.

Having been unmercifully teased for being overweight herself, the author expresses a need for realistic young adult (YA) literature that responsibly deals with obese protagonists. Most YA novels having an obese protagonist present the character with an eating disorder who then recovers, loses weight, and becomes "normal" again.

Solomon, C. Ruth, & Francoise, Serres. (1999, April). Effects of Parental Verbal Aggression on Children's Self Esteem and School Marks. *Child Abuse and Neglect, 23* (4), 339–351.

In a study of 144 French Canadian fifth graders attending four public schools, children who had been subjected to verbal aggression were compared with other children who had not experienced such aggression on four constructs: social acceptance, scholastic competence, behavioral conduct, and global self-worth. Children who reported more verbal aggression consistently showed poorer self-perceptions. The study concluded that verbal aggression, or "yelling and threatening," caused students to be less perseverant, less enthusiastic, and less able to concentrate. It is suggested that this type of abuse could be more harmful than physical aggression and its effects longer lasting.

CHAPTER 3

Escaping the Emotional Hold Using Chris Crutcher's *Ironman* as a Springboard for Discussion

Joan F. Kaywell and Sue Street

INTRODUCTION

Emotional abuse, no matter to what degree, is very detrimental to children's development. According to specialists, emotionally abused adolescents demonstrate many of the same symptoms as victims of other types of abuse, which may entail a wide range of behaviors. Emotional abuse can occur with or without physical abuse, however, Kaplan, Pelcovitz, and Labruna (1999) state that the effects of emotional abuse may have a deeper and more lasting effect on a person's psychological functioning than other forms of abuse. It may sound unreasonable that the emotionally abused child could suffer as many intense negative outcomes from emotional abuse as the child who is sexually or physically abused. One explanation is that emotional abuse usually occurs within the framework of "normal" family relationships and, in fact, that the discipline is "good for you." On the surface, nothing appears to be wrong. While this experience is destructive and painful for the child, the apparent normalcy of it all creates a pervasive sense that all is well. Children experiencing severe violent sexual or physical abuse typically develop extreme responses to their life challenges; thus, they tend to act out more and draw the attention of educators and helpers who initiate efforts to address these children's issues. Emotional abuse is more difficult to define, more difficult to see. In fact, to some extent, emotional abuse is perceptual. Words don't leave you disabled for life. Or do they?

The conflicts within young people that ensue from emotional abuse are not easily resolved. Their authority figures say they are not good enough, but even adolescents sense that they must be better than what their abusers publicly pronounce about them. It is reasonable to determine that emotionally abused adolescents need healthy outlets to release their emotions, especially the anger that erupts so frequently. As a result of being told they are dumb, stupid, or will never amount to anything, they often make poor choices. Psychologists have pointed out that individuals who believe they are locked into stressful situations may compensate through an array of means. Although some may choose to anesthetize themselves through drugs and alcohol, gangs and violence, or rampant sexual activity, others may choose more productive and acceptable outlets such as academics or athletics. One problem that then arises, however, is that these individuals' choice to prove their self-worth through academic or athletic achievement may then be expressed as near-obsessive perfectionism. The child does not pursue achievement for the love of it—although some of that may be present—rather, the person believes achievement can most effectively prove to the world that the world is wrong; that he or she, indeed, is good: so good that he or she is perfect! Anything less than 100% on a test is crippling; training for athletic endeavors is grueling, relentless, and almost as painful as the emotional abuse (although not experienced that way). There is little joy in a triumph, for the child must continue to prove that she or he is worthy. The emotionally abused child is never good enough. The effect that emotional abuse has on children as individuals can last their entire lifetime if it goes unaddressed.

In Chris Crutcher's novel, *Ironman,* several adolescent characters experience various kinds of abuse, but all respond to the abuse differently. As in his other literary pieces, Crutcher's characters are expertly crafted and are very intense. All the students in Mr. Nak's anger management class experience emotional abuse; some also experience physical abuse. At times these adolescents are arrogant, confused, and vulnerable; at other times, they are devoted, caring, and brave. Crutcher does an amazing job bringing in so many aspects of the situations faced by adolescents today. His willingness to tackle a myriad of issues—the ugly events and feelings we would all rather hide away and certainly never discuss—allows readers, regardless of age and gender, to find some acceptance and understanding on the pages of his books. Anyone reading *Ironman* can get a glimpse of what and how emotionally abused adolescents think and feel. It is important for readers to note, however, that the protagonist in this book is very lucky—as the other kids in the novel point out—because he has a rational, healthy significant power figure in his life to balance the insanity.

ORGANIZATION

A synopsis of Chris Crutcher's novel *Ironman,* illustrating the pain and struggles of a high-school senior who is emotionally and verbally abused by a controlling father, is followed by a guidance counselor's comments about Bo's situation with recommended therapeutic objectives and goals. The counselor's piece is followed by an actual dialogue between a professor and a student about the novel. In this way, readers may examine emotional abuse from the perspective of a fictional character and an actual victim with a counselor's help.

SYNOPSIS OF *IRONMAN* BY CHRIS CRUTCHER

Beauregard "Bo" Brewster, the protagonist in Crutcher's *Ironman,* is a 17-year-old high-school student who, like many teenagers, has a problem with his family. Bo has experienced a lifetime of emotional abuse from an overbearing and controlling father. Several adults in the story—outsiders looking in on this all-American family—believe that Bo is not a child in need of help but needs to learn respect and discipline. On the inside, however, readers can see how Lucas has consistently been verbally and emotionally abusive to his elder son. Fortunately, Bo deals with his anger toward his father in healthy ways. Bo chooses writing and extreme athletics—in Bo's case, preparing for a triathlon—as his way of dealing with the frustration the abuse causes; unfortunately, every now and then Bo's own anger gets the better of him. In an emotional outburst, Bo calls Mr. Redmond—his English teacher and ex-football coach—an "asshole." This outburst lands Bo in Mr. Nak's anger management group.

The novel is part epistolary, with Bo writing letters telling his story and feelings to the famous commentator Larry King. Through a series of letters to Larry King, a.k.a. Lar or Mr. King, Bo reveals his thoughts about current issues and conflicts in his life. Bo is dealing with the psychological effects of his father's abuse. His feelings of failure and fear are expressed through his unconscious mind in his dreams. The dreams are so real for Bo that they have a physical effect upon him; he wakes drenched in sweat.

The other part of the novel revolves around the other students in the "Nak Pack," the anger management group that Bo attends before school each morning. Bo finally learns how to deal with his anger toward his father by listening to other people's accounts of abuse and to Mr. Nak's advice. Mr. Nak is a wonderful character: flawed, but caring; wise, but humorous; brave, but small. Throughout the novel, this lovable Japanese cowboy shares pearls of wisdom with the group. When some guys start calling Hudgie names, Mr. Nak comes out with this: " 'Sticks and stones may break my bones,' " he says, 'but names will break my heart.' "…'I want y'all to hear somethin',' Nak says. 'I know you think all those words you're usin' on one another make ya tough. But ya know what I hear? I don't hear tough at all. I hear scared' " (p. 137). Mr. Nak's genuine caring for his "Nak Pack," as well as the wisdom he shares, is sorely needed by each individual group member. His approach transforms them all, and each member has his place in leading Bo to insight and safety. According to the American Academy of Pediatrics, emotional abuse rears its ugly head in the following ways in children: difficulty in making friends, difficulty in learning, being pushy and hostile, and acting falsely grown up. All these behaviors are observable in the anger management group.

By the novel's end, Bo realizes that the way his father has treated him is wrong. Bo is not at fault; he did not do anything to cause his father's abuse. His father is the sick one. With the help of the members of the anger management group, Bo is able to finish a triathlon and learns a valuable lesson about bigotry. He is also able to convince his father to see a therapist. Bo is able to overcome his anger by writing and talking about his abuse. Bo's literacy skills help him to lay the foundation for becoming an emotionally healthy, well-adjusted individual. An adolescent dealing with emotional abuse baggage will benefit from reading this novel.

A Counselor Talks with Bo

Bo: I have this recurring dream based on an experience I had when I was nine years old. My father was sleeping, and I accidentally woke him by slamming a door. My father commanded me to open and close the door quietly 20 times, but I refused. As punishment, my father sentenced me to isolation in my room for six months. My father wouldn't even let me join the family for Christmas. The dream goes like this:

I'm standing by a huge steel door, intent on closing it in absolute silence. My father looms over me, hands on his hips, eyes blood red like some kind of special effect…. I push the door so carefully it doesn't even creak, and get it *almost* shut without a sound. Dad glares; he's *huge,* way bigger than in real life. I handle the doorknob as if it were filled with nuclear waste. Just when I think I've done it, the latch clicks like a shot put dropped in an echo chamber and I freeze, staring back into Dad's scowling eyes, and try again. Tonight I woke up on my third failure, my bedding crumpled on the floor, sweat pouring off me like early spring runoff. (p. 26)

Counselor:	Bo, I don't know if you realize that the amount of control and the unrealistic expectations your father had for you are typical for an emotional abuser. In your father's mind, the severe punishment is justified because it is for "your own good." Those expectations that you must be perfect, must be exactly and precisely what Dad (or Mom) demands—no matter how unreasonable—are internalized, creating intense anxiety. That's what creates those anxiety dreams such as the one you just described: the ones where we keep trying but never get there, never get it right, never reach the goal, drive in circles and more circles. Your dream is your unconscious expression of your sense of futility and worthlessness.
	A big part of your anxiety, and, in fact, your anger, comes from a psychological state we call "cognitive dissonance." One of the most debilitating outcomes of emotional abuse is the creation of cognitive dissonance. Cognitive dissonance is a term that refers to two conflicting truths held by a person. Young people who are constantly berated over a period of years by their most credible authority figures—parents, teachers, coaches, or church figures—as being bad, no good, and never good enough struggle to keep their heads above water. When significant people in your life, who are bigger, older, wiser, and in power over you, tell you that you are bad or not good enough, what else can you think? Are you with me so far?
Bo (nodding thoughtfully):	But they are supposed to know.
Counselor:	And that's what causes the cognitive dissonance. The indomitable human spirit continues to whisper the message, carried by gossamer threads, that "You *are* good, you *are* okay, you *are* right, you are *not* being treated fairly, *you are good!!!*" These filaments persist, sometimes in barely discernible whispers, reminding you that you are really okay. Maybe, just maybe, all these people in power over you are, in fact, wrong when they say you are bad, wrong when they say you are not worthy, and wrong when they say you are not lovable. Do you understand what I'm saying?

Bo (nodding with a small smile):	I had no idea of calling it that, but you've described what I feel exactly!
Counselor (smiling):	Yet all the while, an appearance of normalcy is maintained; indeed, the bulk of public opinion is clearly supportive of the parents who are trying so hard to "get this unruly child in line." From all outward appearances, nothing is amiss except the child's self-esteem, which has been systematically shredded over the years of abuse. Is this how it worked with you?
Bo (with down-turned, tightly pressed lips):	Yeah, that's how it worked all right.
Counselor:	Yet as long as those gossamer threads continue to whisper, there is hope. You may not have realized this, but the fact that you—or any child in your situation—continued to become angry was a good thing; it was an indicator that you were still fighting. While it may have appeared to many folks that you were fighting the external world, it was those internal demons you were really fighting. Yes?
Bo (listening intently):	Yes.
Counselor:	You were fighting the most important fight that anyone ever fights: that is the fight for self-value, self-worth, and self-love. The "world" says you're "bad," but your mind whispers you might, just might, be okay. These contradictions and not knowing which is right fuel that anger, causing the inner conflict, the cognitive dissonance.
Bo (in deep thought about reframing his anger and fighting as a more acceptable psychological process):	Well, again, I hadn't put it in those words. But that's exactly what it was as I think about it.

COUNSELOR OVERVIEW

While professional counselors typically encourage the client to set the goals of counseling, it is realistic to assume that Bo might state his counseling goals as these: sorting out his life thus far, understanding his relationships with family and friends, and figuring out what he wants to do with the rest of his life. The counselor, aware of Bo's counseling objectives, would help Bo to reach those goals. The framework of goals and objectives outlined here is one approach; other strategies could be effective in helping Bo reach his goals. This framework has been used a great deal over the years with emotionally abused youth and has proven very successful. The reader may also see that the objectives are not mutually exclusive; that which addresses issues in one area will contribute to growth in other areas as well. The idea is to address the most fundamental issues that are at the foundation of the symptoms.

Reframing Responsibility and Blame

Bo will need to "reframe blame." Bo and others like him have developed a sense that they are wrong, bad, or not good enough largely because they cannot please the authority figures in their lives. For most kids, those figures are all they know; authority figures certainly exert almost total control over the kids' lives. Parents have tremendous authority over their children. Children are so vulnerable and are largely at the mercy of their major power figures. When the parent says the child is bad, or wrong, or when the parent dispenses an absurdly unreasonable punishment, the child has little choice but to accept it at face value. Children lack the ability to objectively stand outside themselves and evaluate themselves and their family members. They subjectively and unconsciously adopt a view of themselves that is consistent with the significant others in their environment, including parents, close family members, teachers, and any other adults who spend time with them in positions of some power and authority. As a result, the majority of young people grow up mirroring the assessment of them held by their significant others. In the case of those young folks who experience emotional abuse at the hands of their authority figures, their self-esteem is minimal.

An early objective for Bo's counselor will be to begin discussions that will facilitate the development of Bo's objectivity and distance from events that hold great emotional significance for him. This will contribute to positive outcomes in two areas: first, in developing a realistic analysis and understanding that his father carries the biggest portion of the responsibility for the challenges in his life up to this point; and second, in helping Bo begin to address his anger issues.

Discussing Bo's Father's Role in His Life

Several strategies might be effective here. It will be important for Bo to discuss his family life, in particular his father's role in his life. Helping Bo understand the dynamics of healthy families will contribute to his understanding that perhaps his father had some unhealthy issues of his own that he expressed through his parenting role. The counselor could provide some of the information about healthy family dynamics, but it would probably be more effective for Bo to read some of the family systems professional literature—recommended by the counselor—which would allow him to absorb and reason out those theories himself. Every kid on the planet breaks things, drops things, makes mistakes, and generally screws up, with the best of intentions. The purpose of being a kid is to learn, and the purpose of parenting is to teach. In healthy families, children do not have to be perfect; they simply have to try to learn the lessons of childhood.

At the same time, the whole notion of power in the family is an important variable. Bo is a strapping young man, but his father still holds the power. Children are vulnerable and do not exercise the level of power of the parents. When abuse occurs, it occurs with the concurrence of the power figures. Abuse of power is not appropriate. Power is best shared with the developing child, who can assume more power and responsibility with maturity. Understanding this concept will help Bo redirect his own behavior, and he will probably be a healthier parent than his dad.

Discussing Other Men's Roles and Bo's Role in His Own Life

Another strategy a counselor might use is to discuss the relationships other men have developed with Bo. This novel offers a range of positive as well as dysfunctional male role models. The counselor could help Bo realize that there are male authority figures who do value him very highly, providing input that is synchronous with those gossamer threads whispering in his head. Bo could be led to the conclusion that he is not the one entirely at fault, but that certain men in his life and his relationships with them are at the root of some problems.

Next Bo would benefit by learning to objectively analyze his own behaviors, reframing them as the actions of a kid fighting for survival, a kid who is a "warrior fighting for good." A counselor might ask Bo to step outside himself and think about his behavior as though it was the behavior of a kid in someone else's family. What does Bo think about this young man? Is he a bad kid or a good kid? While Bo's dad may be responsible for the negative self-image Bo has carried with him up to this point, it will be important for the counselor to stress that Bo himself will be responsible for his self-image from this time forward. Once Bo realizes that the negativity was generated outside himself, he must exercise the mental acuity to reclaim his sense of "good self."

The first step in helping Bo to reclaim a sense of his "good self" is to help him reframe his self-perception of himself as a misfit to a new perception that he is a good kid. Bo is in the habit of seeing himself as a misfit, and he works hard to make that image a reality. With a counselor's help, he must change that way of thinking about himself. The next step is to help Bo move from his need for perfectionism or high levels of achievement to feeling good about just being himself, imperfections and all. Perhaps athletics will absorb Bo for a few years, but he may decide to follow in the footsteps of Mr. Nak. Bo needs to get to the place where he realizes he is a good person, worthy of respect, and is good enough even when he does not excel to the extreme. A third step is for Bo to realize that he is a person with the skills and ability to make his life what he wants it to be. When external events don't work out exactly the way he planned, Bo will learn that he is in control of his reactions and can make the best of life at all times.

Attention focused on these three areas will enable Bo to begin to step out of his situation and to reframe his own misfit role. Bo can reframe himself as a good kid who tried to do the right thing but whose father made grossly unreasonable demands that even the "best" kid could not fulfill. Bo can reframe himself as a bright, capable young man who is a good person—and always has been.

Managing Anger

The emotional abuse experienced by some young people creates tremendous conflicts in their thinking; the world is telling them they are bad, but something inside keeps saying they are good. And it says it just often enough, just loudly enough for those people to become really angry over the way they are being treated by the world. They are frustrated by the unfairness of it all and by the cognitive dissonance they experience: they really aren't sure whether they are bad or good, but they want so much to believe they are good, and yet the world keeps telling them they are bad, and so on. It's enough to make a person boiling mad, and sometimes it is easier to take it out on people who aren't perpetuating the real ugliness because those people are easier and safer to deal with.

Anger management can be addressed directly, but it will probably be more effectively facilitated through working with some of the fundamental causes. Initially, the counselor may want to work with Bo on direct anger management: identifying his anger cues, his body signals, and then practicing tuning into them and becoming aware of them. Role playing might be one way to practice this, either with the therapist individually or with a group. As Bo becomes increasingly conscious of his external buttons and his internal cues, he will begin to be able to control his angry responses. It will also be important, however, to address the underlying anger issues.

Through Mr. Nak's character, Crutcher emphasizes that fear underlies anger. Bo's counselor will help him explore the source of that fear. While Crutcher does not give us detailed insight into Bo's thinking, it can be assumed that he is fearful that he will not be given the opportunity to control his life; that he is not capable of controlling his life; that he will always be abused by male authority figures; and that life will never really be fair. He will always be controlled by people who, he is convinced, do not have his best interests at heart—no matter what they tell him.

Bo will need to learn that being in control simply means controlling his own responses and reactions to external events. As Bo attends to various issues raised in counseling, he will begin to realize that while he cannot control the events around him or even the way some people treat him, he can control how he reacts to them. Bo can also learn the extent to which he allows external events to impact his own life. Yes, his father tried to control him, but ultimately, it did not work. The only person one is ever totally in control of is one's own "self." Bo can claim that control and begin to exercise it anytime he wants. There is little reason to be angry when one is in control.

It is important for Bo to specifically realize that when he gives others the power to make him angry, it only hurts him. Each of us will have authority figures we must answer to, at least to some extent, all our lives. We all must learn how to communicate effectively with authority figures. Becoming angry with them and calling them names is an ineffective approach to conflict resolution, as Bo learns the hard way. Angry students end up being suspended or getting an F on a paper. Angry adults miss out on bonuses or even get fired. Bo is apparently well on his way to learning that there is nothing sacred about parents and teachers. They are imperfect adults, like all other adults. Included in learning about family systems is the reality that adults may not be mature; biological maturation occurs with or without the accommodation of emotional and social maturity.

Learning to handle conflict in ways that result in positive outcomes for ourselves is the goal. When a teacher is the instigator of conflict with a particular student, the student can choose to become angry and behave inappropriately toward the teacher who is, indeed, taking out frustrations on that student. The student is then kicked out of class, sometimes out of school, which ultimately affects his grades, and he may need to take summer school, or worse, drop out. It is sometimes true, as the student claims, that the teacher wasn't really being fair. The counselor's question is always: "Who is the winner?" The way for the kid to be the winner is for the kid to refuse to allow that teacher, who may well be at fault, to make him behave in ways that are not appropriate. It was clear in Bo's last scene with Mr. Redmond that he had realized the importance of practicing appropriate behavior. Bo no longer saw Mr. Redmond as having a great deal of control over his life. No matter whether Mr. Redmond was still negative toward him, Bo had taken control of his own life, and with that comes maturity and a sense of balance. Something more fundamental than simply preventing anger had transpired—Bo had realized that his power lay within himself and was his for the taking. Bo could afford to be polite and respectful to Mr. Redmond because now Mr. Redmond really didn't matter much to Bo. The kid is the winner when he behaves courteously, does his work, passes the class, and goes on with his life. Kids in control refuse to allow teachers to interrupt their progress toward their goals.

Goal Setting

The counselor will encourage Bo to talk about his goals and to concretize them realistically. Goals are integral to getting kids through adolescence. Clearly formulated goals that are well within the possibility of attainment serve as beacons to guide us through times and situations that are fraught with peril. Keeping an eye on the goal ahead is tantamount to having a light that is showing the way. Crutcher depicts Bo as a person with goals. These goals keep Bo going, give him purpose, and keep him so busy that he does not have to think too much about things that are painful and confusing, about things that suggest he really might be a bad boy.

Goals serve other purposes, too. Goals allow us to define who we are. That is why it is very important for young people to choose their own goals; they are an expression of how young people see themselves. Young people without goals are people who cannot envision themselves as individuals with a future. Having no goals indicates that a person lets life happen to him or her instead of taking control of his or her life and choosing to formulate and direct it. A person without realistic goals may be someone who has given up; he or she is letting the environment be in control, with little hope of making something different happen. Bo had focused so long on his triathlon goal that he was not certain what he would do after high school. A counselor would help him realize that he has options. By the novel's end, Bo seems to realize that he needs some time to think about what he wants to do. This is part of his process of getting to know himself and making decisions for himself—taking control of his own life.

Healthy Masculinity

Bo's masculinity is an important part of his self-concept and identity. Bo has experienced some very negative male behaviors, although they were effectively packaged under the guise of traditional masculinity, or "real manliness." Football exemplifies traditional masculinity; thus playing football is more highly esteemed than competing in a triathlon, which actually requires a far greater range of physical prowess. People who exercise strong masculine dominant roles generally also buy into the idea of submissive roles. Strong dominance demands submission; the two extremes are coupled. It appears that Bo's father also experienced authoritarian, dominant fathering, surely from the submissive perspective. Men who experience this kind of fathering without questioning it will repeat it. This is what they have learned; it is all they know.

Bo fortunately has been mentored by some positive male role models. The fact that one is gay creates some conflict for Bo temporarily, but he realizes his caring for this man is worth more than his trepidation about homosexuality. Bo is already identifying some traits that are more important than sexual preference or race. Bo realizes that integrity, support, caring concern, and wisdom are important masculine strengths. His mentors deviate from traditional masculinity and make decisions that require the courage of their convictions. Bo may not have articulated these specific attributes yet, but it will be helpful for his counselor to talk to him about very specific strengths that contribute to his own concept of masculinity. Bo is beginning to realize that personal power is not about giving others orders in an authoritarian manner; it is about internally adhering to one's values, persevering in the face of adversity, and facing challenges with courage without running from them. As Bo consciously identifies his perception of masculine strengths, he will continue to gain awareness of his own skills relative to these strengths. Identification of that which he admires in others will give him something to which he can aspire. And all the while, his own self-awareness will continue to grow, grounding him and building his internal skeleton of strengths.

A PROFESSOR AND STUDENT DIALOGUE ABOUT *IRONMAN*

Student: Bo's writing to "Lar" is an aspect of the novel that appeals to me on several levels. For one, I think that Crutcher's choice of Larry King as the recipient of Bo's journal entries appeals to anyone with strong opinions. It also makes writing in a journal seem like a pretty cool thing, especially for a young man. Crutcher also shifts the perspective of the story on occasion. Readers get a taste of the same event from two perspectives, reminding us that there are different "realities" in this world.

Professor: It's a very effective literary technique, and Crutcher is certainly a master in its use.

Student: Bo Brewster describes a holiday moment that is a zenith point in his life: "I truly believed my heart would break. So be it. In the wee hours of December twenty-fifth, I lay on my bed reading a Popeye comic book while my parents and sister opened their gifts less than four feet on the other side of the wall, and I felt a cold, stainless steel cage close over that heart" (p. 30). This is the moment Bo's heart decides it will not break again but will protect itself from ever feeling again in order to avoid any pain.

Professor: Those proverbial walls we all have.

Student: Every feeling, that is, except anger. He was being punished for slamming the door during his father's lunch hour nap.

Professor: I hope you can see that the punishment did not fit the crime.

Student: But the punishment becomes a battle of wills. His father's choice of behavior modification backs Bo into a corner. Trapped, Bo follows his animal instinct and lashes out by disobeying. I say "animal instinct" because in the heat of the moment it really is animalistic. The anger seeps over you slowly—waiting, waiting—your heart actually contracting in on itself while your chest seems to draw all the heat from the rest of your body. For me, my ears would begin to tingle, and my breath would come to me like I was breathing through a curlicue straw. I am still working on remembering that anger correctly. I don't want to exaggerate it or reduce it because I am looking at it from my new status as an "adult." Let me try and explain.

Professor: You've already explained anger in great detail. I suspect it's embedded in something very big.

Student: I am in no way abused beyond repair. I really don't consider myself abused at all. Seriously, even writing this I cringe that someone would think that I am, was.

Professor: For whatever it's worth and before I continue reading this piece, it is absolutely natural for children to love and bond with their parents. While working with abused kids, I noticed that they could identify abuse when they read it in a book but had a very hard time transferring the word abuse into their own lives. It was as though a blanket of "does not compute" would cover their faces until an "Oh, my God— that's like what my mother did!" would come out immediately followed by tears. The good news is that once awareness happens, these kids can break the negative patterns and create a much healthier next generation with their own children. Awareness must happen first, followed by a resolve to learn a new way of parenting.

Student: Starting at about 14, I entered a new phase in my relationship with my mother. It was also about this time that my parents' marriage began to crumble. My dad disappeared into work, and my mother never disappeared at all. She was always there and in my face constantly. Sometimes I would laugh that I wouldn't be in the door a minute after school, and I would be grilled about the condition I left the bathroom in that morning or how I didn't rinse my cereal bowl.

Professor: Her life was out of control and she had to control something; it sounds like you fit the bill.

Student: One afternoon I came home to my little sister laughing as I entered my room. On my bed were the remains of my oatmeal from the morning—smeared on my sheets, spattered on my posters of River Phoenix.

Professor: Sorry, but once again, the punishment did not fit the crime.

Student: Honestly, as I started reading this book, I had to wonder how Bo was being abused. He had a tough parent is how I see it. His dad's punishments seemed petty and sometimes a bit twisted, but Bo seemed tough enough to handle it. I couldn't help but compare some of the punishments. Yep, I even started thinking that Bo had a lot of gumption talking back to his dad the way he did. (But I was in awe that Bo— with Chris Crutcher's therapeutic edge—could be so eloquent in the thick, pounding anger that filled him up to cover the shame.) Talking (yelling) at my mother never did any good. I think at some point I realized how terribly she was hurting, and I started to understand that it wasn't me that was the source of her anger.

Professor: For you to realize that as a young adult is amazing!

Student: I'm glad Bo did, too. It's almost like a movie or something when you figure out that the adult demanding control or obedience or respect is clinging to nothing. I would watch the transformation take place as my mother would find something wrong and obsess about it. She just couldn't let it go. Her voice would rise, her anger boiling over, and her desperation making her eyes go wild and unseeing. I knew what Bo saw, but fortunately for me, my mother found therapy on her own.

Professor: Ah, maybe that's why you were able to call it what it was and with such insight.

Student: It wasn't a perfect little American family with the white picket fence after that, but she did ease up. Now, as an adult, I have hugged away her apologies and tried not to look too long into her regret that pierces me when she "goes there" with her memories. I guess I just don't see that as malicious abuse when I look back on it now. At that time in history, my mother was just a sad, lonely, and scared woman who didn't know how to cope for a time.

Professor: Forgiveness is a beautiful thing. It is wonderful to be able to give genuine forgiveness when a person comes to a penitential state; both people win in that instance.

Student: As I continued reading about Bo, I finally realized how it was for him and just how dysfunctional his family life was. I think it was his father giving the $5,000 bike to the CFU students in order to ensure that Bo wouldn't win the Yukon Jack marathon when I fully recognized the extent of the dysfunction. At first I believed that his dad was never leaving "that place"—which is truly scary—but as in many of Crutcher's stories, I sensed a desire in Bo's dad to make it better. What incredibly low self-esteem this man must have. I have already predicted that he experienced a similar upbringing to the one he has given Bo, but how unsuccessful he must feel as a parent. Although I'm sure he blames Bo for that, there must be some level on which he aches to feel success as a father.

Professor: Therapy would probably reveal all of that, but right now Lucas Brewster has no idea of how his own upbringing is hurting his own relationship with his son. And that's what makes them such powerful characters. Readers are encouraged when Bo mentions seeing his dad's Lexus in the parking lot at the therapist's office at the end of the novel.

Student: All the characters in Mr. Nak's "anger management" class were amazing. I felt lucky to witness the healing, and felt even a little healed myself after reading about their individual stories. (Sometimes I just wanted to put the book down, it seemed so overwhelming.) Mr. Nak's drawl was only annoying when he was talking, but it seemed the voice of some great benevolent being speaking when he would spout the truths that had been stolen for so long from those kids. "It ain't love," he had said, when "if what's coming from others don't make you feel better about yourself in the world" (p. 162).

Professor: That's a great line!

Student: Bo's letter to Larry is almost poetic, explaining why many hurting children throw themselves into a sport or activity:

Lately I've been thinking maybe God was behind my self-imposed banishment from team sports, rather than Redmond, because this kind of training feels almost spiritual. There were times in the fall as I hammered over the rolling hills outside town on my bike, pushing my body…somehow I call up this *power,* and it feels like hate and it feels like love, and I simply pull ahead. And I want to tell people, but only a few can hear because if you haven't taken your body or your brain or your spirit down that road, you are deaf to it. (pp. 152–153)

Bo calls it "spiritual" and it is saving grace for abused kids. His confidence seems to be at an all-time high. He has cleared things up with Mr. S, in reference to his sexuality, and so all of his support is back in place. At this point in the novel, he is surrounded by people who encourage him (except Mr. Redmond, who is now really kind of powerless against him). Since he lives with his mom and only sees his father at his choosing, his world is mostly safe. Research supports this as being one of the best scenarios.

Professor: And isn't it nice to be able to read it in a book? I find that people who have not been abused cannot understand some of this stuff even when they want to. Because I'm a communicator by trade, it frustrates me to no end that I cannot find the words to make those people understand. It doesn't stop me from trying though.

Student: There is a scene when Bo is at dinner with Mr. S, and he is trying to explain to Bo about the importance of recognizing that this is a bad point in time with his father but time will pass, and it will become increasingly important for Bo to recognize it for what it was. I like the idea about it being about "connection," but I am sure most adolescents would not be able to comprehend that idea fully. Shoot! Most adults have a hard time with it, but even those who do get it don't find it easy to achieve. It requires both parties to be on the same wavelength and be able to separate histories and baggage from relationship. It's a heavy but wonderful ideal to hold onto.

Professor: It's also good to remind people that bad times do eventually pass, and lessons learned need to be implemented rather than continued by negatively repeating the same mistakes.

Student: I about lost it when I read all that happened to Hudge, a kid in Mr. Nak's anger management class. Hudge is a sad, sad case. His dad actually kills Hudge's dog, and the awful scene of Mr. Nak going to his house to find him hugging his dead dog on the front porch is a heartbreaker. I just wanted to hug Hudge and let him cry it all out. According to all of the reading I've done about abuse, Hudge is the classic abused child: abused by a close family member (his father), blamed for the abuse he receives, lacks self-confidence/self-esteem, and loves the one who abuses him; Hudge screams at the police as they haul his dad off. Hudge does not have any of the items listed for maintaining good mental health:

unconditional love from family, self-confidence, secure sur-
roundings, or appropriate discipline. He does, however,
have the support of Mr. Nak. How scary is that to be a
child's *only* hope?

Professor: The profound impact some teachers have on their students'
lives often goes unnoticed by society at large. Teachers
often do way more than teach students the three Rs. I dis-
agree with you on something you said. I believe if you tried
to hug Hudge, at this point in the novel, it would probably
elicit no emotion from him. In fact, Hudge would be in better shape if he were to cry infinite tears. I suspect that Hudge
has closed off most if not all of his feelings for survival reasons.

Student: Now, as I close, I want to say that revisiting unpleasant
memories is not easy for me.

Professor: I'm sorry—more than you know.

Student: We all need love, right, as well as the mercy that Mr. Nak
speaks of at the end of the novel before leaving. I really
have worked at letting many of those bad feelings go.
Indeed, to get angry—ear-tingling angry—is as foreign as
speaking Chinese to me today. My mother and I have a
healthy (at least by FDA standards) relationship today.

Professor: That's such a blessing!

Student: When she drove away from me for the first time leaving me
in charge of my new life as a college student, I bawled. All
I wanted was her. So when she would call me once, sometimes twice a day the entire first month I was alone, I was
okay with her not disappearing. My mother was the first
person I called when my heart was broken for the first time
as a senior in college. I remember choking on my tears, trying to tell her what happened—that I had invested a future
in someone and had lost any return. She stayed on the phone
with me until 4 A.M. that Monday morning, nursing my
severe disappointment. She is half of me when it comes
down to it. And I am eternally grateful for all the happy
memories I have with her and will have with her.

Professor: She sounds like a great woman.

Student: I'm thankful that Bo's mother acknowledges the role she
played in allowing the abuse to occur in their home. This

would be a cathartic time for an adolescent and a parent in these circumstances. Bo is a pretty mature young man, and I think his character is probably a little less bitter than an adolescent might tend to actually be under these circumstances.

Professor: There's something to be said about a person's willingness to admit his or her being in the wrong. When someone can admit his or her role in the demise of a relationship, then authentic forgiveness can take place, healing can occur, and the relationship can healthily move on.

Student: I am emotionally tired. Actually, I think weary would also describe it right. I am having a hard time concentrating on even writing this. I'm a step off right now, and I don't make any excuses. I really got this book. And maybe that's why driving home today I kept thinking about Mr. Nak saying that "People ain't fair" (p. 226). There is so much bad in this world today. If I stop too long to reflect I won't get this sent off to you. And the assignment is due. And life goes on. But Bo knew he was different, and lucky almost, to have been able to see inside of his father at what the root cause of his anger was. I am trying to see that behind the angry, angry world out there is fear. And I'm working on my mercy.

Professor: Well said, and I think I understand. As an abuse survivor, I can honestly say that I am a better person for surviving the abuse and coming out on the other side. Not that I'd ever wish abuse on anyone, but my life is a lot richer because I have such understanding that I never would have had had I not gone through such trauma. I had to learn to let my perpetrator go *in love*. I suspect you have a clue as to how difficult it is to get yourself to that place when someone has hurt you so badly. As Crutcher says, "We often cannot control the bad stuff that happens to us, but we can *always* control our response to the events." There is a balance between being a doormat and taking the high road.

CONCLUSION

Ironman is a book that shows a young man's personal rite of passage in our modern times. In today's society, most of the rituals for adulthood have vanished, become obsolete, or are scarcely practiced. Spirituality is widely discussed in our society, but is it practiced? Cycles of abuse and addiction, woven through generations, are discussed but seldom put to rest for the individual. Many people stay in limbo between adulthood and adolescence for years—sometimes a lifetime—because they never fully accept responsibility and reality. Many people do not learn what Bo learns in his story. Many people do not have a rite of passage into adulthood, learning that life is sometimes painful and tough but through belief in something greater than oneself and support and assistance from other people, one can succeed and find peace and happiness. The triathlon is Bo's ritual into adulthood, but in order to complete his quest, he can succeed only by asking others for help. There is no shame in asking.

As in adult life, Bo learns that he cannot accomplish anything alone, and his support comes from the most unlikely places—a bunch of misfits in an alternative to detention, a homosexual swim coach, and a Japanese cowboy. The beauty of this book is the story's combination of personal power and community power. Through *Ironman*, Crutcher shows a young man's successful completion of a phase of life; he shows Bo overcoming some of his personal demons. In the end, even though his future is unknown to the reader and to Bo, one knows that Bo will be okay in his adult life because he has learned to ask for help—a powerful message for us all, especially the abused. Reading, writing, church involvement, and positive role models are all outlets that are beneficial for these adolescents and can help them heal their wounds. All of these "misfits" are able to make some beautiful magic for one another. Now, ain't that something?

REFERENCES

Crutcher, Chris. (1995). *Ironman.* New York: Dell Laurel-Leaf.
Kaplan, Sandra J., Pelcovitz, David, & Labruna, Victor. (1999). Child and adolescent abuse and neglect research: A review of the past 10 years. Part I: Physical and emotional abuse and neglect. *Journal of the American Academy of Child and Adolescent Psychiatry, 38* (10), 1214–1222.

CHAPTER 4

Han Nolan's *Born Blue:* Using Self-Expression to Heal the Wounds of Emotional Abuse and Neglect

Danielle Lyons and Candace Odierna

INTRODUCTION

Educators, social workers, and legal and medical professionals most often report child abuse and neglect; unfortunately, very few reports of abuse and neglect come from anonymous tips, relatives, victims, friends, and neighbors (Kaplan, Pelcovitz, & Labruna, 1999, p. 1215). As educators we need to be sensitive to and aware of the causes and symptoms of emotional abuse and neglect so that we can use the appropriate resources to help abused students. Emotional abuse is defined as "verbal abuse, harsh non-physical punishments (e.g., being tied up), or threats of maltreatment, while emotional neglect covers failure to provide adequate affection and emotional support or permitting a child to be exposed to domestic violence" (Kaplan, Pelcovitz, & Labruna, 1999, p. 1214). Victims of emotional abuse suffer from a distorted process of attachment and affective development; the victims of this type of abuse also may not have the ability to develop "appropriate emotional responses" (Hamarman & Bernet, 2000, p. 928). The effects of emotional abuse are far reaching because they may lead to "lifelong emotional difficulties" (Hamarman & Bernet, 2000, p. 928).

ORGANIZATION

A synopsis of Han Nolan's novel *Born Blue,* illustrating the pain and struggles of a survivor of severe emotional abuse, will be enhanced by information from research journals regarding the types of emotional abuse and the effects of emotional abuse and neglect. Candace Odierna, a guidance counselor, will then provide comments about Janie's, a.k.a. Leshaya's, condition and some recommended short-term and long-term therapy goals. In this way, readers may examine emotional abuse and neglect from the perspective of the victim, researchers, and a high-school guidance counselor.

SYNOPSIS OF *BORN BLUE* BY HAN NOLAN

When the reader first meets Janie, she explains, "My first memory of myself I be drowning" (Nolan, 2001, p. 1). Janie's mother left her to drown in the Gulf of Mexico when she was four years old. Her mother, Mama Linda, was lost in the delirium of a heroin high when she committed this unspeakable act but told Janie that she was suffering from a spell of amnesia. After the incident, Janie is placed in foster care and refers to her new home as the "stink house" because of the stench of baby vomit and dirty diapers that permeates the home.

Janie says that the "only thing good about living in that home were knowing Harmon. It didn't take me any time to figure out that Patsy and Pete had no use for either of us 'cept to boss us around and make our lives miserable" (p. 2). Harmon, Janie's foster brother, becomes her best friend. He shares his most prized possessions with Janie—the ladies: Aretha Franklin, Ella Fitzgerald, Odetta, Sarah Vaughan, Etta James, Billie Holiday, and Roberta Flack. They spend their afternoons listening to the ladies' cassettes on a Fisher Price tape player. Janie discovers that she has a natural talent for singing the blues when she imitates the soulful ladies.

Mama Linda visits Janie once a month. Janie explains, "I always know when the visit were gonna be short, 'cause she'd wear something black and sexy that showed off her boobs. On days when she stayed long, she wore baggy jeans and kept her boobs tucked in. I liked her best on her long visit days, even when we didn't get along" (p. 16). The social worker allows Mama Linda to take Janie for a weekend extended visit, so the well-intending mother takes Janie to a nearby hotel. As soon as she unlocks the door to the hotel room, Mama Linda asks Janie to sing for her. Things quickly turn sour when Janie says, "I cain't," and Janie endures another verbal assault all the way back to Patsy and Pete's.

Janie experiences more emotional pain when a wealthy family adopts Harmon. To comfort her in his absence, Harmon gives Janie his treasured music collection. One lonely afternoon, Janie decides to rename herself Leshaya. While riding the school bus home, she rehearses how she will introduce her new name to her foster parents. As she steps off the school bus, she sees someone she hasn't seen in a long while; Mama Linda is hiding in the bushes. Mama Linda kidnaps her and trades her to a drug-dealing couple for a fix.

Although Leshaya knows that she has been kidnapped, she doesn't mind because these new parents have a clean house. Mama Shell and Mitch have plenty of money to buy Leshaya new clothes and whatever else she wants. Leshaya is forced to leave her new home after Mama Shell and Mitch are arrested. She finds Harmon at his adopted parents' home. Mr. and Mrs. James invite Leshaya to stay the night, but she informs them that she will be living with them. When they ask her about what her parents will say about this Leshaya explains:

> They ain't my real parents, first of all, and second of all, they in jail. Maybe they in jail for kidnappin' me, and maybe they in jail for dealin' drugs. But anyways, they in jail, and my Mama Linda put them there. She said yesterday that she were gonna pay Daddy Mitch back 'cause he wouldn't hand her over no heroin, and she way addicted to heroin. She so addicted, she traded me off for it. (p. 81)

Leshaya causes trouble while she stays with the James family. She steals jewelry and clothes from Mrs. James and picks fights with Harmon. While Harmon has grown and changed, Leshaya has remained the same.

Leshaya convinces an older boy she meets at choir practice to take her to Muscle Shoals, Alabama, to meet Etta James. Jaz drives his 13-year-old date to the small town where Etta James is known to record her music. They meet some local musicians and decide to spend the evening jamming with them since Etta is not in town at the time. Jaz and Leshaya stay up all night singing, dancing, drinking alcohol, and using drugs with their new musician friends. Leshaya ends her night inebriated on the bathroom floor with Jaz, "He come down on top of me, and I stopped screaming. And I wanted what he give me, every bit of it" (p. 140).

Nine months later, Leshaya gives birth to a baby girl while she is living at a new foster home. The social worker has told her that she must give up her baby for adoption. Leshaya, however, refuses to allow her child to experience the brutality of living in a foster home. She sneaks out of the doctor's clinic with her day-old baby girl and takes a taxi to Harmon's house. There, she introduces Harmon to "his daughter." Harmon, in a state of shock, calls a taxi for Leshaya and tells her that he wants her out of his sight; she has caused him more than enough grief.

The taxi driver drops her off at a Holiday Inn. She is weak from just having given birth and barely makes it up to her hotel room. All that she has with her is a baby bag stuffed with ten thousand dollars she took from her former drug-dealing parents and the clothes on her back. She is bleeding heavily, in severe pain, and suffering from a high fever and the chills. The hotel maid cares for Leshaya and takes her to her mother's house. While recovering, Leshaya falls in love with the maid's brother, Cliff, who becomes her boyfriend and manager. They decide to live together, Cliff introduces her to a band, and they "got music screaming against the walls and windows, and crowds of people stuffed in on top of one another, bumpin' and grindin', poppin' and smokin', and whatever fell to the floor, we was down on our knees, licking it up like we was dogs" (p. 180). Cliff and Leshaya's relationship does not last very long. When Cliff professes his love to her, Leshaya distances herself from him. She explains to Cliff, "Love is knowin' my soul, knowin' me deep down to my soul and lovin' all the dark corners of it. Ain't nobody ever gonna love that, cause ain't no love there, not for you. Ain't no love for you in my soul" (p. 184). Leshaya never sees Cliff again.

On Leshaya's 16th birthday, she learns that she will be recording a song at a studio in Muscle Shoals. A record producer heard her band perform while they were on tour in Mississippi. The record producer is interested in promoting Leshaya but not the rest of the band. Once she signs a contract with the music producer, he places her with some classically trained, college-educated musicians. The new band is initially outraged by having to work with a singer who cannot read music, but they overlook her lack of formal qualifications once they hear the profitable possibilities of the new talented vocalist. Paul, the keyboardist who is most offended by her, allows Leshaya to stay at his apartment after they complete their tour. He attempts to teach her how to read music by leaving beginning music theory books out for her while he is at work. Leshaya is not the most grateful guest and becomes upset when Paul entertains a female guest for the weekend. She retaliates by inviting Paul's best friend, Jed, for an evening of fun.

Jed offers Leshaya tranquilizers but she does not accept, only agreeing to drink with him instead. Jed overdoses from the combination of tranquilizers and alcohol and dies in his best friend's bed. In his grief, Paul blames Leshaya for the death, but she will not accept this guilt. She tells him, "I didn't kill nobody! He were your best friend, so why didn't you help him? Why did you let him go on all his binges? Why didn't you get him to a rehab place or something if you cared so much?" (p. 237). Paul's response to Leshaya's retaliation is cutting: "You know, you act like you're the only one. Like the whole world is against just you. Just because your life's been tough doesn't mean you're excused from being responsible. Like it or not, you do live in society" (p. 238).

Leshaya leaves Paul's apartment after she is kicked out and finds her mother dying of AIDS. Mrs. Trane, her grandmother's friend, is caring for Mama Linda in a beach house that Mama Linda inherited from her parents. Mrs. Trane forces Leshaya and her mother to reunite. When Mama Linda needs attention, she sends Leshaya into the room against her will. She even locks Leshaya in the room with her dying mother until she cooperates. Leshaya doesn't realize the significance of Mrs. Trane's actions until after her mother's death. Leshaya sets out to reclaim her own daughter so that she can raise her in the beach estate that she has recently inherited. When Leshaya looks into the window of Harmon's house and sees a bright, happy toddler interacting with a loving family, she is moved for the first time in her life. Readers realize that Leshaya has grown when she decides not to take her biological daughter from her loving adopted family.

FACTS ABOUT EMOTIONAL ABUSE AND HOW THEY RELATE TO LESHAYA

Leshaya's first memory of drowning and being abandoned by her mother is an example of emotional abuse. Mama Linda's presence and lack of presence cause Leshaya distress and pain. Leshaya's childhood is deprived of emotional stimulation and responsiveness. Severe emotional abuse occurs when

> actions that inflict emotional harm are performed with malicious intent. The parent is aware that the actions may cause emotional distress and yet the parent continues. Alternatively, the parent may be unable, because of his or her own psychiatric problems, to control his or her actions and thus the malicious intent standard may be impossible to meet. However, in all of these cases the severity warrants legal reporting and removal of the child should be considered. (Hamarman & Bernet, 2000, p. 930)

Although Mama Linda might not have had malicious intent to hurt her daughter when Leshaya almost drowned, due to the fact that she was under the influence of narcotics, she still does damage to her child. As a result, Mama Linda does not have legal custody of Leshaya for the majority of Leshaya's childhood. Mama Linda's visits and lack of visits, combined with the inadequate foster care situation, inhibit Leshaya's emotional development.

Mama Linda's addiction has completely taken over her life and her relationship with her daughter. Researchers explain, "Numerous studies have reported that maternal affective or substance abuse disorders are related to parent-child interactions marked by verbal aggression directed toward children and decreased emotional nurturance" (Kaplan, Pelcovitz, & Labruna, 1999, p. 1219). Mama Linda tells Leshaya that she can call her when she wants to talk in between their visits, but she is never there to answer the phone; she never attempts to call Leshaya at the foster home. Leshaya can predict the length of her mother's visit by the type of clothes the woman wears. Mama Linda exhibits rejecting behavior when she immediately takes Leshaya back to her foster home simply because Leshaya doesn't sing for her. This tirade just happens to occur at the beginning of their extended weekend visit. Using drugs is far more important to Leshaya's mother than spending time with her daughter. Mama Linda happily trades Leshaya for heroin, the drugs being worth more to her than her own daughter.

Leshaya's inability to form relationships and get along with others is a result of her childhood. "There is evidence that the interpersonal problems of maltreated children are related to the difficulty in understanding appropriate affective responses to interpersonal situations and to limited social problem-solving skills" (Kaplan, Pelcovitz, & Labruna, 1999, p. 1216). Harmon is one of Leshaya's only friends throughout her life, but she even has difficulty having a relationship with him. When she visits him at his new home, she has angry outbursts. She is jealous of the love and attention he receives from his new parents. Instead of trying to be a polite and respectful guest in Harmon's home so that she, too, can win the affection of Mr. and Mrs. James, she throws temper tantrums and even steals from the generous family. Mrs. James gives Leshaya numerous chances to confess, but she refuses each time. The Jameses finally decide to make Leshaya leave their household for the sake of their own family dynamic. Although therapists do not have the ability to erase Leshaya's past, they do have the ability to help Leshaya finds ways to build positive relationships with other people and to live a productive life.

A GUIDANCE COUNSELOR'S RESPONSE TO JANIE'S SITUATION

Question: If Leshaya were to come in and see you for counseling, what would be some of your goals for your first sessions?

Counselor: If Leshaya [Janie] were one of my students, one of the first things I would do is establish some kind of trust with her because she has been shuffled around so much; Janie has no roots. Attachments are very difficult for her, so there has to be some sort of level of trust established before anything meaningful can occur. I doubt this will be an easy thing to do.

Question: How will you go about establishing that trust?

Counselor: To establish this trust I would give Janie an environment in which she feels comfortable, an environment that is not threatening. I would allow her to speak openly and freely without criticizing her and constantly reinforce the fact that I am here for her, just to listen. I would always have positive comments to make to Janie and reward the small successes.

Question: After establishing trust, what would be your next goal?

Counselor: The first main goal will be to let Janie know that I am her advocate. My job is to help her in any way that I can, to be there for her as her counselor.

Question: It seems that Leshaya is so maladapted throughout the book. Is there any hope for someone like her?

Counselor: It is true that Janie has never had a constant adult figure show her the right thing, and she is not comfortable with talking about her emotions with anyone. Instead, she puts on a show and pretends that nothing bothers her. Deep down inside, her life situation does bother her, and she really does care, but she doesn't know how to express that feeling. It would be my job to get her to admit and say, "I really do care about me; I really don't want to be just like my mother." Toward the end of the book she starts to realize that she is following in her mother's footsteps, and it is a place that she does not want to be.

Question: Janie has some positive habits such as singing, but she also has formed many maladaptive habits such as drinking and using drugs. What do you think about this?

Counselor: As I mentioned earlier, Janie has never had a positive adult figure show her how to do the right things on a consistent basis. She does not know those alternative behaviors. It is much easier for her to go inside herself and do her singing because that is where her comfort zone is. Her comfort zone is totally within herself. Her use of drugs and alcohol involve interactions with other people.

Question: Harmon is Leshaya's best friend when she is a small child. What do you think about her jealous and rude behavior toward him when she finds him at his new home?

Counselor: When she goes back to see him he is not the same person, probably because of the positive influence of his adoptive parents. Harmon is a member of a family where education is valued, where he is loved every day, and he receives constant support, so he can feel secure. Leshaya, on the other hand, is still living a life on the run. Janie has basically stayed the same, and that realization has to hit her on some level. Even though in her heart she is really happy for Harmon, she cannot accept it. She asks herself, "Why did he get so lucky and get out, and I didn't?" She is very jealous, but of course she can not come out and admit it. She thought that they would continue with the same level of closeness that they once shared, but Harmon has grown up and apart from her.

Question: Leshaya seems to lack a conscience and does not see the consequences of her actions. Can you help someone like her?

Counselor: Janie hasn't developed a healthy social consciousness that most people get from living with people who care about them and vice versa. The poor kid never had anyone to teach her basic right and wrong. The social maladjustment that she has experienced is very difficult to overcome. It is difficult to instill a conscience in someone who does not really have one.

All of the things Janie experienced when she went to live with her mom toward the end of the novel, the things that were said and the things that were unsaid, helped her to grow. When Janie leaves to get her baby and sees little Etta through the window, that's when I knew she had turned a corner. Although Janie selfishly wants her baby, she realizes that it is not the best thing for Etta. It is at this point where I knew she was going to be okay because she could think of another's needs over her own. She would have taken Etta had she not learned and grown from living with Mama Linda. Nonetheless, she will definitely need help to keep her going in the right direction. It is very easy to slip back into what is familiar, one's comfort zone. For Leshaya, it may be using drugs. It is much easier to go back to what one knows than it is to make that corner and keep going in the proper direction.

Question: What kinds of activities would you suggest for Leshaya?

Counselor: I would highly recommend that she keep a journal and think that she would need to continue to get positive reinforcement about the decisions she is making. Whether or not she does something in a peer group, Janie needs an adult mentor to continue to reinforce good behaviors. Janie is starting to make good decisions, but she is still a child. Even when she turns 18 or an age that defines her as an adult, she is still going to be behind in concepts that she forms in her mind. She will need help for a long time. She is not just going to stand up one day by herself and say, "I am fixed." She is still going to have to face the demons of her childhood, and she will need help to do that.

Question: Would you suggest reading adolescent literature that deals with emotional abuse to Leshaya?

Counselor: Yes, definitely. Adolescent literature that deals with these issues is very helpful because it lets kids know that they are not isolated in their problems. They are not the only ones who are going through something traumatic. Even though the situation may not be exactly the same—no two situations are exactly the same—there may be similarities. If there were a forum for kids to talk about the books, that would be even better. Getting kids to talk about problems through book discussions is very helpful.

CONCLUSION

Leshaya finds solace in self-expression. She is able to express her thoughts, emotions, pain, and moods with her strong singing voice. Although Leshaya has not always had someone to guide her to make positive choices with her life, she has been fortunate enough to have an exceptional singing voice. Her songs and love for music comfort her throughout her childhood, accompany her when she is lonely, and guide her through the darkness of her pain. Adolescents experiencing any kind of emotional trauma will benefit from self-expression.

Odierna suggests self-expression in the form of journaling for Leshaya and for other students who have suffered through emotional abuse. The activity of expressing one's feelings on paper is known to be therapeutic for anyone at any age. Odierna also suggests that adolescents read literature that deals with issues that are pertinent to troubled teenagers. Troubled adolescents can be empowered by reading about conflicts that echo their own struggles. Odierna comments that a forum where teenagers can talk to one another about literature is very helpful. Reading adolescent literature is a key that can unlock the door of communication with emotionally distressed teens.

Teachers can provide the place and the safe environment for teenagers to discuss the ramifications of emotional abuse through literature. Whether or not the students have experienced this form of abuse, they will learn how to empathize with a character and have the empowering experience of expressing their thoughts while others listen. Self-expression in the form of music, artwork, writing, and reading is therapeutic for everyone, especially those who are experiencing emotional trauma.

Teacher's Note

The book that I wrote about, *Born Blue,* has greatly helped an at-risk ninth-grade student in my class this year. Being an adopted child dealing with confused feelings of rejection, my student was able to identify with the protagonist of the novel. Instead of indulging her pain in risky behavior, she is now looking for healthy ways to work through her difficult emotions.

REFERENCES

Hamarman, Stephanie, & Bernet, William. (2000). Evaluating and reporting emotional abuse in children: Parent-based, action-based focus aids in clinical decision-making. *Journal of the American Academy of Child and Adolescent Psychiatry, 39,* 928–930.

Kaplan, Sandra J., Pelcovitz, David, & Labruna, Victor. (1999). Child and adolescent abuse and neglect research: A review of the past 10 years. Part I: Physical and emotional abuse and neglect. *Journal of the American Academy of Child and Adolescent Psychiatry, 38,* 1214–1222.

Nolan, Han. (2001). *Born blue.* New York: Harcourt.

CHAPTER 5

Without Witches and Wizards: Surviving Emotional Abuse and Neglect through Journaling on James Deem's *3 NBs of Julian Drew*

Nicole Schaefer-Farrell and Eileen Kennedy

INTRODUCTION

I finally caved. After a semester of emotionally challenging reading in the area of young adult (YA) literature for at-risk youth, I gave into the leagues of friends, family, and students who had been reacting with varying degrees of shock, disbelief, and disdain that I had not read any *Harry Potter* books. I purchased the first in the series and then stared at it sitting on my coffee table for a week. (As an aside, I'm beginning to relate to my students' exasperated pleas that they have no time to read anything for pleasure.) Finally, one Monday night I ignored the loads of laundry waiting to be washed, I switched off CNN (since September 11 it has been a constant background companion), and I set aside student assignments to be graded and assignments due for my own graduate classes. With excitement and a little trepidation that I was about to read a book that would cost me public humiliation if I didn't join the rabid Potter fans after finishing, I sat down to read.

I could tell that I liked such decadent pleasure reading from the first chapter. It was an easy read, fun and light. And then, in chapter 2, I was flabbergasted to discover that Harry Potter might be a wizard destined for great things but is also an emotionally abused and neglected little boy, at the hands of his aunt and uncle caretakers. The book describes his cupboard under the stairs where Harry is forced to live with spiders as companions. Not a line of dialogue passes without his aunt or uncle criticizing or chastising him, and there is an obviously abusive scene where they discuss how they will get rid of Harry for the day so as to not spoil their biological son's birthday celebrations. "I suppose we could take him to the zoo...and leave him in the car," his aunt muses (Rowling, 1997, p. 28).

Maybe I'm more sensitive to abuse now after taking an intensive course in adolescent literature focusing on abuse issues, but I couldn't help but raise an eyebrow that no fans of the *Harry Potter* series had ever landed upon the issue of their beloved Harry as an abused child. Indeed, they wouldn't have to speculate for long on Harry's well-being. The issue of abuse is quickly forgotten amid fantastical adventures and humorous mishaps once Harry is recognized as the famous wizard that could save the magic world from evil. But this chapter isn't about how magic saves children from abuse, despite the long-winded introduction. It's about the insidious nature of emotional abuse and neglect. It will focus on the journey of a rather "normal" boy who shares one abusive chapter with Harry Potter but does not have magic as an escape to fill in the rest of his story. Julian Drew writes from his locked GB (garage bedroom) in three coded journals that stand testament to the monumental struggles facing an emotionally abused teenager.

ORGANIZATION

In this chapter, I will provide a key for some of Julian's code along with a synopsis of the three notebooks that make up the novel. Dr. Eileen Kennedy will then offer a clinical perspective of Julian as well as describe how reading and writing are tools that can be used in clinical therapy for the abused. I will conclude with the definition of emotional abuse, include a list of indicators of such abuse, and stress the role of the educator in identifying and reporting emotional abuse.

SYNOPSIS OF THE *3 NBS OF JULIAN DREW* BY JAMES M. DEEM

Fifteen-year-old Julian Drew keeps a journal that recounts the emotional and physical abuse he receives at home at the hands of 543 (she, "stepnother" or step-not-her) and 43 (he, his biological father). Julian writes to his deceased mother using a strange form of code to protect the information he writes. His obsessive counting of the bricks that make up his locked "GB" (garage bedroom) and the shame of using a "P can" mark the quiet desolation that this severely neglected child suffers. When a teacher does not believe the severity of his problem and despite what could be paralyzing feelings of wanting to "KI77" (kill), Julian runs away to his childhood town in an attempt to travel back in time to see his mother; the memory of her love is Julian's primary source of strength. Alone and free from the tyrannical abuse of his demented stepmother, Julian is finally able to face his past in order to survive the present.

At first difficult to follow because of the chaotic code of the severely abused, the book leads the reader to appreciate the raw intensity that code lends to the action of the novel. At once frustrating and terrible, the "NBs" (notebooks) provide a link into the mind of a child struggling to survive emotional abuse and neglect. The ending leaves room for a variety of conclusions with only the understanding that Julian is going to begin the healing process. A brief explanation of the code Julian uses as he writes in his notebooks is in order.

Dates and Times

Each journal entry is labeled with the date and time. For example, TN8, 432WP translates as Tuesday, November 8, 4:32 P.M. The first letter is the day of the week, the second letter the month, followed by the date. Using his mother's wristwatch, the example time is 4:32 "Watch" time in the P.M. Note that the P is for evenings, and when A is used it is in the morning. When the watch breaks, Julian begins referring to time of day as RP or RA, his bedside radio time.

Numbers as Letters

0 replaces O
1 replaces I
3 replaces E
4 replaces H
5 replaces S
7 replaces L
9 replaces P

Letters and Numbers Stand for Words

D often stands for Day or for Die
4 often stands for For
M often stands for Mad
GB stands for Garage Bedroom
2 often stands for To

Abbreviations

Abbreviations are numerous and are interpreted based on the context. Here is a passage that highlights the intense emotions expressed through Julian's coded journals and serves as a sample of his early expressive writing:

My hand is going 2 WRITE.

My hand IS going 2 write.

My hand is going 2 write U if it K1775 me.

No 1 can stop me.

43 can't stop me.

543 can't stop me.

There are 2 many things 2 write.

2 many. (Deem, 1994, p. 5)

NB #1: THE IMI55U NB

The novel opens with rampant code and abbreviation. Some lines are only one word in length. Julian describes a recurring dream involving "U" (his biological mother) and lapses heavily into debate over how he is going to write in the notebook without getting caught. Julian lists the events that have led up to the moment he is writing to "U" as a series of "things." The reader learns that it has been a little over three years since Julian moved with his new stepmother ("step-not-her" or 543) and father (43) from West Virginia to Tucson, Arizona. He has a biological sister named Emma who is young enough to be sitting in a car seat. There is a mention of two step-sisters—Roxie and Rebecca—and his stepbrother, Roger, who seems to be close to his age.

At this point his age is unclear, but Julian describes his lack of friends and details the effect that changing middle and high schools has had upon him: "They weren't hi schools, they were bye schools" (Deem, 1994, p. 9). Julian gives a painfully detailed description about his living conditions inside a locked garage bedroom—from a stark description of his plywood bed to an eerie counting method for the number of bricks that line the room, wooden beams across the ceiling, and spiders and lizards that share his living space. He expresses his pleasure in being locked in his room because it offers security from his abusive stepmother and father. The section ends with him finding a possible outlet of expression through writings for his curious but unassuming English teacher and a newfound friendship with Susan, a neighbor and classmate from school.

NB #2: THE JUNKMAN IN MCMOP LAND NB

The writing is less coded now but more urgent in tone. This section opens with Julian recounting what happens when his father finds the first notebook. There is a marked change in Julian's voice as he strikes through 4AT3 and writes the word HATE when describing his father. Julian thinks more and more about trusting his English teacher with what is going on but still cannot talk out loud about anything. His teacher encourages him to write in a journal even if he doesn't ever show her what he is writing. Julian celebrates his 16th birthday by rummaging through old papers and boxes while the rest of the family is away. He also makes an amazing declaration and moves from addressing his mother as "U" and begins addressing the journal entries to her by name.

Julian also gets a job at the local McDonald's and begins saving money to get his own food to eat. In the meantime, his relationship with his new friend, Susan, has become an outlet for talking out loud about some of the issues Julian is facing. He has to speak in code, but Susan patiently allows him to share what he can with her. Interspersed throughout this notebook are strange and bizarre dream sequences involving memories of his biological mother. The section ends with a terrible accident involving Julian's English teacher's son. Because of her own pain, she shuts Julian out and is no longer receptive to his visits or writings. Julian is desperate and feels that now there is no one with any kind of power who can help him.

NB #3: THE 9OJ(D) NB

The writing reaches an almost frantic pace but is more complete in thought and more complex in terms of structure. Abbreviations are still used but sparingly. It is apparent that Julian has a plan and is set on enacting it. The reader is apprehensive in the suspense of not knowing what Julian's desperation will lead him to do. He catches rides from Arizona back to West Virginia with only his savings from McDonald's and the clothes on his back. Julian's voice is triumphant that he has escaped his stepmother and father. Fear enters his voice only when he has to explain what he is doing when he arrives at his childhood home. He wants to stay the night with the new residents, whom he had met briefly before moving years earlier. It is clear now that Julian has traveled back to his hometown to reconnect with his deceased mother.

The earlier dream episodes and fascination with a certain book are now evidently linked explicitly with his mother's past. Julian gets an apartment in the same building in which his mother had once lived. As Julian begins to form his mother's memories into his own reality—buying a vase that he remembers from childhood from an antique store, finding a letter that his mother had written 20 years earlier as she contemplated marriage with Julian's father, and discovering his mother's favorite book—it is sadly evident that Julian is slipping into an alternative reality in which he believes he can somehow align all the evidence in order to transport him back in time to be with his mother. He visits her gravesite and makes all the final arrangements to leave reality to find her.

Understanding that Julian is acting out plans of suicide devastates the reader. Finally, after days of fasting and waiting for a magical moment to transport him back in time, Julian slips into a coma-like state. In his euphoria, he thinks he sees his mother reaching for him, but it turns out that Susan has managed to piece together his whereabouts and has come to him instead. The book does not end with rescue, redemption, and happily ever afters but somberly informs the reader that Julian is fully aware of the extent of his abusive situation and that he will seek healing.

DIAGNOSTIC IMPRESSION AND CLINICAL CONSIDERATIONS

Julian Drew, Age 16, November 26th

Julian is dealing with the desperate grief of the loss of his mother, made precipitously worse by the inhumane trauma of neglect and emotional abuse at the hands of his father and stepmother. Within his numbers-into-words writing, Julian tells us early on that his mother Jenny died when he was 11 years old, and that within six months, his father married a seriously disturbed woman with children of her own. The woman becomes Julian's nemesis, beginning one week after the wedding when he is locked in his room all night, the first of innumerable times, for his refusal to eat Brussels sprouts. The action is extreme as she ties his doorknob to the banister to ensure that Julian cannot escape.

The family leaves Julian's home in West Virginia soon after this incident, and in three and one-half years in Arizona live in five different homes. Julian attends four different junior high schools and is in his second high school as a sophomore when we meet him. His father's work includes travel every other week, and his stepmother is especially insidious when his father is away. Her specialty is maltreatment involving clothing and especially food, such that Julian, at almost 5 feet 10 inches, weighs only 115 pounds. She infuriates him by regularly calling him "Julie-Ann" and by treating all the other children with reasonable care and kindness.

Julian's problems are very serious and might never have come to light without the writing he did for his English teacher. His symptoms include social withdrawal, interrupted sleep, and emotional numbing as evidenced by his use of code for words that are too emotionally laden for him to bear. He tends to retreat into a safer mental and emotional world, as seen in his fantasy of living better on an alien planet and in his dreams of running away. He has episodes of paranoia, as in the episode when he perceives a glass of apple juice as a glass of urine. He is grief-stricken and plainly overwhelmed, yet he is also resourceful. Julian has a resolute ability to take care of himself as best he can in a rather survivalist mode, and he eventually begins tentative relationships with an adult and a peer.

Children like Julian are difficult to identify because until they speak up, there are no visual signs of distress. Families in which abuse occurs are notoriously closed to letting outsiders in. Psychological care for children like Julian is essential, and someone must advocate for proper safety and support with extended systems as necessary. In cases like Julian's, a therapist has to reeducate such children about their worth, to help them understand their harsh experiences within a developmentally appropriate context, to teach them strategies for coping and asking for help, and to develop active roles in relationships that can be safe and meaningful.

READING AND WRITING IN THERAPY

Bibliotherapy, the practice of assigning recommended reading to a client, is a well-established adjunctive strategy within the process of psychological therapy. This is as true in the care of school-age and adolescent clients as it is in adults who are in therapy. Often, the most helpful books are those that offer a first-person account, whether fiction or a true-life story, that parallels the issues inherent in a person's therapy. Experienced clinicians, or teachers, cull the best-written books across a range of topics and may offer selected titles to clients or students with specific areas of concern.

Why is bibliotherapy helpful? First, reading about another person who has problems similar to one's own decreases one's sense of isolation. Many times, children and teens with challenging life situations or psychological problems do not know of others with similar difficulties, and it is very helpful to the children or teens to know that they are not alone. Second, reading about a similar situation has the potential to increase self-understanding. It is always illustrative to help children or teens understand which aspects of their own behavior, thoughts, or feelings are caused by their illness or problems or disorders. Awareness of similar problems through literature can help sharpen that picture. Discussions about how the book's protagonist is similar to and different from the child or teen in therapy can be especially fruitful in the effort to increase self-knowledge. Finally, reading in therapy is also extremely useful as the reader learns of the resolution or self-management strategies employed by the protagonist. These strategies often can be used as effective models for creating change.

The role of writing in therapy is especially helpful when working with children and adolescents who, like Julian Drew, have a history of being traumatized. This is true for several reasons. Keeping a journal helps the writer maintain a safe place as well as safe pace of self-disclosure. This is clearly seen in *3 NBs of Julian Drew,* as Julian begins with highly coded language that becomes less so as his issues emerge and his intense feelings rise to the surface.

Children and adolescents with histories of trauma can be characterized as being markedly avoidant of revealing the events, circumstances, places, people, or sensory conditions associated with the trauma. Writing in the context of therapy, over a period of time, with the therapist integrating entries into the therapy work, can help a child more fully integrate the experience of the trauma in order to put it into its proper, less overwhelming place in the life of the child.

Similarly, the use of writing in therapy helps the traumatized child or teen move gradually from indirect expression of issues to more direct communication with others. We see this in the case of Julian Drew. Though he is not in therapy in the book, note that his initial writing is only for himself, thoroughly protected and vigorously hidden from others. Over time, very slowly, he comes to trust two others sufficiently to begin dealing with them with increasingly direct interactions and disclosure about himself.

DEFINING AND IDENTIFYING EMOTIONAL ABUSE

According to Prevent Child Abuse America, emotional abuse can involve words, actions, and indifference along with rejecting or dominating the individual (Prevent Child Abuse America, 2001, p. 1). Parents who inflict emotional abuse often repeatedly deny life experiences, discount the child, invalidate feelings, and displace blame for adult and family problems (Keith-Oaks, 1990). Every expert worries about the lack of information available to the general public and how training in public schools often focuses on physical and sexual abuse as prevalent forms of which to be wary. The result is an astonishingly low percentage of substantiated emotional abuse cases (Romeo, 2000) and the misconception that physical and sexual abuse are more prevalent than emotional abuse.

Imagine reading a journal entry like the following:

> Sometimes my brain is so unhappy it doesn't know what 2 do at all. My body sits in my GB + my brain wishes me D. Would the police investigate? My brain says no. THEY don't leave marks. THEY don't B me w/cigarettes, THEY don't S me in the bathtub with boiling water, H me w/electric cord, or T me in a plastic bag. Those kids are in the newspaper. But all you have 2 do is look at my face + U can see it. My eyes see it when they look at myself in the mirror. It is hard 2 look 4 long. (Deem, 1994, pp. 25–26)

The educator's role in reporting emotional abuse is crucial. This type of abuse is more difficult to detect, however, because the abuse is considered internal. Because emotional abuse is often learned and passed from generation to generation, developing more and more angry, hostile adults, and because victims often enter into abusive relationships in adolescence and adulthood, resulting in tragic consequences in many situations, reporting emotional abuse is paramount to a child's or adolescent's present and future well-being.

Clinical psychologist Dr. Felicia F. Romeo outlines the passive and aggressive indicators for educators to watch for in a recent issue of the *Journal of Instructional Psychology*. Along with grades and achievement far below academic ability, the following is a compilation of those indicators:

Passive Indicators

- Difficulty in forming relationships
- Inability to relate to and bond with other children
- Lack of self-confidence and emotion
- Extreme shyness
- Being victimized and exploited by other children
- Fatigue and listlessness
- Helplessness and hopelessness
- Feelings of inadequacy
- Pessimism
- Difficulty in concentrating on school activities
- Self-denial

- Inability to engage in and enjoy pleasurable activities
- Self-injury—hair pulling and twisting, nail biting, accident proneness
- Self-deprecating remarks, such as "stupid," "no good," and so on

Aggressive Indicators

- Bullying and hostility toward others
- Intimidating and threatening
- Defiance
- Ridiculing others
- Cruelty to other children or animals
- Destruction of property and fire setting
- Repeated truancy or tardiness
- Reluctance to go home
- Constant attention seeking and hyperactive behavior

Educators have the opportunity to observe student behavior and have the legal and ethical responsibility to report suspected abuse of all forms. Because emotional abuse often leaves no marks, as Julian discussed in the journal entry quoted earlier, educators must look beyond the traditional indicators of physical and sexual abuse to notice abnormal behaviors.

CONCLUSION

Whether an educator chooses to read YA literature for emotionally abused youth for personal growth and education or for classroom study, it is clear that education needs literature and training involving this much understudied area of abuse. Julian Drew presents a sometimes harsh, sometimes poignant rendering of the journey of an emotionally abused youth seeking help. There are no magic ogres to come rescue him, and he can't fly away from his problems on a broom. Harry Potter and his magic certainly appeal to the masses, but his abuse survival story is not based in reality. *3 NBs of Julian Drew* by James M. Deem offers a perspective into the mind of an emotionally abused adolescent and the coping mechanisms that children develop as a result of severe emotional abuse and neglect. For a more detailed breakdown of the code used, teacher's guide, and author commentary about the novel, visit the author's Web site, "A Narrator Named Julian Drew" at http://www.jamesmdeem.com/juliandrew.main.htm (Deem, 2001).

REFERENCES

Deem, James M. (1994). *3 NBs of Julian Drew.* New York: Harper Tempest.

Deem, James M. (2001). *A narrator named Julian Drew.* Retrieved from http://www.jamesmdeem.com/juliandrew.main.htm

Keith-Oaks, Judy. (1990, September/October). Emotional abuse: Destruction of the spirit and the sense of self. *Clearing House, 64* (1), 31–35.

Prevent Child Abuse America. (2001). *Emotional child abuse.* Retrieved from http://www.preventchildabuse.org

Romeo, Felicia F. (2000). The educator's role in reporting the emotional abuse of children. *Journal of Instructional Psychology, 27* (3), 183–187.

Rowling, J.K. (1997). *Harry Potter and the sorcerer's stone.* New York: Scholastic.

Part III

Physical Abuse

Definitions, indicators, and statistics on physical abuse have been compiled by the sources listed.

DEFINITION OF PHYSICAL ABUSE

Physical abuse, which makes up 22% of all substantiated cases of child abuse, is the most visible form of abuse and may be defined as any act that results in a nonaccidental trauma, harm, or physical injury. Most physical abuse incidents occur when a parent strikes, shakes, or throws a child out of anger or frustration. Inflicted physical injury most often represents unreasonable, severe corporal punishment or unjustifiable punishment. http://www.preventchildabuse.com/physical.htm

Physical abuse occurs when a person responsible for a child's or an adolescent's welfare causes physical injury or harm to the child. Examples of abusive treatment of children include, but are not limited to, hitting a child with an object, kicking, burning, scalding, punching, and threatening or attacking with weapons. http://www.aacap.org/about/glossary/Physical. htm (American Academy of Child and Adolescent Psychiatry, 1997)

The legal definition of battery is touching someone in a rude or insolent manner. If it hurts you and if you're unwilling, touching you is a crime. Following are some signs that may signal the onset of physical abuse in an intimate relationship: threats of violence, breaking or striking objects, any force during an argument, and past battering. http://www.bloomington.in. us/~mwhouse/physicalabuse.htm (Middle Way House, 2000)

When an adult leaves a bruise or mark on a child or teenager, it is considered physical abuse. Spanking isn't against the law; however, if a bruise or mark is left, it *is* child abuse. http://www.childhelpusa.org/child/ kids_only.htm

Public recognition of physical abuse has yet to reach the same level as public knowledge of sexual abuse. Unless the public is made aware of the nature of child physical abuse cases, prosecution and conviction will remain difficult. Jurors, for example, tend to believe that parents or care-takers do not intentionally harm their children. They tend to see the injuries as the accidental result of discipline that parents can, and often should, impose. http://www.ncjrs.org/txtfiles/pcphysab.txt (Prosecuting Child Abuse Cases: Lessons Learned from the San Diego Experience, 1995)

An eight-year-old boy defines child abuse this way: "That's when they hit you and make you bleed and you can't stop crying and they tell you they'll kill you next time because you don't deserve to live." http://www.pasa.org/resources (Positive Attitudes Solutions and Actions, 1998)

EXTENT OF THE PROBLEM

Physical abuse or severe neglect caused the deaths of an estimated 1,215 children in 1995, according to the survey conducted by the National Committee to Prevent Child Abuse. NCPCA reports that child abuse fatalities increased 39% from 1985 to 1995. http://www.casanet.org/library/ abuse/survey-facts

In 1996, approximately 1 million children were confirmed victims of maltreatment, and 1,185 children died from their injuries. http://www.aafr.org

Physical abuse, which normally takes place when an agitated or angry caregiver physically and intentionally injures a child in his or her charge, manifests itself in 22% of all substantiated cases of child abuse. http://www.preventchildabuse.com/physical.htm (National Exchange Club Foundation, 2000)

According to a study released in March 1999 by Prevent Child Abuse America, formerly the National Committee to Prevent Child Abuse, 3 in 10 Americans have witnessed an adult physically abuse a child, and 2 in 3 Americans have seen an adult emotionally abuse a child; yet nearly half these Americans failed to respond to the incident. http://www.childabuse.com/brandrelease.html

More than two-thirds of all child physical abuse is to children under 3 years old. http://hlthed.uregina.ca/cni/units/9.5/tbabu205.html

Almost 25% of all babies with shaken baby syndrome die, and it is esti-mated that 25%–50% of parents and caretakers aren't aware of the effects of shaking a baby. http://www.preventchildabuse.com/shaken.htm

Each day in the United States more than three children die as a result of physical abuse in the home. Child abuse is reported every 10 seconds on average. www.childhelpus.org

WHO DOES IT

Parents who have many personal or marital problems, are undergoing economic stress, have a history of childhood abuse, are highly moralistic, have a history of drug abuse, are easily upset or frustrated, and/or are fearful of other people are more likely to abuse their children physically. http://www.stopabuse.com

Some indicators of adult behaviors that point to possible child abuse include the following: harsh punishment of the child in public; reference to the child as "difficult, different, or bad"; unconcern about a child's conflicting stories about injuries; defensiveness when asked about the child's health; belief in excessively strong male authority; and extreme religious and/or fundamental beliefs. http://www.project-care.org/child-abuse.html

Parents who were abused as children often become abusers when they punish their own children. Being poor, sick, or on drugs increases the risk of abuse. http://www.aap.org/advocacy/childhealthmonth/ABUSE2.html (American Academy of Pediatrics, 1995).

Twenty-five years after domestic violence became widely recognized as one of America's most deadly and vexing social pathologies, the damage it does to children is being studied as never before. There have been journal articles, conferences, and new laws. But much less has been achieved when it comes to practical help, making certain that children get the counseling and intervention they need in schools, at domestic violence organizations, and from police, prosecutors, judges, and social welfare agencies. In families where adults are violent with each other a couple of times a month, children stand a 50% chance of physical injury. The odds get worse when adult violence is more frequent. http://www.washingtonpost.coe=article&node=&contentld=A36445-2001Jun7 (*The Washington Post*: Online, 2001)

Female parents were identified as the perpetrators of neglect and physical abuse for the highest percentage of child victims. http://www.calib.com/nccanch/prevmnth/stats.htm

Men who batter their wives are likely to assault their children, the severity going hand in hand. http://www.minicava.umn.edu/hart/risks&r.htm (Minnesota Center Against Violence and Abuse, 2001)

Children from homes where domestic violence occurs are physically or sexually abused and/or seriously neglected at a rate 15 times the national average. http://www.aaets.org/arts/art8.htm

According to the U.S. Department of Justice, a parent is the perpetrator in most homicides of children under age five. Data between 1976 and 1997 indicate that 27% of these children were killed by mothers, 27% were killed by fathers, 24% were killed by acquaintances, 6% were killed by other relatives, 3% were killed by strangers, and 12% were killed by perpetrators whose relationship to the child was unknown. http://ican-ncfr.org/MurderedChildren.html

Despite myths about its prevalence among lower-income populations, child abuse occurs throughout all strata of society. Physical abuse does appear more frequently in poor families. Because middle-class and wealthy families are more likely to have their children treated by a sympathetic personal physician who may be less likely to diagnose and report injuries as child abuse, numbers reported may be biased. Even with such reporting bias, however, poverty seems strongly linked to abuse. www.findarticles.com (*Gale Encyclopedia of Psychology*, 2001)

Child abuse is also linked to parental use of alcohol or other drugs. Several studies during the 1970s confirmed that nearly 70% of substantiated cases of abuse were related to alcohol. www.findarticles.com (*Gale Encyclopedia of Psychology*, 2001)

Abusive parents often stay away from other mothers and fathers in the neighborhood, do not take part in school activities, may have a drinking or drug abuse problem, don't want to talk about the child's injuries, or seem nervous when they do. http://www.aap.org/advocacy/childhealthmonth/ABUSE2.HTM (American Academy of Pediatrics, 2001)

Abusive parents might seem unconcerned about their child; seem overwhelmed by their child's needs; take an inordinate amount of time to seek medical attention for their child; fabricate varying, inappropriate, or inadequate explanations for injury to their child; and probably misuse alcohol or drugs. http://www.kidsafe-caps.org/physical.html (Child Abuse Prevention Services, 1999)

Abusive caretakers often conceal children's injuries; do not seem concerned about children's needs; describe children as bad, different, or selfish; have unrealistic expectations; have low self-esteem; abuse alcohol or drugs; are markedly immature; were maltreated as children; and project blame on others. www.capcenter.org/CONTENT (Child Abuse Prevention Center, 2001)

Abusive parents are particularly sensitive to threats to their ability to maintain control over their children. Thus, when their children approach the developmental tasks of the "terrible twos," which involve learning autonomy and beginning control over their environment, their normal behavior is often seen by abusive parents as willfulness that must be controlled. Because abusive parents often have inaccurate ideas about the capabilities of toddlers, normal soiling of clothes that occurs with eating and toileting are seen as deliberate misbehaviors. If the child is punished inconsistently for behaviors that he or she cannot help, the child feels helpless, angry, and confused about how he or she is supposed to respond. With abusive parents as models, the child begins to react aggressively and with *tantrums* to parental discipline, responses which actually serve to heighten the potential for abuse. It is not surprising that 60% of the major physical injuries inflicted by caregivers occur in children under age 4. http://www. findarticles.com/cf_dls/g2602/0001/260200128/print.jhtml (Published in the *Gale Encyclopedia of Childhood and Adolescence*: Child Abuse, Physical, 1998)

According to the juvenile justice system, exposure to multiple forms of family violence doubles the risk of self-reported youth violence. http://www.ncjrs.org/txtfiles/fs-9421.txt

Hundreds of studies of the effects of television violence on children and teenagers have found that children may become "immune" to the horror of violence; gradually accept violence as a way to solve problems; imitate the violence they observe on television; and identify with certain characters, victims, and/or victimizers. http://www.aacap.org/publications/factsfam/violence.htm

According to the Minnesota Center Against Violence and Abuse, adolescents who make direct statements about committing violence are sending red flags. Verbal statements include talking about harming or killing others, idolizing violent heroes, and providing specific details of how the violence will take place, including who the intended victims are and when and where the violent events are to take place. Writing poems and stories about killing people could also be a warning sign in combination with other indicators. One or more of the following increases the likelihood of acting out the talk: preoccupation with violence and its glorification, possession of weapons, history of bullying or being bullied, psychological vulnerability, participation in a violent gang, history of violence in the families of origin, a sense of entitlement, emotional closing up, antisocial behavior, and abuse of drugs and/or alcohol. http://www.mincava.umn.edu/jgilgun/detect.htm

RECOGNIZING PHYSICALLY ABUSED CHILDREN

Following are the physical indicators of child physical abuse: unexplained bruises, welts, or abrasions in various stages of healing, in clusters

or unusual patterns, or on several different parts of the body; unexplained
burns in the shapes of cigarettes, rope, an iron, or a sock or glove (due to
immersion in hot or boiling water); unexplained cuts to the mouth, lips,
arms, legs, or torso; unexplained skeletal injuries; stiff, swollen joints;
multiple fractures; missing or loosened teeth; human bite marks; bald
spots; and appearance of injuries after school absences, weekends, or
vacations. http://www.pasa.org/resources/ica_physical.html

Children get bumps and bruises over bony areas such as knees, elbows,
and shins when they play. A child who is being physically abused has
injuries on other parts of the body, such as the stomach, cheeks, ears, but-
tocks, mouth, or thighs. Black eyes, human bite marks, and round burns
the size of a cigarette don't come from everyday play. http://www.aap.org/
advocacy/childhealthmonth/ABUSE2.HTM

Following are the behavioral indicators of child physical abuse: avoids
physical contact with others; is apprehensive when other children cry;
wears clothing to purposely conceal injury (long sleeves); refuses to
undress for gym or for required physical exams at school; gives inconsistent versions about the occurrence of injuries, burns, and so on; seems
frightened by parents; is often late or absent from school; comes early to
school and seems reluctant to go home afterward; has difficulty getting
along with others; shows little respect for others; is overly compliant and
withdrawn; gives in readily and allows others to do for him/her without
protest; plays aggressively, often hurting peers; complains of pain upon
movement or contact; has a history of running away from home; and
reports abuse by parents. http://www.safechild.org/childabuse2.htm
(Coalition for Children, Inc., Sherryll Kraizer, Ph.D. and The Levi Company, 2001)

Children who have been physically abused may exhibit any of the following behaviors: fear of adults, parents, and other children who cry;
destructiveness toward themselves or others; extreme mood swings;
delays in learning; short attention span; delays in language; tendencies to
run away from home; delinquent behavior; an ability to fabricate incredible explanations for injuries or an aura of being accident prone; a tendency
to wear clothing inappropriate for the season; and a fear of going home.
http://www.pasa.org/resources/ica-physical.html (PASA, Inc., 1998)

Physical abuse is associated with psychiatric disorders such as post-
traumatic stress disorder, conduct disorder, ADHD, depression, and
impaired social functioning with peers. http://www.surgeongeneral.gov/
library/mentalhealth/chapter3/sec2.html#risk

The most common physical indicators include bite marks, unusual
bruises, lacerations, burns, high incidence of accidents or frequent injuries,

fractures in unusual places, injuries, swellings to face and extremities, and discoloration of skin. http://www.safechild.org/childabuse2.htm (Coalition for Children, Inc., 2001)

Among child injuries consistent with child abuse are bruises and fractures in places on the body not likely to be accidentally injured, bruises shaped like objects, and burns with clear circumferences. http://www.find articles.com/cf_dls/m3225/10_61/62829175/p1/article.jhtml

According to Prevent Child Abuse America (2001), children who are physically abused may be nervous around adults; be watchful, as though preparing for something bad to happen; have difficulty playing; act aggressively toward adults and other children; be unable to concentrate at school; suddenly underachieve—or overachieve—at school; find it difficult to trust other people and make friends; and arrive at school too early or leave after the other children. http://www.preventchildabuse.org/family_community/index.html

Children who have been abused physically might also display a poor self-image, exhibit a need to "act out" sexually, suffer from an inability to form trusting relationships, or abuse drugs and alcohol. http://www. aacap.org/publications/factsfam/chlabus.htm (American Academy of Child and Adolescent Psychiatry—*Child Abuse: The Hidden Bruises—AACAP Facts for Families #5*)

Perpetrators have abused animals in order to frighten their partners and as a form of retaliation or punishment. Children's witnessing both parent and pet abuse may increase their propensity for interpersonal violence and make children's cruelty to animals more likely to emerge as a symptom of their distress. http://www.vachss.com/guest_dispatches/ascione_1.html

Abuse causes more abuse. Children who suffer from physical abuse are likely to inflict injury on animals. http://www.healingspecies.org.html

Cheri Brown, the founder of the Healing Species—an organization that takes rescued dogs into classrooms—discusses the link between animal abuse and violence against children. She encourages all of society to stop turning a blind eye toward "the link" between animal and child/human abuse. http://www.healthyplace.com

A large number of animal cruelty cases also involve some form of family violence. http://www.calib.com/cbexpress/articles.cfm?issue_id= 2001-07&article_id=316

Results of a year-long study showed an extremely high number of intentional animal cruelty cases committed by male teens under the age of 18. Of those cases, a large number also involved some form of family violence: either domestic violence, child abuse, or elder abuse. http://www. hsus.org/firststrike/2001week/fs_2000_report.html

Youth who report homosexual or bisexual romantic attraction are more likely to have been in a fight that resulted in the need for medical treatment, according to a 1999 study that reviewed national data. http://www. hrw.org/reports/2001 (Human Rights Watch, 2001)

In efforts to prevent physical abuse, children need to learn that it is not acceptable for someone to hurt them physically, that punishment that leaves bruises or marks the next day is excessive, and that they need to tell someone if they are being hurt. Children also need to be made aware of who to tell and how to tell it. http://www.safechild.org/Program4htm ("Prevention of Child Abuse," Safe Child Program by the Coalition of Children, Inc., 2001)

RESULTS OF PHYSICAL ABUSE

Shaken baby syndrome occurs most frequently in infants younger than six months old, yet can occur up to the age of three. Resulting injuries can include brain swelling and damage, cerebral palsy, mental retardation, developmental delays, blindness, hearing loss, paralysis, and even death. http://www.preventchildabuse.com/shaken.htm

Children and adolescents who have been abused may suffer from depression, anxiety, low self-esteem, inability to build trusting relationships, alcohol and drug abuse, learning impairments, and conduct disorder. http://www.aacap.org/about/glossary/Physical.htm (American Academy of Child and Adolescent Psychiatry, 1997)

Among behavioral indicators suggesting child physical abuse are avoidance of physical contact with others, apprehension when other children cry, reluctance to go home, lack of respect for others, compliance, aggressiveness, and a history of running away from home. http://www.safechild. org/childabuse2.htm#Family%20or%20Parental%20Indicators

Often the severe emotional damage to abused children does not surface until adolescence or later, when many become abusive parents themselves. Without proper treatment, physically abused children can be damaged for life. Adolescent psychiatrists can help families learn new ways of supporting and communicating with one another. http:www.aacap.org/ web/aacap/publications/factsfam/chldabus.htm (American Academy of Child & Adolescent Psychiatry)

The physical abuse of children causes both immediate and long-term damage, as it impacts the healthy transition of children to adulthood. Apart from the physical damage caused to the child, children who are assaulted or rejected by their parents experience a sense of worthlessness, badness, and self-hatred that forms the nucleus for subsequent self-destructive behavior. http://www.kidshelp.com.au/info9/physabus.htm (Kids Help Line, 2000)

Dissociation is a post-traumatic stress condition consisting of a sort of self-hypnosis by which abused children defend themselves when they can neither avoid being abused nor reveal the secret of the abuse. Extreme dissociation is dysfunctional and can make living successfully impossible. http://www.hc-sc.gc.ca/hppb/familyviolence/pdfs/welfare.pdf

Research strongly suggests that the single most common element in the lives of abusive or violent adults is the experience of having been neglected or abused as children. Consider these two facts: (1) Two out of every three prisoners convicted of first-degree murder report being physically abused as children; and (2) hard-core juvenile delinquents experience a history of severe physical punishment and assault in the home. http://www.ojp.usdoj.gov/ovc/publications/infores/clergy/chld abus.htm

According to *Reason to Hope: A Psychosocial Perspective on Violence and Youth Reason to Hope,* the 1994 report by the American Psychological Association's Commission on Violence and Youth, it is possible to predict from an eight-year-old's aggressive behavior in school how aggressive that child will be in adolescence and adulthood—including whether he or she will exhibit criminal and antisocial behavior. This is why prevention programs that start early in childhood and continue throughout adolescence have the best chance for success. http://www. apa.org/pi/pii/isyouthviolence.html

Some children demonstrate a resiliency, almost from birth, that protects them from becoming violent or that makes them less vulnerable to the effects of violence. Psychological research suggests that resilience can also come from early experiences that counter the negative effects of violence. These experiences include

- Positive role models; exposure to a greater number of positive than negative behaviors
- Development of self-esteem and self-efficacy
- Supportive relationships, including those with teachers and friends
- Sense of hope about the future
- Belief in oneself
- Strong social skills
- Good peer relationships
- A close, trusting bond with a nurturing adult outside the family
- Great empathy and support from the mother or mother figure

- The ability to find refuge and a sense of self-esteem in hobbies and creative pursuits, useful work, and assigned chores
- The sense that one is in control of one's life and can cope with whatever happens. http://www.apa.org/pi/pii/isyouthviolence.html

YOUNG ADULT NOVELS INVOLVING PHYSICAL ABUSE

Throughout the following sources, RL: MS = Reading Level: Middle School and RL: HS = Reading Level: High School.

Byars, Betsy. (1986). *Cracker Jackson.* New York: Puffin Books. 146 pp. (ISBN 0–14–031881–X)

Jackson Hunter was nicknamed "Cracker"—because of his sweetness and surprises—by a former baby-sitter, Alma. Alma stopped baby-sitting Cracker after she got married and had a daughter, Nicole. Cracker didn't remember seeing bruises on Alma before she got married, and suddenly he finds himself in a world unfamiliar to most 11-year-olds. All of the manners his mother had so painstakingly taught him were useless with an intimidating, abusive man like Alma's husband Billy Ray. Cracker tries to stay away from Alma and her problems as his family demands, but when Alma calls crying one day, finally admitting to the physical attacks on her and her infant, he just can't stay uninvolved. After a final ordeal with Billy Ray, Cracker's family understands the severity of the situation and why she needs their help. This winner of the Parents' Choice Award, an IRA-CBC Children's Choice, and ALA Notable Book is interspersed with fond memories of Alma's innocent baby-sitting days when the love between Cracker and Alma developed. RL: MS (physical abuse)

Coman, Carolyn. (1995). *What Jamie Saw.* New York: Puffin Books. 126 pp. (ISBN 0–14–038335–2)

Nine-year-old Jamie worries about things he has no control over, like protecting his mother and baby sister, Nin, from his mother's abusive boyfriend, Van. After they finally do leave his house and face homelessness, Jamie tries hard to keep his mom moving and his little sister safe. Jamie makes plans in case Van finds them. He punches holes in the drawer Nin sleeps in so that his baby sister can still breathe when he slides the drawer into the bureau to hide her. Young children, both those who have experienced abuse and those who have not, can see themselves in Jamie. Their fears can be validated by Jamie's reaction to his fears. In addition, the reaction and help of adults such as Jamie's teacher and his mother's longtime friend, Earl, can help children realize that there are adults who can help people living in fearful and desperate circumstances (a 1996

Newbery Honor Book, an ALA Notable Book, a Booklist Editors' Choice). RL: MS (physical abuse)

Crutcher, Chris. (1990). *Stotan!* New York: Dell Laurel-Leaf. 192 pp. (ISBN: 0–440–97570–0)

Four young men—Nortie, Lion, Jeff, and Walker—are on the high school varsity swim team and are preparing for a week of hell, called Stotan Week, during their Christmas break senior year. Their swim coach has a week of intense training in store for them, but all four boys survive an intense emotional workout as well. They learn that Nortie's mother has endured countless beatings, and so has Nortie while trying to defend her. When his father ends up putting Nortie in the hospital, the guys go to his house to pick up his stuff so that he can stay with Lion. Lion tries to help Nortie's mother get away from the situation, but she returns to the abuse she has grown accustomed to. As the novel closes, the abuse is still going on, but Nortie has managed to find a way out through swimming, his coach, and his band of friends. RL: HS (physical abuse)

Flinn, Alex. (2001). *Breathing Underwater.* New York: HarperCollins. 263 pp. (ISBN: 0–06–029198–2)

The topics of date rape and physical abuse are usually written from the abused person's point of view, but this novel takes the perspective of the abusing male. Nick Andreas, a wealthy and popular teen of Greek descent, is in trouble—legal trouble. The judge sentences Nick to attend Mario Ortega's Family Violence class and requires him to keep a journal, writing at least 500 words per week. Readers are privy to Nick's way of thinking as he chronicles, in his journal, the events that led to his sentence, and also discusses his life in therapy. Nick writes about his relationship with his girlfriend Caitlin, his confusion about what love is, and his obsession with Caitlin's obeying him. In therapy, with the other "losers," Nick talks about his abusive Greek father and how he wrestles with his perceived destiny to become just like his father. In the end he makes some very clear and insightful conclusions about his father, his friends, and moving on. He also embraces a newly discovered talent, thanks to one of his teachers. The book's message is clear: Although there may be people who have caused us pain growing up, it is within our power and control to break the cycle of abuse and take responsibility for our actions. RL: HS (emotional and physical abuse)

Howe, James. (1999). *The Watcher.* New York: Aladdin Paperbacks. 174 pp. (ISBN: 0–689–83533–7)

One summer, a lone girl sits and watches families on vacation. From her perch at the top of the steps that lead to the beach on Fire Island, she records her observations in a notebook while everyone else plays. She never walks onto the beach; instead, she is just a shell of a person who feels invisible. She becomes particularly enamored of watching Evan and his family playing on the beach and is envious of this seemingly perfect family. She sneaks into their beach house and takes a family portrait. She carefully cuts out a photograph of herself and places it inside the frame of the stolen family picture. When her parents discover the tampered photograph, the origins of her feelings are revealed, and "Margaret" emerges (an ALA Best Book). RL: MS (emotional and physical abuse)

Hunt, Irene. (1976). *The Lottery Rose.* New York: Charles Scribner's Sons. 185 pp. (ISBN: 0–684–14573–1)

As is typical in families where the abuser is someone known by the family, seven-year-old Georgie's abuser is his mother's boyfriend Steve. His mother does nothing to stop it, instead, simply warning Georgie to fear Steve because he's "not goin' to stand for a kid whinin' on him. He'll kill you if you ever say anything against him so you be smart Georgie. You keep your mouth shut." Georgie is failing in school, and his teacher Miss Cressman doesn't bother to find out what might be causing Georgie's peculiar behavior. The day Georgie wins a rose in a grocery store lottery is the day Steve inflicts his last blow. Georgie goes to a home for boys and does a lot of growing, but what he is when he goes in is a far cry from what he is when the story ends. RL: MS (physical abuse)

Klass, David. (2001). *You Don't Know Me.* New York: Frances Foster Books. 262 pp. (ISBN 0–374–38706–0)

In speaking directly to his mother ("You don't know me"), John takes the reader on his flights from reality into a surreal, hilarious, and often painful world. Although it is actually a very serious subject, John analyzes his life in high school and with his stepfather ("the man who is not [his] father") with humor, an obvious survival skill he has learned. His sarcastic descriptions of the students, teachers, and events of a typical high school (anti-school) are reminders of the feelings of isolation and pain John carries inside. Then, to John's surprise, he encounters a teacher, Mr. Steenwilly, the band director, who just might know him a little bit. Through talks with his tuba "frog," arguments with his locker (in which the locker always fights back), and fantasies of the sad life his despised algebra teacher must have, John reveals the hopes and fears of a teenager of divorced parents who lives with an abusive stepparent. In the end, a violent evening with his stepfather shows John that he is wrong to think that no one "knows" him. RL: HS (physical abuse)

Marsden, John. (1987). *So Much to Tell You.* New York: Fawcett Juniper Books. 119 pp. (ISBN: 0–449–70374–6)

Fourteen-year-old Marina hasn't talked or interacted with others since an abusive incident that put her father in prison. She communicates by writing in a journal at the boarding school she attends after a stay at a psychiatric hospital. Marina struggles with unacknowledged and conflicting feelings of anger, guilt, love, and hate. As she writes, however, Marina (and the reader) begin to understand the event that changed both her life and her appearance forever. In spite of her resolve to not feel, Marina starts wanting to get to know Cathy, the girl she trusts the most. Finally, Marina stops hiding in corners trying to be invisible, but occasionally smiles and writes notes to others in a conversational way. Marina's journey toward health, however, is not without obstacles. With feelings come a period of regression and another stint in the hospital. Adolescents who have suffered abuse will relate to the way Marina deals with the ordeal in her life and might then see their own coping strategies in a more objective light. (Australia's 1988 Book of the Year Award, the 1990 Christopher Award) RL: MS (physical abuse)

Mazer, Norma Fox. (2000). *When She Was Good.* New York: Scholastic. 228 pp. (ISBN: 0–590–31990–6)

Life for Em is pleasurable only when she is able to create positive moments in her mind. After her mother's death, she and her sister Pamela have to deal with their father's abusive, alcoholic rages. The sisters, both young teens, decide to leave their father and try to make it on their own. Unfortunately, Em then endures years of ever-increasing emotional and sometimes physical abuse from her sister. Pamela eventually receives disability for her psychological condition, and Em quits school to go to work wherever she can. When Pamela unexpectedly dies of a stroke, Em must learn to live on her own. The long-lasting effects of the severe emotional and physical abuse Em has suffered make it difficult for her to function in society. Readers see how the damaging effects of abuse linger even after the abuse stops (an ALA Best Book for Young Adults, SLJ Best Book, and ALA *Booklist* Editors' Choice). RL: MS (emotional and physical abuse)

McNamee, Graham. (1999). *Hate You.* New York: Random House. 119 pp. (ISBN: 0–440–22762–3)

The day eight-year-old Alice's father grabs her by the throat as she tries to protect her mother from another outburst of his rage is the day Alice's mother banishes him from the house and their lives forever. Unfortunately,

Alice's mother is too damaged herself to see the damage Alice has suffered. Alice's turtleneck sweater hides the physical bruises, but the emotional bruises continue to grow for the next eight years of her life. Alice is a gifted musician and is able to release her anger when her boyfriend helps her see the beauty in her gravelly voice. Her friend, Rachel, also helps Alice realize that others, including her own mother, have their own difficult burdens to carry. RL: MS (emotional and physical abuse)

Miklowitz, Gloria D. (1995). *Past Forgiving.* New York: Simon and Schuster Books for Young Readers. 153 pp. (ISBN: 0–671–88442–5)

Jenna knew how it would go. She would forgive him when he sent her flowers and gifts and treated her lovingly, like he did in the beginning. Then it would start again. She would say or not say, do or not do something, and he'd get mad. He'd call her names, belittle her, embarrass her in front of friends, humiliate her so that she felt like a nothing, and finally he would hit her. Maybe next time, he would beat her up, so the hurt would be permanent. Like Jenna, some girls have the notion that they need a boyfriend to be noticed at school. They may even allow themselves to be abused by their boyfriends. It is very clear to readers that Jenna would be better off without her abusive boyfriend. This book might help teenage girls who are abused or even teenage boys who are budding abusers see their abusive relationships in a new light. RL: HS (emotional and physical abuse)

Paulsen, Gary. (1977). *The Foxman.* New York: Puffin Books. 119 pp. (ISBN: 0–14–034311–3)

After his alcoholic mother tries to kill him with a butcher knife while his father lies passed out, the teenage narrator is finally sent by the courts to live with his uncle's family in the Minnesota woods. There, the narrator heals by becoming friends with an elderly hermit—The Foxman—whose face had been badly damaged in the war. Gary Paulsen paints vivid pictures of his characters, both young and old. Although the boy in the book is a hero because of his actions, his motivations and feelings are like those of most boys his age. In the end, the reader knows that this boy will grow up intact in spite of his family history. RL: MS (emotional and physical abuse)

Pelzer, David. (1995). *A Child Called "It."* Deerfield Beach, FL: Health Communications, Inc. 184 pp. (ISBN: 1–55874–366–9)

How could a family home of holidays, special memories, and compassion evolve into an abyss of terror, danger, and shame? Sadly, Dave Pelzer was a child in such a home. In this true account of "one of the most severe child abuse cases in California history," Dave tells his story through the eyes of the child his alcoholic mother tried so vehemently to destroy. The reader learns that caregivers often inflict physical and emotional abuse or neglect upon a "target" child while treating other charges adequately. Dave was such a "target" and was denied food, decent bedding, clothing, and affection from his mother. Dave's will to survive is uplifting in spite of the book's graphic details of this young boy's unimaginably horrific life. The author gives ample credit to those who "rescued" him, including a moving account written by the elementary-school teacher who reported his case. The book also includes an author's epilogue as well as the perspectives of a social worker and Glenn A. Goldberg, the former executive director of the California Consortium to Prevent Child Abuse. RL: MS (emotional and physical abuse)

Peretti, Frank. (2000). *The Wounded Spirit.* Nashville, TN: Word Publishing. 220 pp. (ISBN: 0–849–91673–9)

Growing up with a medical condition that left him disfigured was not easy for young Frank. His underdeveloped frame and the fact that he was different led to constant persecution, verbal slings, and physical abuse at school—especially in gym class—but also in the halls, on the school grounds, and even in his own neighborhood. Being at the bottom of the schoolyard food chain led to Frank's dreaming of exacting a bloody revenge on his tormentors. If not for a teacher's loving intervention, he might have destroyed himself and others. This ECPA Gold Medallion Winner is a call for teachers and other adults to stand up to bullying and stop thinking of abuse as "normal" even among kids. It's a call for those in authority to pay attention to the violence being done to the vulnerable in our midst. It's a call for bullies and victims alike to seek healing and forgiveness. It's a call to heal the wounded spirit before the next Columbine occurs. RL: MS (emotional and physical abuse)

Williams, Carol Lynch. (1997). *The True Colors of Caitlynne Jackson.* New York: Yearling. 168 pp. (ISBN: 0–440–41235–8)

Caitlynne Jackson is a 12-year-old girl living in poverty with her single mother and sister in a lake community in Florida. She is thought of as "white trash" by many of the girls at school, but that doesn't matter because Brandon thinks she is cute. When her lifelong pal and neighbor asks her to the end-of-the-year dance instead of to play baseball as usual, Caitlynne decides her life must not be so bad. The night of the dance, however, Brandon is confronted by Caitlynne's mother, a mean and violent woman who has decided Caitlynne cannot attend the dance. At this point,

Caitlynne's secret life of physical and emotional abuse becomes visible to an outsider. Caitlynne's and Cara's mother decides to abandon the girls for the summer, and the sisters get a taste of life without their hateful and abusive mother. Although they are scared at times, like when the money starts to run out and the phone service is turned off, they cherish the peace her disappearance offers them. They know that they cannot return to life as it was before and must do something before their mother returns. These resourceful young ladies find support from a special person. RL: MS (emotional and physical abuse)

NONFICTION TEXTS EXPLAINING THE PROBLEM OF PHYSICAL ABUSE

Anda, Robert F., Felitti, Vincent J., Chapman, Daniel P., Croft, Janet B., Williamson, David F., Santelli, John, Dietz, Patricia M., & Marks, James S. (2001). Abused Boys, Battered Mothers, and Male Involvement in Teen Pregnancy. *Pediatrics, 107* (2). http://pediactrics.org/cgi/content/full/107/2/e19

This article points out that during both adolescence and adulthood, respondents who had a history of childhood physical or sexual abuse or had battered mothers were more likely to have been involved in a teen pregnancy than those who did not. Compared with respondents reporting no abuse, boys who experienced frequent physical abuse or battering of their mothers had a 70% increase in the risk of involvement in teen pregnancy. Boys who were sexually abused at age 10 years or younger showed an 80% greater risk of impregnating a teenage girl. Sexual abuse with violence increased the risk by 110%. Because physical and sexual abuse are often interrelated, boys and adult men who have experienced any of these types of abuse should be counseled about sexual practices and contraception. Such efforts may help prevent teen pregnancy and the perpetuation of child abuse and domestic violence.

Anderson, Stephen A., & Cramer-Benjamin, Darci B. (2000, April). The Impact of Couple Violence on Parenting and Children: An Overview and Clinical Implications. *American Journal of Family Therapy.* http://www.giorgio.catchword.com

If caretakers fail to intervene to stop children's aggressive behavior, children are allowed the opportunity to adopt and practice violent interpersonal skills and develop inadequate problem-solving and communication skills. This research supports the view that children who are exposed to domestic violence as well as to violence in the community are at greater risk of becoming either a perpetrator or victim of violence.

Borrego, Jr., Joaquin, Urquiza, Anthony J., Rasmussen, Rebecca A., & Zebell, Nancy. (1999, November). Parent-Child Interaction Therapy with a Family at High Risk for Physical Abuse. *Child Maltreatment, 4* (4), pp. 331–342.

The authors point to research that clearly indicates that the social sciences focus considerable attention on the problem of documented child abuse. They argue, however, that there has been little study of parent-child interaction before physical abuse occurs. The article highlights a single-case study in which a mother-child relationship suspected as high-risk for physical abuse is the sole focus of treatment. Parent-Child Interaction Therapy, or PCIT, indicates that intervention in the form of redirected parental behavior reduced the likelihood of abuse and increased the amount of positive parent-child interaction. The purpose of PCIT, according to the authors, is to teach parents to use positive reinforcement with their child while offering positive social reinforcement for the parent. The authors attribute the success of PCIT to the therapy method's concrete, nonblaming, and relatively short treatment duration. The authors maintain that the monitoring and intervention of behaviors leading to physical abuse should be as much of a focus of social science as the aftereffects.

Garbarino, James. (1999). *Lost Boys: Why Our Sons Turn Violent and How We Can Save Them.* New York: Free Press. 274 pp. (ISBN: 0–684–85908–4)

This book provides analyses of the causes of young men becoming violent and offers recommendations in the form of providing "anchors" (spiritual, psychological, and social) and offering resources. Throughout the book, Dr. Garbarino includes excerpts of interviews with "lost boys" (many of whom have been in the news for school rampages and murder), and the boys reveal stories of emotional and physical abuse and neglect at the hands of their caregivers.

Hecht, Debra B., & Hansen, David J. (2001, September/October). The Environment of Child Maltreatment: Contextual Factors and the Development of Psychopathology. *Aggression and Violent Behavior, 6* (5), pp. 433–457.

This article asserts that child abuse and parental stress are linked, with the specific components of stress including low socioeconomic status, maternal depression, negative life experiences, and low marital support. Economic trouble is related to anxiety, depression, and hostility. Single-parent homes tend to experience economic hardship as well as the additional stress of increased child-rearing responsibilities. As a result, children of single parents have a 77% greater risk of experiencing physical abuse and an 87% greater chance of experiencing sexual abuse than children in two-parent families.

Kaplan, Sandra J., Labruna, Victor, Pelcovitz, David, Salzinger, Suzanne, Mandel, Francine, & Weiner, Merrill. (1999). Physically Abused Adolescents: Behavior Problems, Functional Impairment, and Comparison of Informants' Reports. *Pediatrics, 104,* pp. 43–55.

The results of this study involving 99 white, middle-class adolescents between 12 and 18 years of age suggest that even mild abuse causes clinical internalizing and externalizing problems and functional impairment. The adolescents were more likely to rate themselves as aggressive, suggesting that children reared around violence are less likely to perceive it as inappropriate. Additionally, abused adolescents self-reported fewer internalizing problems, possibly because abuse leads to difficulty in labeling emotions and feelings, as past studies have suggested.

Kurland, Morton, M.D. (1990). *Coping with Family Violence.* New York: The Rosen Publishing Group, Inc. 134 pp. (ISBN: 0–8239–1050–4)

This text, which contains a table of contents and an index, specifically provides information to adolescents who have been abused. Each chapter describes a type of problem, from sibling rivalry to sexual abuse, experienced by children. Throughout the book, the author stresses the need for children to talk to others about their problems. Dr. Kurland also emphasizes that children are never responsible for the actions of adults because of the very fact that they are children. Finally, he points out that although children are not responsible for others' problems, they have the power to act to help themselves by recognizing the inappropriateness of the behavior of the abusive adults and by talking and listening to adults who can act objectively.

Pressell, David M. (2000). Evaluation of Physical Abuse in Children. *American Family Physician, 61,* pp. 3057–3064. http://www.aafp.org/afp.20000515/3057.html

According to this article, physical abuse of children in our society is a serious problem that has only recently been recognized by the medical community, and it is evident that anyone involved in the care of children has been in contact with some who have been abused. The first published report in contemporary medical literature was in 1946, and the term *battered-child syndrome* was coined in 1962. Since then the numbers of reported cases of child abuse have increased annually. In 1996, approximately 1 million children were confirmed victims of child abuse, and 1,185 children died from their injuries. When considering a diagnosis of physical abuse, Pressell warns doctors to be cautious and aware of conditions that can mimic signs of physical abuse yet be mindful of the following: an inconsistent pattern of bruising, fractures in areas unlikely to be injured, patterned bruises, and circumferential burns. Documentation must be done with great care because it may be used in court; errors could bring disastrous results for the family or the child.

Ritter, A. William. (1996). The Cycle of Violence Often Begins with Violence toward Animals. *The Prosecutor, 30,* pp. 31–33.

In a study of 57 families being treated by New Jersey's Division of Youth and Family Services for incidents of child abuse, researchers found that animal cruelty was the "sign of a deeply disturbed family." In 88% of the families where children had been physically abused, animals in the home had also been abused. Further, in one-third of those cases, the children were the abusers, using animals as scapegoats for their anger.

Taylor, Lauren R. (2001, October). Bad Girls: Violence among Young Women Keeps Rising, and Interventions Designed for Boys Just Don't Cut It. *Teacher Magazine, 13* (2), pp. 14–17.

This article reports that according to the U.S. Department of Justice, the arrest of girls for aggravated assault increased 57% between 1990 and 1999. This increase is attributed to a rise in the number of girls victimized by abuse. In a 1998 California study of nearly 1,000 female offenders ages 17 and younger, 92% were abused as children.

CHAPTER 6

Staying Fat for Sarah Byrnes: A Counselor Picks Up Where Crutcher Leaves Off

Sue Street and Joan F. Kaywell

INTRODUCTION

Life is precious, yet too many people take it for granted, while others wish they did not have it at all. Chris Crutcher's book *Staying Fat for Sarah Byrnes* presents an excellent picture of the complexities that some adolescents experience in their lives. True to Crutcher form, this book addresses some hard issues that many of today's adolescents encounter: the harm caused by teasing and being the outcast in school, growing up in single-parent homes, the conflict between abortion and religion, physical and emotional abuse, and suicide. Through an eclectic cast of memorable characters and a brilliant blend of comedy and tragedy, Crutcher makes readers both laugh and cry while addressing these important problems.

SYNOPSIS OF *STAYING FAT FOR SARAH BYRNES* BY CHRIS CRUTCHER

Eric Calhoun, better known as "Moby," and Sarah Byrnes, also known as "Scarface," are best friends. As their nicknames imply, Eric is severely overweight and Sarah has been badly burned. Because of their very special friendship—it takes one to know one—they believe that they are unstoppable for a while. For example, they fight the people who tease them by writing incriminating satire in an underground school newspaper, *Crispy*

Pork Rinds. If this were their only fight, however, readers might believe these smart students would overcome the cheap shots thrown at them. They even manage to convince the school bully, Dale Thornton, to join in their cause for a while. Tragically, it is Sarah's father, Virgil Byrnes, who is behind Sarah's downfall. Sensing imminent disaster, Sarah becomes catatonic in class one day, is hospitalized, and stays there until she can figure out what to do. It is through Eric's visits that readers learn what has contributed to Sarah's fear and silence.

Sarah Byrnes lives with her father. Her mother abandoned them both when Sarah was three years old. Sarah's mother left after Virgil intentionally burned Sarah's face and arms during an argument. Sarah finally confides to Eric and tells him the truth about her scars and about her mom's disappearance: "My dad accomplished what he wanted when he ruined my face. Mom didn't want me anymore" (Crutcher, pp. 103–105). Further, Sarah's father refuses to let her have plastic surgery to fix the scars, believing that she needs to toughen up and live through this on her own. Virgil is a man out of control; he can't control his anger and he can't control his drinking. Sarah knows when he is particularly dangerous by watching how much alcohol her father ingests.

Talking to Eric was a wise choice for Sarah. Although Eric's father abandoned him when he was just a baby, Eric's mother absolutely adores him. Like Sarah, both Eric and his mother have a void in their lives, but Eric realizes his obsessive relationship with food was an unhealthy attempt to cope with his feelings. His trying to stay fat when he starts to slim down, after joining the swim team, is based on his devotion to his friendship with Sarah. Eric sensibly solicits the help of both his mother and his swim coach to help him help Sarah.

As it is with all of Crutcher's stories, there is at least one caring adult who assists the adolescents in their journey through life and the hardships they endure. Mrs. Lemry is one such caring adult who helps to put important issues in life into perspective, such as abortion and suicide, through the "Contemporary American Thought" (CAT) class that she teaches at the high school. A subplot of the novel involves the character of Mark Brittain, a self-righteous perfectionist who doesn't allow weakness in himself or in others. Ironically, many of the adults consider Mark to be a paragon of teen virtue, but Mark has no joy or whimsy; he is not fun to be near. As Mark's own personal infidelities become exposed, Mark lashes out, as his own family dynamic has taught him. Mrs. Lemry helps her students see how their actions affect others, and she plays an important role in saving Sarah Byrnes.

MOVING BEYOND THE TEXT

Many events happen before Mr. Byrnes is finally imprisoned for his horrific actions. As the book ends, readers are left wondering how Sarah will adapt to life without a mother or father. Further, it is obvious that her trauma left not only the scars on her face and arms, but even more severe scars on her emotional psyche. Plastic surgery will help to repair the physical harm, but there is no doubt that Sarah will have difficulty developing self-esteem and confidence. This next section explores how an anonymous reader responded to the novel, and then how a mock counseling session might help Sarah to address these issues.

A READER RESPONDS TO THE TEXT

Follow my thoughts for a moment. The human body is made up of bones, tissue, water, hair, and cartilage. Basically, our bodies are composed of a physical organization of billions of cells. We are the most exquisite beings on this planet. Our parts work together in amazing synchronicity and complexity, run by an organ no bigger than your average metal lunch box. When we die, this entire machine deteriorates into dust, leaving nothing behind.

But somewhere in the essence of our being is a will—a soul, a drive—that is inextricably entwined with our physical self. It is the spiritual part of us. And the tug-of-war rages on between these two sides of our existence until we breathe our final breath. The two fight against each other. Our will forces itself upon our body, causing it to do things good or bad.

Our will also sends us messages about the way it feels about our body. We don't feel good about the way we look, so we try to change it, or feel guilty about not changing it, or even get angry if we can't change it. If we had no will, would it matter what we looked like? Why would we care? If we had no spirit, the things that happen to our physical body would be of no importance other than preserving life. But it does matter, and our spirit is deeply enmeshed with our body. This is why the physical act of holding a young girl's face to a stove and burning it leaves scars far more damaging than the ones we can see. The word *fatso* leaves its imprint in the mind of an overweight person, like the smell of cigarettes in your clothing.

If our will is out of control, then it propels our body into action. Blood pressure rises. Our system is stressed and the Mark Brittains and Virgil Byrneses and Dale Thorntons of the world strike out. A bruise will heal. A broken bone will mend. But the memories never die. The body gets better, but the spirit takes much more work.

When I was younger, I was physically abused.

For many years, when my brother and I would fight or misbehave, my father would go into a rage and hit us with whatever he could get his hands on—two-by-fours, ping-pong paddles, his hands. Many times he would lift my brother and me off the ground by our hair, smack our heads together, and scream with seething anger. I have seen the rage that consumed Virgil Byrnes. I turned inward, just as Sarah did when she "took a mental vacation," and it is our soul's way of preserving itself. She turned tough because her scars were visible. I withdrew because my scars were invisible. I admit that it wasn't the most healthy way to deal with the pain, but it worked for a while.

I was also a small kid. So the way I looked, my physical appearance, affected my spirit deeply. I was dissatisfied with myself, and I understand what "Moby" felt. Being stripped of confidence, your ability to act and interact with the world around you, is severely influenced. This fleshy shell that temporarily holds my spirit is part of who I am. Now I am struggling with feeling a little overweight. I feel guilty for eating Oreos. I pound on myself for not working out. I feel down. Why? Because we are somehow led to believe that the body part of us is the most important part; the visible person is what matters. Fortunately for Sarah, Moby is able to see past Sarah's burns and remains friends with her from their work together on *Crispy Pork Rinds* to helping her deal with her abusive dad. And now we begin to see the way out.

It is through our fellow humans that we can become free of the emotional and spiritual pain by sharing our experiences with like-minded people: talking with counselors, confiding in a friend, and participating in groups with people who have shared similar experiences. By reading truthful information, we can also empower ourselves. Eric hits the pool and pounds out his frustration. I hit the weights and rage on iron rather than people. And we can break the cycle of abuse by stopping it with us. Sarah's dad, I'm confident, was abused. Eric's father wasn't in the picture. Neither of them addressed their "stuff," but Eric and Sarah have decided to put an end to the pain by not repeating the mistakes of their fathers— just like I have done!

A COUNSELOR TALKS WITH SARAH: TRANSCENDENT FIRE

Counselor:	Hello, Sarah. How's it going this week?
Sarah:	Hi there. (The smile on Sarah's face when she walked up to sit down at the counselor's desk faded into a

	thoughtful, almost puzzled mode, as her voice trailed off.)
Counselor:	What's up? (In acknowledgment of the change in affect she observed.)
Sarah (with a smile):	It's just really hard to get used to being called "Sarah." It seems so weird. I know you explained it and it makes sense, but I've been called "Sarah Byrnes" for so long it almost seems like it's not me you're talking to.
Counselor (also smiling warmly):	I understand why it would be hard to get used to. But I think we agreed that you are starting a new time in your life, that you do want to feel differently about yourself than you used to, that you no longer want to define yourself in terms of your challenges but in terms of your strengths.
	(Sarah nods silently but is actively listening, waiting to hear more.)
Counselor:	I see your strengths as being who you are, Sarah, a very strong and beautiful and smart person. You are just like everybody else, only perhaps a little stronger and a little smarter. Everybody else gets called by their first name and so should you. We did agree on that at our last meeting, didn't we?
Sarah (nodding vigorously):	Yes. And actually, it was my friend Moby who first called me "Sarah." It is just so hard to think about myself differently after thinking about myself as a monstrosity, as someone who is worthless, for so many years. I'm having to get to know myself as a completely different person.
Counselor (nodding slowly):	Yes, I can see that. We grow up seeing ourselves through the eyes of our parents, our significant others, or the people we are around the most. When those people reflect back to us a picture of ourselves that is ugly, that is bad, that says we are no good, then we adopt that same sense of ourselves. When our parents talk to us, or scream at us, and the looks on their faces are angry, or ugly, children translate those looks as meaning, "I am bad. I am worthless."
Sarah:	Yeah, you're right about that. The only looks I can remember from my father are looks of rage and disgust, looks that seemed to say he hated me. I thought

that meant I was an awful person. I knew I looked awful on the outside. I guess I also just thought it meant I was awful on the inside, too.

Counselor: Well, as a child you are so vulnerable. And you have no other data against which to compare the data you are getting. We all assume that because people are our parents, they are good and kind and loving...Not! Unfortunately, there is no license required for parenting. There aren't even any required courses, like Parenting 101. All you have to do is biologically become a parent, and—presto!—you are invested with all this power over a small and helpless child who looks up to you like you're truly a special being. It really doesn't make good sense. Parenting should be a privilege, not a biological imperative.

Sarah (smiling coyly): I agree. I think someday I will campaign for a law that makes parents get a license before they can become parents. They have to pass tests and prove their goodness and kindness.

Counselor: Good idea. I'd vote for that law, too! Actually, though, I think it must be very hard to develop a new picture of yourself. But, I also think it must be exciting, too. You have a clean slate! You had bad data—wrong data—before. Now you have much more accurate data, and you have a chance to create a whole new picture of yourself. That's a neat creative project: a challenge that very few people get to undertake!

Sarah (sadly): Yeah, I think that's the story of my life. I get to have the challenges no one else gets to take on. (After a brief silence and a brave change of affect.) My friend Moby says it's like loading a new program onto my computer. Then I put my new data about myself into the new program and come up with a completely different answer than I ever had before.

Counselor (trying to keep things upbeat): I like it. Your friend Moby must be pretty clever.

Sarah: Yeah. I used to give him a real hard time, back when I was pretending to be so strong, but now I don't have

	the heart to slam him anymore. He saved my life. I wouldn't have made it without him. I miss him so much now that he's away at college.
Counselor:	It does sound like he was a wonderful friend. But you know, I am surprised to hear you refer to the time when you "were pretending to be strong." What is different now? Are you no longer strong? And since when were you PRETENDING to be strong?
Sarah:	Being strong and tough was my major defense. There was nothing and no one I wouldn't stand up to. I think I told you about the time I let a real bully just physically beat the crap out of me. I was too tough for words. It was dumb. And it was pretense. It was an act, a persona. It wasn't the real me. The real me was hiding deep underneath, buried so far down I almost couldn't find me. I thought I was safely hidden forever.
Counselor:	I understand how you think that wasn't the real you, and I would agree with that. But I have to tell you that you are one of the strongest people I know. I am amazed at how you survived the cruelest and most gruesome of odds. You have done super well in school, you have drawn people to you who love you, and you have shown tremendous courage in getting through all the things you have told me about in your life. I think you are truly a very remarkable, *strong woman* in many ways.
Sarah:	But underneath there is still this very frightened and scared little girl!
Counselor:	Sarah, you were the one who told me about how you went on, year after year, living with *The Beast,* as you call him, and surviving. Not just surviving, but taking care of yourself. You did an outstanding job of doing your very best to honor the Sarah inside, the Sarah who could not come out yet because it wasn't safe, but you were still taking care of her.
Sarah:	How do you mean, I was taking care of her?
Counselor:	Heck, Sarah, you did exactly the right thing to take care of yourself by "checking out" when you did. What a smart thing to do! What a strong thing to do! That

took intelligence—and courage—and you are loaded with both! Then you went to Reno to find your mother, and when she didn't come back to support you, you picked up the pieces and went on. People who are not strong or who don't have a strong sense of wanting to take care of themselves might have really broken down after that. In one sense, you might have said, "What is there to live for now?"

But you carried right on. You even tried to get away completely and start a new life, knowing very little about where you were going. Not many people have that kind of courage, Sarah. And I have to tell you that I believe that all the things you did to take care of yourself, to look out for yourself—even the strong macho woman persona—were all your ways of fighting back. They were all your ways of taking care of a person who you knew, deep inside, was a really, really good person, even though nobody but your friend Moby seemed to think so.

Sarah: Hmmm. Well, I had to do those things. There was no other way. (Pause.) But are you serious? Do you really think I cared about myself all along and didn't realize it? How can you tell that?

Counselor: Well, Sarah, I believe that because you were a fighter the whole way. I believe that somewhere inside you, you knew there were good things about you that deserved protecting. Maybe you were not consciously aware of it, but I think you did whatever you had to do to take care of you. You did not always have a lot of choices. Sometimes in life when we look back on ourselves, we forget that we only have so many choices and options. You made the choices you needed to make to take care of yourself. You maybe weren't really sure who you were, but it is clear you never believed you were the person your father made you out to be.

Sarah (thoughtfully):   You are right about that. I guess I never thought it through really clearly, but it is true that I never really believed I was who he said I was or acted like I was. I didn't have much good to think of myself, but I knew I wasn't as bad as he said.

Counselor:	And now you are getting that missing data, the parts about how very good you are in many ways. That data has always been there, but you couldn't access it because there was just too much negativity. Plus, I think we all need permission from somebody somewhere to go ahead and believe, "I'm okay. I'm good. I'm lovable and deserve to be loved by other good human beings."
Sarah (still thoughtful):	Yes, I see what you mean. (Pause.) I think you're right. Moby always believed in me, but in some ways, I was stronger than he was back then, so he didn't really have the credibility I was looking for in support. I really needed someone like an adult I respected to say I was an okay person—like Mrs. Lemry.
Counselor:	In your case, I think it was also a matter of an adult you trusted. And you know, Sarah, you and I haven't known each other long, but I've heard your whole life story. From you. And while I know it is hard to trust people you don't know well, I want you to know that I think you're a good person, too. You definitely have my permission to believe in Sarah, to accept Sarah, and someday, to love Sarah.
Counselor (noting Sarah's silence and warm glow, taking the tactic of reinforcing the issue of strength one last time):	Sarah, you have done everything you possibly could do to take care of yourself. You have developed some real strengths and skills along the way. And now you've even found that people really do love you, and there is a whole new world out there for you! But don't forget those strengths, Sarah. Yes, you were forced to learn them to survive, but that doesn't make them any less strengths or any less real. You are a very special person, Sarah.
Sarah:	I hadn't thought of myself as strong. This talk today has really given me a different picture of myself.
Counselor:	You know what I think, Sarah? I think you could use those strengths to beat this thing, too. You've always had such a determined spirit; now use that spirit to beat those old tapes playing in your head that say you're no good. Use that spirit to tape new tapes and construct new ways of seeing yourself. You used that spirit before to hide your *secret,* to protect that sweet little

girl within. Now that you no longer have the need to protect her, use that spirit to build on her. Allow her to have your strengths, now that you no longer have to hide her. Let "strong macho woman" meet "sweet little girl" and maybe you'll end up with a strong but sensitive and caring woman.

Sarah: I hadn't thought of myself that way. You seem to be suggesting that there are two of me, and that I need to put them together into one.

Counselor: Good insight, Sarah! That's exactly what I am suggesting! Perhaps there is a very vulnerable girl underneath there, waiting to be integrated into the mix. But you *are* a mixture of both strong and vulnerable. Don't make the same mistake again of emphasizing one part of you and ignoring the rest. This time maybe you would want to figure out how to honor *both* parts of yourself—the strong part *and* the vulnerable part. Each part of you has traits you want to keep, and each has traits you want to leave behind. For example, you want to keep the strengths you learned but probably want to let go of the heavy sarcastic attitude you used, largely as a defense. As well, why not keep the kind and caring aspects of the sweet girl, but leave behind the passive vulnerability? Your job is to figure out which parts of you, you want to keep, and then figure out how they can work together!

Sarah: That makes sense. I've been seeing myself as this vulnerable person, unsure of who I am or where I want to go from here. I've lost my cutting edge. I used to know how to survive, how to talk to people, how to get along. You know. How to get them before they get you! I always used my words and my sharp tongue to make sure nobody ever got the best of me. I think it is safe to say I was a master of sarcasm. But then when I realized that was part of my old persona, macho strong woman, I gave it up. (Obviously frustrated.) But I am really floundering when it comes to knowing who I am now. All the old ways are no longer useful. And I have to admit that I am not the sweet little girl within, either. I mean, I can't just be sweet to people. Yuck! But I'm not the sarcastic bitch anymore either. I don't know who I am!

Counselor: Do you think there might be a compromise somewhere? How about a composite that turns out to be "sweet bitch?" (At this they both chuckle, but there is a shared understanding that something of this sort of compromise may be possible.)

Sarah: There is so much new stuff to learn. This really is a completely different way of thinking than I am used to. (Silence, then a woebegone expression.) I think the hardest thing is to change my value of myself, my feeling that I'm still not good enough. I keep seeing my dad's face twisted in rage at me. I keep hearing his voice and the words that say I'm an awful person. They constantly replay like a video that won't stop rewinding.

Counselor (with keen sensitivity and tenderness): It has to be very hard for you. You've had a very ugly and sick influence all of your life. Your father mirrored back to you his own anger with himself, not who you really are. It is hard for children to know how to stand back and say, "He's nuts! His anger and rage are not my fault! I did not make him the angry person he is today! I didn't teach him to address all his problems with anger! What he's talking about has nothing to do with me!" But you know, you can say those things to yourself today. You're an adult now, and now you know those things are true. Say them today—all day long—to yourself. Eventually, you'll believe them.

If you step outside yourself to look at your life, you will know that is true. You will see that his abuse, his sickness, was not your fault. But children don't have the cognitive capacity to see that. They think that because it is happening to them, because their parents are angry with them, it is their fault. So when you were a child, you could not say to yourself, "I do not deserve this abuse. I am a good person. I am a child who trusts this older person, who wants to do what is right and wants to please this older person. Healthy families do not hit their children or hit each other. My family is not a healthy family. This is not my fault. I am not in charge. The adults are in charge and are making the decisions. I am doing the best I can to survive and take care of myself."

Sarah (after a long silence, while trying to absorb the truth she knew lay in those statements):

You know, now I can see exactly what you're saying. And I guess I'll have to give it a lot of thought. Knowing those things still doesn't get rid of the tapes. It still doesn't make things any different. I still feel the same way I did when I believed the tapes were real.

Counselor:

I know. The tapes and the feelings that go along with them won't go away quickly because you have believed them—you have lived them—for many, many years. You cannot erase the tapes or the feelings by simply knowing it was wrong, because all of your life experiences—your belief systems—have been built around that foundation about yourself, right or wrong, true or not true. But as you continue to learn new material—and believe it—you will tape over the old tapes. They will lose their power if you continue to film and record new interpretations and new information.

Use your words! The tapes are actually given meaning by your words. You have told me how good you are at verbal challenges. You told me about that terrific newspaper you and Moby put out that really caught the edge of truth about most of the people you were writing about. You are excellent with your words. Now use them to your own advantage! Practice saying to yourself the kinds of things I just suggested. Or figure out your own truths, then use your words and your powerful reasoning ability to reconstruct the reality of your life and your responsibility in that life.

Sarah:

I used to tell Moby that words are the only way people like us, like him and me, can fight back the creeps and bullies of this world. But I'm not sure about using my words to forget about the things *The Beast* said.

Counselor:

I don't think you forget, Sarah. What you do is reconstruct reality. You once believed in a reality largely constructed by your father. Now you know that reality was not valid. You must use your words to remind yourself that what you grew up believing from home was not

	accurate, and that there is a very different reality in which you can participate. You may choose to participate in this reality by using your words to affirm who you are, to affirm your value. This you must do, Sarah. You will never feel really different about yourself until you use your words to very specifically redefine yourself. Nobody can make you feel better about you but you. No matter how much those of us who care about you try to help you, nothing will really change until you change you. That is, until you step forward and claim your birthright: a valuable and lovable human being.
Sarah:	This is awesome! (A long period passes while the counselor's caring words hang in the air.)
Counselor (breaking the comfortable silence):	Why not try this when you are doing your evening meditation? Pretend you are someone else looking in on your life. Look at the little girl Sarah and the ways she found to survive, to take care of herself over the years. How would you describe this person? What is she like? Does she have many strengths that many other people don't have? Does she have courage? Is she weak? I think once you do this a few times, you will see that she is a remarkable young woman who has all kinds of personal resources to carry her into the next stage of her life!
Sarah (with hesitation):	I think I can do that.
Counselor:	Doing so will at least give you a more objective picture of what you have been through. Whenever you start feeling blue, try seeing yourself from the perspective of reality—as though you were someone on the outside looking in. Then you can use that perspective as a foundation for your words to say to yourself, "This was not my fault. I was a young child who loved her mom and dad. I did not deserve to be treated badly. That was my dad's problem, not mine."
Sarah:	That part won't be too hard to do, but it won't be fun to look back on my life.
Counselor:	No, it won't. But over time, as you keep looking at it and reframing it, it will no longer have the power to

hurt you—at least not as much. You are a strong woman, Sarah, and you must not let the evil you have experienced be the winner. You be the winner! Do not let the evil dominate your life. Instead, make your own dreams, beliefs, and values control your life.

Sarah (smiling): You're right. I've never let a bully come out on top, whether it was my father or the jerks at school. I'm not going to let any bully come out on top of this one, either!

Counselor: That's the spirit! We cannot let the adversities in life win. (Slowly, after a long silence) You know Sarah, you were burned by a fire. Fire can be very deadly. But fire can also be purifying, cleansing, renewing. In Eastern religions, fire has always symbolized spirit, and that is true even in some Western thought. Turn the sword of fire the other way! Allow it to be your transformative agent—that which inspires you to transcend the old ways, the old self-perception, and become a person reborn, transfigured. Make fire your friend rather than your nemesis.

Sarah: Where do you come up with this stuff? I never in five thousand years would have thought of it that way, but I think I get it. It's a way of saying that all swords have two edges; one is good and the other is a real problem. It's the same thing you are showing me about how I can look at myself as damaged goods or as a good and caring person. Fire can be that way, too. I never thought of that. Will you help me find some reading on it?

Counselor: I surely will. Let me find books about fire and about helping you see your strengths. Let's check my bookshelves first, and we'll go from there. And I'll see you again next week.

Sarah: Yes, thank you. You know, I've really enjoyed our meeting today. You've given me a lot to think about!

CONCLUSION

Life is taken for granted by people who act carelessly and is abused by those who have no concern for the destruction they cause. Adolescents need to be encouraged in their lives. If they are not taught or modeled how to appreciate their lives, then most likely they won't. Many adolescents, especially those who have suffered abuse at the hands of their own parents or guardians, do not see the value of their lives. When children are abused in any way, it has devastating and long-lasting effects on their outlooks on life and on themselves. The cycle will continue, even to their own children, until a caring adult helps them to break it. Although abuse is devastating to read about and to see around us, teachers have a precarious role because they see adolescents every day in their home away from home. Not only do teachers have the responsibility to educate, but they also have the added responsibility to be positive and caring role models who notice when things aren't quite right.

REFERENCE

Crutcher, Chris. (1993). *Staying fat for Sarah Byrnes.* New York: Harper Collins.

CHAPTER 7

Precocious Teacher Encounters Professional Social Worker: Conversations toward Understanding Physical Abuse through Chris Crutcher's *Whale Talk*

Shannon D. Dosh and Carolyn T. Royalty

INTRODUCTION

During the seventies, when I was a teenager in high school, the word *abuse* never entered my conversations with peers. Growing up in a typical middle-class family at a time when sexual freedom and drug experimentation were on the rise, I realize now that our small community reveled in the Andy Griffith and Brady Bunch ideals. Highly controversial issues were shied away from in an effort to protect the illusion of innocence that society strove to maintain. Parents valued public opinion and kept private problems enclosed within the walls of their respective homes. I remember my father spanking me with his fraternity paddle signed by all the brothers and my mother chasing me around the house with my father's belt — but only a couple of times. "Wait till your father gets home," was a familiar phrase. I learned early on in my adolescence to abide by the rules because the consequences could be painful. This punishment was not considered child abuse when I was growing up. "Spareth the rod, spoileth the child" echoed in my ears. I respected my parents and followed the rules set forth by my dominant father, whom I love very much.

Now that I am a parent myself, I am faced with trying to discipline my young, impetuous son, who constantly challenges my authority, without resorting to the traditional measures taken by my parents. As a teacher, classroom behavior increasingly challenges my resolve as I struggle to maintain composure while adhering to county-adopted discipline guidelines. As an educator, I grow increasingly concerned about many of my students who are simply out of control. On the other end of the extreme, two girls admitted to being physically abused by a parent, gave a short explanation without a flinch about the impending legal action, and moved on in regular conversation as though it were no big deal. As a compassionate teacher, I often feel ill equipped to respond to these students who swing at two polar ends of emotion.

Very few teachers are trained in counseling techniques, yet all face troubled young people searching for answers to help resolve emotional questions in their lives. While there is no one right answer in any given situation, I have learned through writing this chapter that professional assistance for teachers and parents is readily available. Students need teachers who genuinely listen to what they have to say. Teachers are required by law to report any suspicions about abused children, but actively researching prevalent issues increases any teacher's confidence toward addressing delicate situations and then guiding troubled youths to seek professional help. Considering the fact that the majority of teachers do *not* have the educational background to deal professionally with abused adolescents, we must utilize readily available tools; reading is one option. Abused adolescents must realize that they are not alone in their world of pain and that help is available.

ORGANIZATION

Chris Crutcher's *Whale Talk* (Crutcher, 2001) details the life of a multiracial protagonist who, during his senior year of high school, combats prejudice and assists abused adolescents in finding the inner strength to battle their abusers. A trained social worker responds to teacher-generated reader responses to *Whale Talk*. The questions posed to the social worker throughout the responses are guided by daily experiences in a suburban high-school classroom, heightening a genuine concern for students growing up in a troubled society.

SYNOPSIS OF *WHALE TALK* BY CHRIS CRUTCHER

Fourteen-year-old The Tao Jones, better known as T.J., is "a rainbow-coalition kid" primarily because of his multiracial background as well as his being adopted by "two white, upwardly mobile ex-children of the sixties." Throughout his own childhood, The Tao has stood his ground on racial injustice, having had his own fair share of confrontations considering his looks as well as his name. Being an avid swimmer, however, has given T.J. some advantage in size and stature, although he shuns organized sports and the ruling gung-ho athletes at his high school. When T.J. witnesses several Wolverine football players harassing Chris Coughlin, a student who is mentally challenged, for wearing his dead brother's letter jacket, T.J. challenges the tradition upheld by these Cutter High bullies and the *Wolverine Too* alumni who enforce the code surrounding the wearing of letter jackets. With the help of swim coach Mr. Simet, T.J. organizes a rag-tag swim team comprised of some of the social misfits of the school and pushes them into a quest for the coveted letter jackets worn by varsity athletes. Tension mounts from all perspectives, with T.J.'s parents standing behind the measures necessary to combat the social stereotypes and assist those emotionally unable to stand their ground. Intermingled in this challenge is the story of Heidi, a girl who's abused by her adoptive father. Coincidentally, he is an alumnus of Cutter High who is actually the main bully behind the rigid football tradition. T.J. must decide how to respond to some pretty tough adversity, and through his experiences we learn that the world does not need more hatred but rather more compassion and understanding.

A TEACHER CONVERSES WITH A SOCIAL WORKER ABOUT THE NOVEL

Teacher Response #1

After meeting T.J., I began to think about all the stigmas in our society and how people are judged by the color of their skin or even by what they wear. T.J. takes a different attitude, one that I admire. He believes that all people are simply that—people. Despite his inner strength, T.J. still feels unsettled whenever he thinks about his birth mother, Glenda; she gave him up when he was two years old. Do all adopted kids yearn to find their birth parents and find out the circumstances behind their adoption? Even though T.J. worries about filling in the gaps from his past, he definitely lucked out by having wonderful adoptive parents. The Joneses nurture T.J.'s strong positive opinions of himself, making him more adept in dealing with his multi-ethnicity in a racist society.

Glenda not only gives him away but also gives him additional baggage: his name. His legal name is "The Tao," pronounced "The Dow," Jones. T.J. guesses that his birth mother went through a spiritual phase during the sixties when he was born. Growing up with a controversial name only heightens his ethnic awareness, shown through the constant battles he has with peers. Most multiracial adolescents I know have uncommon names that their peers think are weird. As an adult, I see their names as unique, but I can remember as a child picking on kids who had strange names, just like the boy Ronnie picks on in the book. Defending yourself against your peers must be a lot easier than defending yourself against adults, whom T.J. must eventually face.

Social Worker Response to #1

It would be difficult to say whether all adopted kids want to find their birth parents; however, most would be curious. Whether adoptive children have the permission, explicit or implied, from their adoptive families to explore this subject raises several points. Until recently, most states sealed adoptive records from children until adulthood. Furthermore, for various reasons, not all biological parents are eager to have communication with children from their past. Reconnecting and remembering the past only reminds them of a painful period in life. In some cases, an adult child has located a biological parent only to be rejected from contact. This is very disappointing to the "child." Many biological parents need time to get used to the idea, to determine what form and frequency any future contact will take. Nowadays, arranged "open adoptions" have become more common. In these situations, the adoptive and biological parents already know each other and are determined to have ongoing contact with each other, often limited to well-defined situations such as special occasions and birthdays. Of course, this is not practical or advisable in all situations, especially if the biological parents were not in agreement with the circumstances of the removal of the child from their care. Some parents would be too detrimental to the child's well-being for ongoing contact with either the child or the child's adoptive family.

T.J.'s real name—"The Tao"—is interesting, perhaps a symbol for his "philosophical" approach to and understanding of his life. T.J. is probably correct in assuming Glenda's choice was attributable to the spiritual phase during the sixties. Eastern philosophies, along with the "mind-expanding" drugs of the time, were embraced by the younger generation as a new way of understanding our Western culture and society. Many multiethnic children are given unusual names because in some African cultures, it's considered important to have a unique name. Unfortunately, there is a great shortage of ethnically diverse therapists. A teenager faced with defending himself with peers is in a difficult situation, and it is harder still for anyone to assist this adolescent who is "different" to realize that the best strategy may be a nondefensive one. This seems to be a theme with T.J. Note again the Eastern philosophical influence here of nonresistance. As the book progresses, T.J. increasingly demonstrates an ability to overcome his initial impulses to act out violently on his anger.

Teacher Response #2

T.J.'s account of the coaches trying to get him to play sports is all too familiar. My students constantly complain about coaches pressuring them into playing on school sports teams. Just like T.J., these kids know their athletic capabilities on or off the field/court. Sometimes personal reasons, whether a past bad experience while playing a certain sport or a verbal confrontation with a particular coach, influence the decision not to sacrifice one's own self-worth and participate. T.J., however, gives in to Coach Simet, the English teacher who broaches the subject of forming a Cutter Swim Team. T.J. admires Simet's teaching strategies, and the two of them connect with similar viewpoints about other characters in the novel. Students naturally cling to Simet because he takes time to get to know them as individuals. T.J. realizes that everything Simet does, whether in class or outside of school, teaches students something. T.J. thinks through the situation, resolving that Simet's proposal benefits them both. Simet's offer prompts T.J. to reminisce about his old swimming days, the way burning off the energy kept him feeling in control. At what age do people begin to realize their own power of self-control?

I admire T.J. for standing up for Chris, the mentally challenged boy who is harassed by the football players for wearing his dead brother's letter jacket. Chris idolizes his brother and wants to preserve his memory by donning the jacket, but the jocks believe only the athletes themselves are entitled to wear a letter. Why can't people just let those who are less fortunate or different alone? Honestly, I don't know many students who I believe would jump in and confront the brutes. Why do adolescents, and adults too, just stand by and do nothing?

Social Worker Response to #2

Simet gave me the impression that he knew exactly what he was doing. He was very aware of T.J.'s strength as a swimmer, but he also knew of T.J.'s well-established resistance to participating in organized sports. Simet ingeniously comes up with a way to engage not only T.J. but others of the school, the underdogs and disenfranchised students. Their shared experience of creating something together develops a sense of belonging over time. Not only do they end up developing friendships, but this "team" stimulates their academic learning, which is a necessary part of participating on the team. The age of realizing self-control probably has more to do with the individual's development of having some sense of mastery over his or her personal situation or circumstances. Adolescents who have been separated or removed from their families of origin typically feel very out of control.

People pick on others for a variety of reasons. Think of Heidi's father and his adult sidekick and how they behave at the high school. Typically, those who pick on those who are in some way handicapped or unable to defend themselves do so because of their own poor self-esteem or self-mastery. Others stand by, watch, and do nothing more often out of fear than for any other reason. Fear of retaliation may be a very real emotion in these instances, as well as not wanting to take the time or risk to get involved. In an ideal world, kids could simply turn to the school administration or the police to help address such things without fear of retribution. It's the fear of the consequences that holds everyone back.

Teacher Response #3

When T.J. accepts Simet's challenge to join the swim team in hopes of receiving a letter jacket, T.J.'s mind begins to work overtime. T.J. envisions gathering all the "suckers" of the school to join along with him. T.J.'s motivation is revenge against Mike Barbour and all that this football brute represents. My first impression is that T.J. is guilty of using students who don't fit in for his own advantage because he refers to them as "suckers." I can't help but wonder whether this is what he really feels toward these outcasts of the school or whether T.J. feels these kids need someone on their side, someone with determination to stand up against those who believe they are better than everyone else. Can one person with a strong will and confidence make that much of a difference for the weakest in a society?

Social Worker Response to #3

T.J.'s use of the word "suckers" could be true to how he's feeling at this point in the novel. Sometimes, for example, the oppressed can take on the attitudes of the oppressor. This idea is illustrated in the Nazi concentration camps, where officers sometimes awarded authority to selective captives in controlling their fellow captives. In T.J.'s case, however, I believe he simply thinks that gathering these "misfits" for a sports team will be a great way to get back at Cutter High School and its athletic policies! Later, he comes to understand the barriers that each guy has to overcome and develops respect for all of them. One person with a strong will and confidence can have tremendous power and influence over a community. Think of the profound ways Mother Theresa, Martin Luther King, and Princess Diana have affected people and even history.

Teacher Response #4

The "Wolverines Too" that T.J. describes could fit the description of any stereotypical small-town alumni organization made up of die-hard fans or ex-athletes who thought they'd make the big time but ended up sticking around town with no real future. These graduates probably headed out of town for a short period after high school but were not as popular anywhere else as they were at home. Missing the cheer of the crowd and the ego boost from their popular status in high school, they return home, stirring up trouble in order to renew the familiar rush of adrenaline. In my county, we label them the "good old boys."

Rich Marshall, the leader of "WT," is a man you can't help but dislike. He and his friend, Mike Barbour, make up two of a kind—a pair always looking for trouble. The story that T.J. tells about these men and some of their friends attacking him is incredible. T.J.'s sympathy for the innocent fawn standing over its dead mother erupts from his feeling of loss for his own mother, and this ordeal must have been dreadful. Watching my grandmother die of cancer and not being able to help her as she lay on her death bed gasping for air, drugged on morphine to deaden the pain, helps me in a way to understand why T.J. put his life on the line to save the fawn. Marshall and his gang acted out of pure selfishness. They wanted to have the fawn stuffed for a prize, to have something to gloat about while drinking beer. These guys were actually contemplating shooting T.J. for standing in front of the poor, defenseless fawn. How can people be so insensitive and cruel?

T.J. stands up for his beliefs in front of the entire school by wearing bloody clothes five days straight to protest Rich Marshall's interference at the school. Remarkably, T.J.'s parents back him up when the principal tries to stop the protest. I can think of only a handful of parents who would defend their child or even allow these soiled clothes—a symbol of the abusive tactics—to be worn to school in the first place. Most parents would just let the incident pass in order to avoid publicity, but the Joneses are different from most parents in today's society. I know that I would never have the courage to do what T.J. did, but if I had chosen to advertise the abuse, my parents would have backed me. Our relationship thrives on our mutual trust and respect for each other's opinion. Like T.J., I am fortunate in having supportive parents, but I know that many kids these days suffer without this bond. In a world where most kids grow up with only one parent, the pressure on that parent to fill both roles is enormous. Sometimes my heart breaks listening to the sad stories kids tell me. I wish there was something I could do to help.

Social Worker Response to #4

These are very sensitive observations on your part, especially about the significance of the poor little innocent fawn standing over its killed mother and what that represented to T.J. The pressures endured by single-parent families in which one parent tries to fill both roles worsen when there is no real role model for the gender of the absent parent. Usually kids will base their understanding of that role on the popular, stereotypical media icons: pop stars, seductive actresses, rock stars, and sports figures. These over-publicized entertainers live outside the norm. Unfortunately, these images are readily available to most families where the television is the usual baby-sitter. In most cases, no parental interaction with the child occurs to sort out the meaning of what is actually portrayed in movies and situation comedies. Furthermore, unavailable parents, forced to work multiple jobs, cannot effectively enforce or prescreen the adolescent's viewing habits.

Steven Covey's *The Seven Habits of Highly Effective Families* (Covey, 1998) discusses the great importance of instilling family values in our rapidly increasing external society. The materialistic values held at the extreme affect the psychological development of our youth. Years ago, if a parent were absent or the family failed, the external society's influence was considered a model for adolescents and actually increased the chances they would grow up to become contributing members of society.

Teacher Response #5

As a nurturing human being, I could never imagine leaving my children without food or attention. I cannot imagine becoming so depressed that I would resort to taking drugs, hindering my ability to function. What possesses a person like Glenda, T.J.'s biological mother, to lose control, knowing her child depends on her for care and responsible decisions? T.J.'s intuitive reaction to the abuse Chris Coughlin receives creates a natural bond between them. T.J. reacts from his soul, and his alter-ego forces his actions in standing up for Chris. Is this the norm for children who are abandoned and neglected? Does instinct take over, creating a sort of "spiritual Robin Hood"?

Social Worker Response to #5

Most parents give up as a result of their own deprivation, neglect, and/or abuse from their own experience in childhood. Glenda probably experienced such poor parenting when she herself was a child. Abandoned and neglected children may not necessarily identify with another's pain. Fortunately, T.J.'s adoptive parents have encouraged his involvement in therapy, which has enhanced his development and strengthened his capacity for insight and self-awareness. Is it a natural instinct for such a kid to become a spiritual Robin Hood? I tend to think not unless a child has the capacity to identify and relate to others' feelings. Even with this capacity, it still takes courage to stand up for an underdog or for one's own principles. T.J. has an unusual amount of maturity and insight for the "typical" (if there is such a thing) abandoned child. T.J. has most definitely benefited from his supportive adoptive parents and a good therapist.

Teacher Response #6

When T.J. was first adopted at two, he had frequent outbursts of rage. Georgia Brown, a therapist, helped T.J.'s adoptive parents cope with the transition and assisted T.J. in managing these outbursts. Georgia also assisted T.J. with the rejection he experienced with girls during his adolescent years. Finally, the one girl he eventually hooks up with comes from an abusive family. Carly is not afraid to stand her ground against her father's outrages, has talent beyond most normal teenagers, and shows up at the school dance with T.J.'s nemesis—Mike Barbour. T.J.'s amazing control in not blowing his cool over Mike showing up with Carly seems unreal to me, but I suppose his control has a lot to do with his therapy. What about those teenagers who do not get help? Where do they end up? Does the state provide free counseling for those without the income?

Social Worker Response to #6

Most communities offer a mental health board, providing free counseling or therapy to those who do not have the income or the insurance to cover costs. The drawbacks to free services, however, are long waiting lists, only a few selected therapists, and other sorts of limitations. Children such as T.J. who do not get professional help usually wind up acting out their emotions without knowing why they are doing so. Often they have self-destructive tendencies that get them in trouble at school, possibly leading to expulsion. Because their emotions can interfere with learning, they may not do well in school and are susceptible to falling in with those who are negative influences. Involvement with alcohol and drugs may seem attractive. This in turn may lead to sexual encounters that cause them to become parents long before they are ready. Becoming a parent too soon may preclude finishing education, and thus the cycle perpetuates itself.

Teacher Response #7

In an intense and memorable scene, Mr. Jones tells T.J. about a zenith event that occurred in his own life. Mr. Jones's life was forever changed the day he stopped at a diner for a meal while a toddler crawled under the wheel of his semi. It took a lot of courage for Mr. Jones to tell T.J. the story about the death, revealing his continuous agony in thinking the death was somehow his fault. Deep conversations such as this reveal this father's trust in his son's ability to understand and increases their emotional bond. T.J.'s father doesn't deserve to be punished because it wasn't his fault, but this man is tortured by the memory. Explain how some people just don't seem to care what they do to children. There are far too many news events recounting *intentional,* horrific, and tragic deaths of innocent children at the hands of an adult, sometimes even a biological parent. What happens to young adults who commit heinous crimes and are sent to prison for numerous years?

Social Worker Response to #7

People who hurt children are acting out on impulses of which they may not even be aware, or they may be blindly parenting in the same way they were parented. Dependent mothers, with little ego strength of their own, may allow others—such as a stepfather or a boyfriend—to abuse or inflict extreme punishments on their children. Sometimes a parent or caregiver may even know better, but there is something about a particular situation—usually one that is highly emotionally charged—that provokes the person's internal unresolved child to act out. These people have not learned how to control their impulses, nor have they learned that it is possible to refrain from acting on one's emotions. Without therapy, they may not know they have a choice about how to behave in response to a certain stimulus. Drugs and alcohol are often in the mix. Sometimes after the incident is over, they realize they have gone too far with their discipline and may even experience extreme remorse. The remorse is similar to the way perpetrators of domestic violence will swear that they'll never do such a thing again, begging forgiveness of the victim. When someone is sentenced to prison for violent acts, rehabilitation is possible, but it doesn't happen overnight. Unfortunately, our prisons and jails are usually places where criminals learn to be better criminals. It is especially detrimental to place children in adult jails, where they are further victimized and exploited; too often this is true of juvenile rehabilitation centers as well.

Teacher Response #8

T.J. works overtime keeping the morale high on the swim team. Accomplishing his personal goals as a swimmer and standing up for the other team members takes great resilience, considering the verbal abuse from what seems to be the entire school. Nothing is worse than public humiliation, especially from your peers. I think T.J. pulls strength from the thanks he gets from Chris Coughlin's aunt, who says she's noticed a significant positive change in Chris since he's been on the swim team. I feel particularly outraged by the teacher, Sanford Davis, who purposely places Chris in the back of the room and plays mind games with him. Do kids report teachers who verbally and psychologically abuse students? We hear about teachers involved in sexual indiscretions, but rarely do we hear of the ones who abuse their students in other ways. Do kids simply take verbal and emotional abuse from teachers as though it is the norm? What can good teachers do to help kids who appear to have given up?

Social Worker Response to #8

Reporting an abusive teacher would be too threatening for most students. The teacher holds the power in the classroom. A young adult who is developmentally delayed, such as Chris, would be less likely to stand up for himself or to the teacher. Realistically, a discriminatory teaching situation would come to light only if the child's parents or some other concerned parent or teacher complained to the principal or school authorities. Adolescents who fail to try obviously need teachers who take time to get to know them, including their parents or caretakers. A phone call home often sheds light on the student's background, issues, and interests. These days parents or caretakers with busy schedules do not make time to visit their children's school. Requesting a referral to the school social worker is a viable resource in helping teachers understand students who demonstrate real problems. More gray areas occur when students refuse to open up. Without the benefit of the family's input, teachers can simply try developing a rapport with a troubled student by offering genuine praise for something positive noticed at school or by sharing something from personal experience. In most cases, this recognition assists an adolescent in opening up. A visit to the home is worth thousands of words. Often, a teacher can gain more information in a single observational visit to the adolescent's home than in several parent-teacher conferences, where family members sometimes cannot effectively express themselves. Observing the cultural situation, the ethnic composition of the neighborhood, or the proximity to external influences and risks—such as drugs peddled on the street corner—are just a few of the key clues to silence or unwillingness to participate.

Teacher Response #9

When T.J. goes home for lunch and finds his father sitting in the dark, watching humpback whales swimming across the screen, I thought for sure that Mr. Jones was going to commit suicide. The death of that little boy surely has taken its toll, even after 30 years. Is this depth of grief normal?

Social Worker Response to #9

For anyone who has experienced a huge loss and been through the grieving process, I think Mr. Jones's grief is understandable. Try to imagine the additional difficulty he has in forgiving himself for being the one who caused the death, even if indirectly. Even if Mr. Jones had worked through this trauma successfully, the anniversary of the event or reminders of the tragedy could cause him to revisit it, even if only briefly.

Teacher Response #10

The title of this book, *Whale Talk,* means something significant. Mr. Jones tells T.J. that a whale voices her "anguish, rage, and despair" if one listens carefully to her truth. Each character must find his own truth in this novel, and T.J.'s father has found this insight by identifying with the whales during his search for inner peace.

Social Worker Response to #10

T.J.'s father simply projected onto the female whale what he assumed she would verbalize in her anguish at losing a child or being separated from her offspring. In my opinion, the more powerful notion of the whale talk is the distance of the thousands of miles in the ocean that it travels. Metaphysically speaking, the power of the word—whether spoken or thought—has wide-reaching ramifications. Words or thoughts held in the mind become very real and eventually manifest externally in physical and material forms. All that is in our own personal worlds first originated in thought and words. The spoken word is part of understanding and controlling the ocean of our emotions.

Teacher Response #11

Why doesn't Kristen, Mike Barbour's on-again, off-again girlfriend, tell an adult about Mike hitting her for not submitting to his sexual advances? T.J. is so fortunate to have parents who reason with him and help him understand the difficulty in dealing with violent people. T.J.'s mother says that Mike probably goes home and regrets his actions but then tries to justify them by blaming Kristen in some way. She then goes on to say that Kristen's own father probably blames Kristen for things that go wrong in their home. Does Mrs. Jones's account hold true in most cases? According to T.J.'s mother, T.J. used to react violently in certain situations until he "played it out" in therapy, proving that therapy must work. What can be done to stop these people before they react? Can't they be made to go to therapy?

Social Worker Response to #11

Abused individuals develop their sense of selves at the hands of an older perpetrator, usually an adult or a parent who doesn't have a clue. Adult victims of domestic violence were typically abused as children. Children with low self-esteem are often taught to believe they are "bad" or "worthless" and thus deserving of the abuse received. This false belief may give the child a sense of mastery over the situation, giving the child a perceived sense of self-control in order to get attention from the parents. Even though the abuse is hurtful to the child, many times the parent is remorseful and tries to make it up to the child by extending special privileges or gifts. So the child begins to recognize some "benefits" to the situation. For instance, a child may think, "I had this beating coming because I did (whatever), which made Daddy or Mommy mad." Without some sort of therapeutic intervention, the individual will gravitate to relationships in which the same dynamics are played out into adulthood, where the thought is replayed as: "I had this beating coming because I did (whatever), which made my significant other mad."

In response to your last question, all therapists and counselors are ethically bound to hold in confidence all information their clients share, unless the therapist is aware that someone's life is at grave risk. Even the authorities usually cannot intervene unless the person actually breaks the law.

This can be so frustrating, especially when you can see that a client is a walking time bomb. The law is on the side of "innocent until proven guilty," which is part of the benefits and risks of living in a free society. Treatment may be court ordered, but often it's not considered very effective unless the participant truly wants to change. Change is hard, as any of us knows who may have tried to stop smoking or lose weight. Also, many of the perpetrators involved in treatment don't have the capacity for insight into their problems due to their own limitations, nor do they have the support systems to continue to reinforce or practice the new learned behaviors from the therapy. I believe in the potential benefits of therapy, but it's just not as easy as forcing someone to go.

Teacher Response #12

Because the Cutter High swim team might actually meet the school board requirements for receiving letter jackets, the "WT" requests a special reevaluation session to discuss the current prerequisites for lettering. Principal Morgan, who also happens to be a coach, joins forces with the traditionalists and harasses T.J. for confronting Mike Barbour about the incident. In our faculty meetings, one teacher always challenges the principal's discussion, asking key questions concerning teachers' welfare. I admire this man. His courage to say what no other teacher dares, and the fact that he knows and understands all the underlying issues, deserves recognition. T.J.'s swim coach reminds me of this brave person who chooses the perfect moment to speak up. Even though the administration and other sports members are too proud to admit the "mermen" into the merit system of their own accord, the confidence among the swim team members evident in their spoken revelations comes from deep inside these boys; they each acquired their personal truths. Everyone has to admire this group of misfits, who start out as nobodies in the eyes of the in-crowd and prove that underdogs can be winners. At least those who put forth the effort can be winners. I wonder what goes through the heads of those misfits who only sit in class and pass the time.

Social Worker Response to #12

Fortunately, the swim team realizes that the letter jacket symbolizes very little. The thrill of belonging and believing in oneself are the most important lessons learned through this effort in proving themselves. These kids are winners all the way around. Satisfaction comes when a person decides to take control of his life and chooses his own destiny; T.J. does that superbly, despite the letter jacket. Admiring this group of "misfits" who win has got to be one of the most inspiring aspects of this book to engage the type of reader being targeted.

Outside of the usual adolescent daydreaming and sexual fantasies, certainly there are some kids who aren't able to concentrate on the assignment at hand due to worry about some troublesome situation at home, with a girlfriend, or with peers. When you observe a student who appears to "check out" frequently, it would be good if you could try to find out what's going on. It may take some repeated tries and effort for a kid to open up to you. In some situations, you could suggest that the student talk with someone other than you, such as the counselor or another trusted adult. Even just reporting your observation in a nonjudgmental way so that the individual can "hear" you is good feedback. Even if the student doesn't appear to take it in at the time, he or she may reflect on it later.

Teacher Response #13

A subplot of the novel that I haven't discussed much is Heidi's story. Heidi is ethnically mixed, and Rich, her stepfather, abuses her and her mother terribly. Heidi's mother, Alicia, stays with the Joneses for a while, but Rich becomes clearly out of control and starts harassing the entire family. Mr. Jones bonds with Heidi, perhaps filling the void that the little baby left after the accidental death. I suppose it is natural for Mr. Jones to intervene and confront Rich, setting up another person for this abuser to add to the long list of victims. I doubt that most foster parents would ever go to this extreme. Are there guidelines for intervention from the proper authorities in cases like this one?

Social Worker Response to #13

The Child Protective System (CPS) is in place to protect children, and sometimes this means the child must be removed from the family of origin. Nonetheless, the CPS agency's first effort is always to try to avoid placing the child outside the biological family. If, however, removal is the only recourse, then the agency is obligated to construct a time-limited plan for reuniting the child with the biological family as soon as possible. The guiding mission should be to determine what's in the best interest of the child.

Another dynamic, and a very real problem, is that most communities have a shortage of foster homes, especially good ones. Because removing a child from his or her family can also be emotionally detrimental to the child—even in the best of placements—most agencies will try to do what they can to keep the family together. This may include giving the parent a "break" if he or she has otherwise been doing well in meeting the terms of the reunification plan. The reunification plan or agreement is a type of contract signed by both the CPS agency and the parent(s). Some of the typical terms of this type of agreement might include participating in therapy, with and/or without the child present; attending drug rehabilitation and/or AA programs; attending and participating in parenting classes; attending all opportunities for scheduled visitation, often "supervised" with an agency representative present with the child; and demonstrating appropriate parenting in that situation. There may be other terms for the contract, depending on the unique needs of the particular family, such as lining up appropriate child care if the parent works outside the home and severing destructive ties of negative relationships.

CPS agencies have policies, guidelines, and practices in place for foster families to adhere to in dealing with the estranged parent figures or family. All foster and adoptive families are expected to participate in initial training classes to prepare them for the sorts of situations they might encounter; many topics are covered. Experienced foster families are also expected to participate in a required number of training hours each year to keep their licenses current. Even outside of required training, there are other less formalized and more immediate opportunities for learning through local support groups for foster and adoptive families. These families need all the training and support they can get. This novel demonstrates exactly how difficult and challenging their roles can be.

Teacher Response #14

Because Mr. Jones personally takes over the legal and verbal stance against Rich, refusing him the right to see Alicia and Heidi, Rich ends up shooting Mr. Jones with the deer rifle. Because of our ineffective laws, an innocent and courageous man's life is lost. Television shows seem to always end this way, with the good guy losing his life so that the bad guy can be put away. Our laws are ineffective if they don't protect the innocent. What can we do to change the system?

Social Worker Response to #14

Changing the system always feels so monumental, doesn't it? But to effectively impact even one student's life is really quite a victory when you think about it. No one can ever know how many more lives that individual will positively impact as a reasonably well-functioning, thinking person who will influence others—including his own children. This is how our system can be changed at a fundamental level, and teachers are in one of the most important pivotal positions to play a part in it! Laws and rules can be useful to effect change, but there will always be that certain element of people who have no regard for the law.

CONCLUSION

In an effort to help students cope with the situations in their lives, English teachers offer hope and guidance through books. Reading about characters who struggle through similar dilemmas creates a connection for troubled students, fosters understanding from healthy ones, and can comfort unstable children. Teenagers thrive on books that speak their language and offer the key ingredients to life. By immersing themselves in a fictional world full of choices and consequences, students can be led toward self-fulfillment and sound solutions for their own problems. Certainly, it is Chris Crutcher's (1999) intention in writing books like *Whale Talk* to help teachers and counselors to engage teens in therapeutic conversations in the hope that such talk will enable students to overcome their own troublesome or disturbing situations.

REFERENCES

Covey, Steven R. (1998). *The seven habits of highly effective families.* New York: St. Martin's Press.

Crutcher, Chris. (1999). My three faces: The writer, the therapist, and the man. In J.F. Kaywell (Ed.), *Using literature to help troubled teenagers cope with family issues, Volume one* (pp. 1–15). Westport, CT: Greenwood Publishing Group.

Crutcher, Chris. (2001). *Whale talk.* New York: Harper Collins.

Part IV

Sexual Abuse

The following sources offer information on defining sexual abuse and understanding its pervasiveness, causes, and deleterious results. Web links for these organizations are indicated at the end of the brief summary.

DEFINITION OF SEXUAL ABUSE

Child sexual abuse is any sexual contact between a child and another person, from fondling to rape, with or without force. The offender is always 100% responsible for child sexual abuse. Child sexual abuse is *never,* not in whole or in part, the victim's fault. Informed consent is not possible. http://www.duhaime.org/childsex.htm

Sexual abuse includes fondling a child's genitals, intercourse, incest, rape, sodomy, and commercial exploitation through prostitution or the production of pornographic materials. Because of the secrecy or "conspiracy of silence" that so often characterizes these cases, sexual abuse is the most underreported form of child maltreatment. http://www.focusas.com/Abuse.html

Sexual abuse is any unwanted sexual intimacy forced on one individual by another. It may include oral, anal, or vaginal stimulation or penetration, forced nudity, forced exposure to sexually explicit material or activity, or any other unwanted sexual activity. http://www.aaets.org/arts/art8.htm

Sexual abuse occurs when a child is exploited for the sexual gratification of an older person. This abuse may be in the form of fondling, penetration, or exposing sexual body parts. http://www.stopsexualabuse.com

Nontouching sexual abuse offenses include indecent exposure/exhibitionism, exposing children to pornographic material, deliberately exposing a child to the act of sexual intercourse, and masturbation in front of the child. http://www.preventchildabuse.com

Sexual abuse can take many forms, but it usually begins by eroding the emotional and physical boundaries of a child needy for attention and affection; this process is referred to as "grooming." Over time, contact can begin with indecent exposure, making sexual comments, intruding into the child's room or bathroom, and then progress to include fondling, touching sexual parts of the child, and encouraging or forcing the child to touch the offending adult. Sexual abuse also includes showing a child pornographic material. http://www.crosscreekcounseling.com/sexual_abuse.html (Cross Creek Counseling Center, 2001)

Any sexual contact between a child and a trusted adult, from flirtation to sexual intercourse, needs to be dealt with assertively. Sexual abuse scars all aspects of victims' lives and robs them of their self-esteem. http://www.siawso.org (Survivors of Incest Anonymous)

EXTENT OF THE PROBLEM

After investigating hundreds of studies and making statistical adjustments for what is known about additional factors, Lloyd deMause after 30 years of research concludes "that the real sexual abuse rate for America is 60 percent for girls and 45 percent for boys, about half of these directly incestuous." http://www.psychohistory.com/htm/05_history.html (*The Journal of Psychohistory 25* (3), Winter 1998)

According to D. A. Regier & R. W. Cowdry's 1995 research on violence and traumatic stress, about 1 in 5 female children and 1 in 10 male children may experience sexual molestation. http://www.aaets.org/arts/art8.htm (National Institute of Mental Health)

An estimated 1 in 5 women and 1 in 10 men report having been sexually abused in childhood. http://www.kidshealth.org/parent/positive/talk/sexual_abuse_prt.htm (KidsHealth, 2000)

A rape survey conducted by the National Victim Center in 1992 showed that 29% of all rapes occurred when the victim was less than 11 years of age, and another 32% occurred between the ages of 11 and 17. http://www.designm.com/protectkids/pages/guide.html

A nationwide poll commissioned by the National Committee to Prevent Child Abuse in 1995 indicated that 23% of parents (30% of mothers and 9% of fathers) reported that as a child, they had been "forced to touch an adult or older child or had been forcibly touched by an adult or older child in a sexual way; or that they had been forced to have sex with such an individual." http://www.cdc.gov/epo/mmwr/preview/mmwrhtml/00049151.htm (Centers for Disease Control, 1997)

In regard to sexual victimization, the National Incidence Study of Child Abuse and Neglect (NIS) survey concluded that girls are sexually abused three times more often than boys, whereas boys are at greater risk of emotional neglect and serious injury than girls. http://www.acf.dhhs.gov/news/ press/1996/nis.htm

Socially permissive attitudes about gender-based violence have been internalized by our youth. According to Advocates for Youth (2000), 62% of students surveyed believed that a male is not at fault if he rapes a girl who dresses provocatively on a date, and males were less likely to believe that the male is totally at fault. A large percentage of teenage girls (29%) who experience dating violence or date rape do not tell anyone. It is important that people involved with youth help to shatter misconceptions about gender-based violence and help to create environments and opportunities where young girls and boys can feel comfortable talking about their experiences and obtaining needed services. http://www.naswde.org (National Association of Social Workers: What Social Workers Should Know about Gender-Based Violence and the Health of Adolescent Girls, 2001)

Between 25% and 50% of adolescent girls with mental and/or physical disabilities have been sexually violated. In spite of these high percentages, few women receive treatment from victim services specialists. http://www.vaw.umn.edu/Vawnet/disab.html (Violence Against Women Online Resources, 1998)

Two-thirds of sex offenders in prisons victimized a child, and 60% of convicted sex offenders are on parole or probation. Half of the women raped were younger than 18 years of age. http://www.prevent-abuse-now.com/stats.htm

There are an estimated 60 million sexual abuse survivors in the United States. Thirty-one percent of women in prison state that they were abused as children. http://www.prevent-abuse-now.com

This site lists several myths and facts about sexual abuse. For example, two myths are that children make up stories about abuse and that only strangers or "dirty old men" sexually abuse children. The facts are that children rarely make up stories about sexual abuse, and most sexual offenders are people the children know. http:// www.casat.on.ca/handindx.htm

Gerri Gribi, an award-winning musician and historian, compiled an extensive list of annotated "Songs Related to Domestic Abuse and Sexual Assault." The bottom line is this: The crime of rape remains the least reported, least indicted, and least convicted of any major felony. http:// www.creativefolk.com/abusesongs.html

In *Desert Flower: The Waris Dirie Story,* the author self-reports being brought up in Somalia, where she was taught "that there are bad things between a girl's legs, a woman is considered dirty, over sexed and unmarriageable unless those parts—the clitoris, the labia minora, and most of the labia majora—are removed." The practice of infibulation, performed on 80% of the women in Somalia, is the removal of the genitalia, leaving only a small opening and a scar. Village women in primitive environments perform the operations using knives, scissors, or sharp stones with no anesthetic. Although female genital mutilation (FGM) is practiced predominantly in Africa, cases have been reported among girls and women in the United States and Europe where there are large numbers of African immigrants. Approximately 6,000 girls per day face this dangerous practice, which eliminates all possibility of their having personal sexual enjoyment. http://www.fgmnetwork.org/articles/Waris.htm

WHO DOES IT

According to a study focusing on the kinds of people who harmed 1,011 children in 2000, abusers were most often people the children knew and trusted; only 5% of the alleged perpetrators were strangers to the children. Seventy-seven percent of all alleged perpetrators were male, and 23% were female, with the average case being 7-year-old white females sexually abused by a father figure. http://www.carecenter-okc.org/statistics.html (Child Abuse Evaluation and Response Center based in Oklahoma City)

Male parents were identified as the perpetrators of sexual abuse for the highest percentage of victims. http://www.calib.com/nccanch/prevmnth/stats.htm

Following are some of the characteristics of molesters: can have adult sex partners, but children are the primary sex object; often target a specific gender, age, hair color, and eye color; have easy access to children; use threats to manipulate and control victims or bribe them with gifts, love, or promises, luring victims into their confidence before victimization takes place; shame children into not telling anyone of the abuse; may commit their first offense when in their teens and continue the behavior even after conviction and treatment; are mostly male but can also be female; may videotape or photograph sexual activity with children to exchange with other molesters; and have some network with pornographers. http://www.designm.com/protectkids/pages/guide.htm

Rape is a crime primarily committed against girls and young women. Adolescents are considered to be at highest risk for sexual assault, with more than half of reported assaults occurring in dating situations. Overall, 12.5% of teenage girls in grades 9 through 12 reported being forced to have sexual intercourse. http://www.naswdc.org/practice/update/ ah0102.htm

Incest and sexual abuse are prevalent among drug-abusing adolescents. The incidence of incest and sexual abuse among adolescent girls who are in chemical-dependency treatment is estimated to be two to three times higher than for adolescents in general. http://www.fadaa.org/resource/ justfact/sexualabuse.html

Having a history of past sexual abuse or prior sexual victimization appears to be one of the most important risk factors for date/acquaintance rape. Adolescents with a history of sexual abuse are five times more likely to report date/acquaintance rape than nonabused peers. http://www.etr.org/ recapp/research/journal200009.htm

Approximately 15% of students will be sexually abused by a member of the school staff during their school career. http://www.ncweb.com/org/ rapecrisis/sesameresearch.html (Survivors of Educator Sexual Abuse & Misconduct Emerge: S.E.S.A.M.E., 1998)

RECOGNIZING SEXUALLY ABUSED CHILDREN

Following are the behavioral indicators of child sexual abuse: unusual interest in or avoidance of all things of a sexual nature; sleep problems or nightmares; depression or withdrawal from friends or family; seductiveness; statements that their bodies are dirty or damaged or fear that there is something wrong with them in the genital area; refusal to go to school; delinquency/conduct problems; secretiveness; aspects of sexual molestation in drawings, games, and fantasies; unusual aggressiveness; and suicidal behavior. http://www.aacap.org/publications/factsfam/sex abuse.html (The American Academy of Child and Adolescent Psychiatry, 1998)

Sexually abused children may have nightmares or develop sleep problems; exhibit signs of depression; and/or show aspects of sexual molestation in drawings, games, and fantasies. http://www.aacap.org

Following are warning signs and indicators of a sexually abused 9- to 13-year old: withdraws socially, avoids close peer relationships, displays promiscuous sexual behavior, exhibits manipulative behavior, is often truant from school, and/or sexually victimizes younger children. http://www. rasac.org/warning.html (Rape and Sexual Assault Center, Nashville, TN, 2000)

Sexually abused adolescent girls are more likely than nonabused teens to report more physical complaints, including headaches, asthma, spastic colitis, and heart palpitations as well as gynecological symptoms. http://www.familymanagement.com

RESULTS OF SEXUAL ABUSE

Child sexual abuse, more than child physical or emotional abuse, seems to be a risk factor for earlier pregnancy among African American adolescents according to Fiscella. http://www.ama-assn.org/special/womh/library/scan/vol_4/no_12/fiscella.htm (Published April 1998 in *The Journal of the American Medical Association* by Kevin Fiscella, MD)

Many survivors (estimates are as high as 50%) do not remember the abuse until years after it has occurred. Usually something in adulthood will trigger the memory, causing "flashbacks" where the survivor re-experiences the sexual abuse as if it were occurring at that moment. "Re-victimization" refers to women who were sexually abused as children getting involved in abusive, dangerous situations or relationships as adults. This Web site lists numerous reports, books, and booklets that can be downloaded and printed from there and includes the children's book *The Secret of the Silver Horse*. http://www.hc-sc.gc.ca/hppb/family violence/childsa.html

The effects of sexual abuse are numerous and can be long term. They range from depression and low self-esteem to post-traumatic stress disorder (PTSD) and include multiple-personality and borderline syndromes. Longer duration and higher frequency of abuse have been correlated with greater trauma. http://www.ncvc.org/infolink/info05.htm (National Center for Victims of Crime, 1997)

Group treatment is often an ideal therapeutic setting because trauma survivors are able to risk sharing traumatic material with the safety, cohesion, and empathy provided by other survivors. As group members achieve greater understanding and resolution of their trauma, they often feel more confident and able to trust others. As they discuss and share ways of coping with trauma-related shame, guilt, rage, fear, doubt, and self-condemnation, they prepare themselves to focus on the present rather than the past. Telling one's story (the "trauma narrative") and directly facing the grief, anxiety, and guilt related to trauma enables many survivors to cope with their symptoms, memories, and other aspects of their lives. http:// www.ncptsd.org/facts/treatment/fs_treatment.html

Research has revealed that prostitutes report histories of sexual abuse as children. http://www.ojp.usdoj.gov/ovc/publications/infores/clergy/chld abus.htm

YOUNG ADULT NOVELS INVOLVING SEXUAL ABUSE

Throughout the following sources, RL: MS = Reading Level: Middle School and RL: HS = Reading Level: High School.

Anderson, Laurie Halse. (2001). *Speak.* New York: Puffin Books. 198 pp. (ISBN 0–14–131088–X)

Melinda Sordino begins her freshman year of high school as an outcast, an almost invisible student without a voice. "Nobody really wants to hear what you have to say" (p. 9). None of her friends wants to hear why she called the police during that summer party; no one even asks. The novel, narrated by Melinda and alive with characters we may all recognize from our own high-school experiences, realistically portrays Melinda's struggle to recapture her voice and her strength, to speak up and tell the world what happened. Her quest to express her pain, to tell her truth, metaphorically weaves itself into Mr. Freeman's assigned art project to turn an object (for Melinda, a tree) into a piece of art. "This is where you can find your soul, if you dare. Where you can touch that part of you that you've never dared look at before" (p. 10). Through Melinda, Anderson shows the courage of a young adolescent girl conquering the "Beast" in her life. At the end, Melinda's growth as displayed through her metaphoric tree, gives the reader hope for Melinda's recovery. Her growth, her tree, breathes hope. (Winner of the 2001 Heartland Award for Excellence in Young Adult Literature, a 2000 Printz Honor book, an ALA Top Ten Best Books for 2000, a 1999 National Book Award Finalist, Edgar Allen Poe Award Finalist, Winner of the Golden Kite Award, an ALA Top Ten Best Books for Young Adults, an ALA Quick Pick, a *Publishers Weekly* Best Book of the Year, a *Booklist* Top Ten First Novel of 1999, a *BCCB* Blue Ribbon Book, an *SLJ* Best Book, & a *Horn Book* Fan Fare Title) RL: HS (sexual abuse)

Atkins, Catherine. (1999). *When Jeff Comes Home.* New York: Putnam. 231 pp. (ISBN: 0–399233–66–0)

Bright and handsome, 13-year-old Jeff Hart is the star pitcher on his school's baseball team and the apple of his father's eye. Everything changes the day Jeff is kidnapped at knifepoint and is held captive for over two years by a man who routinely rapes him. Jeff's first-person account begins the night he returns home after his ordeal and chronicles the adjustments he must make to try and regain his life. Jeff won't talk to the FBI agent or his family about what occurred during the time he was away because his feelings of self-hate, shame, and guilt overwhelm him constantly. Jeff's father arranges for him to start school as a junior and pushes him to pick up where his old life ended by encouraging him to pick up sports again. Jeff can barely hold a normal conversation with his brother and sister, and the thought of anything ever being "normal" for him again is unimaginable. When Jeff's kidnapper is arrested, he asserts that Jeff was a runaway participating in a consensual relationship. Jeff must make the decision to face his abuser with the truth or forever be a victim, living in the horror of those two and a half years. Jeff breaks his silence and begins to tell his father what happened to him, relieving himself of some of the burden of his guilt and shame while finding acceptance among the people who love him. Details of Jeff's rape and abuse unfold slowly and are not explicit, but the mental and emotional torture that sexual abuse and rape victims endure after the abuse is center stage in this page-turner. While the situation of a kidnapping may not relate specifically to most sexual abuse victims, this book is one of the few that deals with male sexual abuse, and Jeff's feelings of self-blame and hopelessness are common to all abuse victims. The story confronts many issues that male sexual abuse victims must deal with, including subsequent rumors of the victim's homosexuality. RL: HS (sexual abuse)

Block, Francesca Lia. (2000). *I Was a Teenage Fairy.* New York: HarperCollins. 192 pp. (ISBN: 0–064408–62–0)

Once upon a time in Los Angeles there was a girl named Barbie Marks who was forced by her aging, beauty-queen mother into the ugly, adult world of modeling. Mother manages Barbie's career and life with an iron fist while allowing Barbie to become prey for a child-molesting photographer. To cope with the abuse and the life of glamour she does not want, Barbie dreams of becoming a photographer herself—to be the one who is in charge, who creates the beauty. Her only hope comes from two sources: Mab, a pinkie-sized, blue-skinned fairy with deep red hair whom Barbie met about the time when the molestation began; and two new friends, Griffin Tyler (whom she remembers seeing years earlier, being forced into the studio of the molester by his mother) and Griffin's roommate Todd Range, who encourages Barbie's own ambitions. Mab thinks the thoughts that Barbie is not allowed and speaks them to her. Together, Barbie and Mab experience a host of adventures where Barbie learns what Mab and her friends have been trying to get her to believe all along. Barbie must believe in and take care of herself and know that she can rebuild her life with love, acceptance, and a new name. With her signature language and writing motifs, Block creates a fantasy world with very real problems and emotions experienced by young people. Block writes to the adolescent audience in this "postmodern fairy tale," revealing the ugly, realistic side of people and sexual abuse, but offering strength and hope to her characters and readers. (Los Angeles Times Best Sellers) RL: MS (sexual abuse)

Block, Francesca Lia. (1994). *The Hanged Man.* New York: Harper Collins. 137 pp. (ISBN: 0–06–440832–9)

After her father dies, 17-year-old Laurel drifts through her dreamlike, stylized Los Angeles world trying to heal. Years of sexual abuse are over, but Laurel feels the scars left by her father's abuse and her mother's ignorance. Laurel's anger at her father turns inward, and Laurel becomes anorexic in an attempt to disappear. Drug abuse and careless sex color Laurel's Los Angeles world, which Block draws as a magical fantasy world. Tarot cards begin each chapter to help both Laurel and the reader follow her attempted self-destruction and her eventual recovery. This book offers a sensual, symbol-laden journey through one young woman's attempt to recover from years of abuse. RL: HS (sexual abuse)

Lauck, Jennifer. (2000). *Blackbird.* New York: Pocket Books. 406 pp. (ISBN: 0–671–04255–6).

The house on Mary Street was home to Jennifer, her older brother B.J., their hardworking father who smelled like aftershave and read her *Snow White,* and their mother, who called her little daughter "Sunshine" and dressed like Jackie O. But Jennifer's perfect world begins to crumble as her mother's mental illness and eventual tragic death shake Jennifer's foundation. Her father remarries into a bad situation; Jennifer is abused by her stepmother and molested by her stepbrother. In the midst of her loneliness and loss, Jennifer learns to transcend her landscape of pain and mistreatment to discover her richest resource—her own unshakable will to survive. Readers will get caught up in the innocent narrator's perspective on the abuse and her eventual triumph. RL: HS (sexual abuse)

Luna, Louise. (2001). *Brave New Girl.* New York: Pocket Books. 197 pp. (ISBN: 0–7434–0786–5)

Doreen Severna's summer before entering high school is filled with cleaning the garage, hanging with her one friend Ted, listening to the Pixies, and being raped by her sister's 21-year-old boyfriend. The story, told through Doreen's eyes, outlines a young girl's transition into adulthood amidst a family that doesn't understand her, doesn't see a predator's moves, and doesn't protect her in her own house, where any child should be safe. An outcast among her peers, Doreen looks forward to a different future. "I wish I was a big reader, though. When you hear about people who everyone hated in junior high but then became a movie star or a famous writer or Nobel Pulitzer winning whoever, they're always saying stuff like they were always in a corner, reading book after book while all the cool kids laughed" (p. 19). No one laughs, though, when Doreen becomes the "brave new girl" and stands up for herself by telling the truth about her attacker. As Doreen confronts her feelings and speaks the truth, she impacts her life, her family's, and her best friend's. This book is a great testament to the courage to tell the truth, no matter how evil that truth is. RL: HS (sexual abuse)

Mazer, Norma Fox. (1994). *Out of Control.* New York: Avon Books. 218 pp. (ISBN: 0–380–71347–0)

Valerie is a quiet, artistic teenager. The Lethal Threesome is a group of three boys who have been friends since grade school. One day, Valerie snubs one of the three boys in front of his friends, and The Lethal Threesome impulsively decide to get revenge. Their sexual harassment and intimidation of Valerie are quickly exposed, however, and all pay a price for their vicious, thoughtless actions. Readers will see that actions can get quickly out of hand among peers and that the consequences for those actions may be much more devastating than anyone could imagine. RL: MS (sexual abuse)

Reynolds, Marilyn. (1996). *Telling.* Buena Park, CA: Morning Glory Press. 160 pp. (ISBN: 1–885–35603-X)

Twelve-year-old Cassie begins baby-sitting for a young couple only to have the father of her charges begin making sexual advances toward her. Although she is never actually raped, she is definitely intimidated by him. He corners her on several occasions and sexually assaults her with his hands. The book deals with Cassie's feelings of guilt, fear, and worry about "telling." Readers become engaged in a realistic account of what happens when Cassie does tell. RL: MS (sexual abuse)

Sparks, Beatrice. (2000). *Treacherous Love: The Diary of an Anonymous Teenager.* New York: Avon Books. 162 pp. (ISBN: 0–380–80862–5)

At the age of 14, Jennie's life is beginning to fall apart, largely due to her parents' failing marriage and emotional abandonment. Her father is rarely home, and her mother is taking pills. Jennie's two best friends are also unavailable now that Marcie has moved away and Bridget spends all her time with her new boyfriend. Jennie doesn't even have a boyfriend to talk to, and she knows why: she is short, flat-chested, and looks like a baby. The only true friend Jennie has is her diary, where she records the loneliness of her life. At the lowest point in her self-esteem, she meets Jonathon Johnstone, a substitute math teacher who is full of praise for her abilities in class. Soon he asks whether she might like to be his student aide to help him grade papers because he has an eye injury. She develops a crush on her math teacher and is surprised and delighted when Mr. Johnstone reveals his feelings for her. They begin a relationship, but over time her loneliness returns and she begins to feel trapped. *Treacherous Love* graphically shows how a young girl may become prey for a molester, a "how not to" book for girls. RL: MS (sexual abuse)

Talbot, Bryan. (1995). *The Tale of One Bad Rat*. Milwaukee, OR: Dark Horse Comics, Inc. (ISBN: 1–56971–077–5)

In an effort to make this graphic novel explore a sensitive issue that concerns the author, Bryan Talbot has created a new genre. In this beautifully drawn comic, readers follow teenage runaway Helen Potter through the cities and countryside of England as she escapes sexual abuse. The name Potter and the rat are both homage to Beatrix Potter, herself an emotionally abused child, whom Helen admires as a person and as an artist. The text is minimal and the drawings tell most of the story, but the story of pain, anger, and guilt caused by sexual abuse is clear. Helen's ability to confront her father and begin healing makes the reader cheer. (an Eisner Award winner, a Comic Creators' Guild Award winner, and Internet Comic Award for Best Graphic Novel) RL: HS (sexual abuse)

Turner, Ann. (2000). *Learning to Swim*. New York: Scholastic Press. 116 pp. (ISBN: 0–39–15309–3)

This book is a series of touching narrative poems that tell the story of little Annie. The lyrics convey the feelings of a girl whose sense of joy and security at a family's summer house is shattered when an older boy who lives nearby sexually abuses her. This haunting story juxtaposes the beautiful summer Annie is supposed to have—picking blueberries with her mother, playing with her brothers, learning to swim with her dad—with the terrible secret she bears. RL: MS (sexual abuse)

Voigt, Cynthia. (1994). *When She Hollers*. New York: Scholastic. 177 pp. (ISBN: 0–590–46714-X)

This novel chronicles one day in the life of Tish, a teenager who decides to stand up to her stepfather after years of rape and sexual abuse. Influenced by the recent suicide of Miranda, a girl at school, Tish decides she doesn't want to face the same desperation herself. Miranda, six months pregnant, hanged herself naked from a tree in the front yard of her house. The rumor mill at school said Miranda was "easy" and asked many boys to sleep with her, but Tish knows the truth. Tish knows that Miranda was a victim of incest and that the baby was Miranda's father's. Tish begins her morning by showing Tonney, her stepfather, the hunting knife she has bought to protect herself. As she warns him to stay away from her in the bathroom and her bedroom, Tish's mother and siblings ignore her outburst. Tonney warns her about the consequences of slander and informs her he will deal with her that night. Tish has one chance to help herself or end up pregnant and/or dead like Miranda, but finding someone who believes her proves to be unimaginably difficult. One adult after another refuses to get involved or doesn't believe that her stepfather is violating her. Tish's inner thoughts are filled with the common feelings of sexual abuse victims: confusion, self-doubt, guilt, and shame. Tish even questions her own memory of the abuse, wondering whether she asked for it or whether her stepfather is telling the truth about her being worthless and a liar. After running away from school, Tish breaks through her shame and guilt and reaches out to a lawyer who is her last hope. RL: HS (sexual abuse)

Weinstein, Nina. (1990). *No More Secrets.* Seattle: Seal Press. 157 pp. (ISBN: 1–878067–00–1)

Much of Mandy's life seems relatively normal for a teenager. She likes to hang out with her best friend, has difficulty communicating with her critical parents, and feels terribly alone. Mandy, however, lives with a dreadful secret—when she was nine years old, she was raped by an acquaintance of her mother. This secret has been suppressed by her parents, and for years Mandy struggles with her memories and her sense of identity. Finally, persistent health problems force her and her family to confront the past. Slowly, with the help of an understanding therapist and her best friend, Mandy learns to accept what happened to her and begins the process of healing. Readers may be able to identify with Mandy's struggle to communicate with her parents and come away with insights into the roles and responsibilities that various family members may assume when dealing with a crisis. *No More Secrets* has a gritty, realistic flavor, as Mandy slowly resolves many of her internal and external conflicts. RL: MS (sexual abuse)

NONFICTION TEXTS EXPLAINING THE PROBLEM OF SEXUAL ABUSE

Angelica, Jade Christine. (2002). *We Are Not Alone: A Teenage Boy's Personal Account of Child Sexual Abuse from Disclosure through Prosecution and Treatment.* Binghamton, NY: Haworth Press. 94 pp. (ISBN: 0–7890–0927–7)

Jade Christine Angelica, the Director of The Child Abuse Ministry in Scarborough, Maine, sheds light on the emotional ordeal a sexually abused teenage boy must face. Told in first person, the book is Joe's story of the process he goes through after a neighbor molests him. Angelica also offers *We Are Not Alone: A Guidebook for Helping Professionals and Parents Supporting Adolescent Victims of Sexual Abuse* "as a companion volume for therapists, teachers, legal and law enforcement professionals, and parents of the victim."

Alpert, Judith L., Brown, Laura, & Courtois, Christine A. (1996, Feb. 14). Symptomatic Clients and Memories of Child Abuse: What the Trauma and Child Sexual Abuse Literature Tells Us. *Working Group on Investigation of Memories of Childhood Abuse: Final Report.* American Psychological Association, pp. 1–91.

This final report is written in the form of a debate. The first group (three therapists) presents its beliefs/findings, the second group (three scientists/researchers) responds, and then the first group responds back. The second group then presents its findings and beliefs, the first responds, and the second responds back. Together they develop a conclusion, discussing their agreements and disagreements. Following are some of their observations.

- Child sexual abuse is a complex stressor that carries a multiplicity of potential meanings for the child victim; furthermore, the child's age and stage of development are critical to the child's reactions and ability to understand.
- Developmentally intolerable emotional and physical arousal can lead a child victim to utilize numbing and/or dissociative coping strategies.
- Numbing and/or dissociative strategies used to cope with sexual abuse may interfere with or impair coding, storage, or retrieval of memory.
- Numbing responses may lead to delayed recall.
- Adult survivors may use pathological and dysfunctional coping strategies.
- A consensus has developed among experienced clinicians regarding post-traumatic therapy. Symptom management, containment, and safety and

stability are important goals for the preliminary phase of treatment. Discussion of traumatic material for post-traumatic resolution optimally is undertaken after stabilization is achieved.

Brown, Jocelyn. (1999, December). Childhood Abuse and Neglect: Specificity of Effects on Adolescent and Young Adult Depression and Suicidality. *Journal of the American Academy of Child and Adolescent Psychiatry, 38* (12), pp. 1490–1496.

Beginning in 1975, more than 700 children between the ages of 1 and 10 were studied for a 17-year period. As adolescents and young adults, those who had suffered some form of maltreatment (as determined in separate interviews with the children and their mothers as well as information obtained from New York State records) were three times more likely to suffer from depression or suicidal tendencies. Those who had endured sexual abuse as children were eight times more likely to attempt suicide repeatedly. It is unlikely that neglect alone is responsible for depressive disorders or suicidal behavior, but coupled with sexual abuse, it places a youth at greatest risk. The study estimates that 16.5%–19.5% of attempted suicides may be linked to childhood sexual abuse. It also suggests that clinically depressed youths be screened for the presence of different types of abuse. Finally, the study "suggests that children who have been neglected are less likely to become depressed or suicidal if the contextual risks that comprise their lives could be changed."

Dersch, Charlotte Alyse, & Munsch, Joyce. (1999). Male Victims of Sexual Abuse: An Analysis of Substantiation of Child Protective Services Reports. *Journal of Child Sexual Abuse, 8* (1), pp. 27–48.

Researchers attempted to understand why Child Protective Services reports involving female victims of sexual abuse are substantiated at a significantly higher rate than reports involving male victims. The study analyzed the investigative process, related variables of reports involving both genders, and concluded that the reports yielded few differences. In fact, reports involving male victims had a greater reliability, specifically concerning the source of the complaint. The study suggests reporters and investigators require education regarding sexual abuse signs in males.

Foshee, Vangie A., Bauman, Karl E., Greene, Wendy F., Koch, Gary G., Linder, George Flether, & MacDougall, James E. (2000, October). The Safe Dates Program: 1-Year Follow-Up Results. *American Journal of Public Health, 90* (10), pp. 1619–1622.

As a result of providing community activities such as a play and a poster contest about date rape to rural adolescents, researchers found after a year that adolescents were less accepting of dating violence, more knowledgeable about where to go for help, able to list more negative consequences to dating violence, and less likely to respond destructively when angry.

Garneski, Nadia, & Deikstra, Rene F.W. (1997, March). Child Sexual Abuse and Emotional and Behavioral Problems in Adolescence: Gender Differences. *Journal of the American Academy of Child and Adolescent Psychiatry, 36* (3), pp. 323–330.

Seven hundred and forty-five 12- to 19-year-old Dutch boys and girls who, according to a self-report questionnaire, had experienced sexual abuse were matched for age and sex with adolescents who did not have a self-reported history of sexual abuse. Comparison of results indicate that adolescents with a history of sexual abuse have significantly more emotional problems, behavioral problems, and tendency toward suicide than adolescents without a history of sexual abuse. When looking at differences between girls and boys, suicidality was reported almost five times more often by sexually abused boys than by sexually abused girls. Also, sexually abused boys reported higher rates of additional risk behaviors and aggressive criminal behaviors than girls. Although in the general population emotional problems are reported much less in boys than they are in girls, the reporting of emotional problems in sexually abused boys and girls was about the same.

Gothard, Judge Sol, & Cohen Ivker, Naomi A. (2000, May). The Evolving Law of Alleged Delayed Memories of Childhood Sexual Abuse. *Child Maltreatment, 5* (2), pp. 176–190.

Court cases based on recovered memories raise serious ethical and legal issues, and the authors offer a general warning: The issue of delayed memories has formed two "recognizable and organized camps," and allegiance to one or the other (citing one as enlightened and the other as perverse) could lead to a danger of polarizing the findings of either group. Because many states are allowing delayed memory cases to come to court, the plaintiff must meet the burden of proof by a preponderance of evidence to support the claim. In some cited cases, the "repressed memories" are often compared with "hypnotically refreshed testimony," and courts do not accept such testimony. Cases are cited that indicated that some patients believe that therapists "planted" such memories. General practices and safeguards for therapists are then outlined. The authors conclude that "courts must be careful to balance the interests of victims with their judicial function to critically test the validity of all evidence presented" on a case-by-case basis.

Holmes, William C., & Shep, Gail B. (1998, October 2). Sexual Abuse of Boys: Definition, Prevalence, Correlates, Sequelae, and Management. *Journal of the American Medical Association, 280* (21), pp. 1855–1862.

The researchers found that studies and definitions for sexual abuse concerning boys varied greatly; yet 8%–16% of the male population has experienced sexual abuse. The highest at-risk group is younger than 13 years old, nonwhite, of low socioeconomic status, with the father absent from home, and with known but unrelated male perpetrators. Abuse typically involved penetration and occurred more than once. Male sexual abuse is "under recognized, underreported, and under treated," and the authors warn that "such a wholesale societal shunning" of sexual abuse of boys plays a part in psychosocial problems in adult male victims. Drug abuse as a form of self-medication is a popular option for victims because our culture does not encourage male victims of sexual abuse to speak out or seek help.

Jones, Rebecca. (1999, November). I Don't Feel Safe Here Anymore. *American School Board Journal,* pp. 26–31.

The U.S. Department of Education's Office for Civil Rights has said that public school districts must protect homosexual students from sexual harassment, just as they protect heterosexual students. The U.S. Supreme Court Decision *Aurelia Davis vs. Monroe County Board of Education* says that under Title IX, school districts must protect homosexual students from "harassing conduct of a sexual nature" but not from "simple heckling." Unfortunately, gay youth who have been harassed usually refuse to name their harassers for fear of reprisal. Administrators therefore cannot punish those who are responsible. On-campus support groups (SAGA or GSA) and discussions of homosexuality when appropriate to the curriculum may help to lessen harassment of gay and lesbian youth.

Krahe, Barbara. (2000, September). Childhood Sexual Abuse and Revictimization in Adolescence and Adulthood. *Journal of Personal and Interpersonal Loss, 5* (2/3), pp. 149–166.

After a summary of leading research regarding the effects of sexual abuse upon children, the author expounds upon the lasting effects such abuse has on a person's psychological development in adolescence through adulthood. In women, there is a link between childhood sexual abuse and number of sexual partners, failed marriages, and self-esteem dependent upon social relationships as a source of self-worth. In men, some research points to confusion about sexual orientation, sexual aggression, and difficulty in maintaining an intimate relationship. Another effect of childhood sexual abuse is the recurring evidence of revictimization. Physical, emotional, and sexual abuse during adolescence and adulthood within interpersonal relationships occurs more frequently among those who report childhood experiences with sexual abuse. The author concludes by pointing out the need to focus on the tendency for revictimization in order to provide appropriate therapy when an adolescent or adult is treated for repeat abuse—noting that rape in particular causes more severe trauma in a patient who had previously been sexually abused as a child.

Lev-Wiesel, Rachel. (1999, May). The Use of the Machover Draw-a-Person Test in Detecting Adult Survivors of Sexual Abuse: A Pilot Study. *American Journal of Art Therapy, 37* (4), pp. 106–112.

In this pilot study, subjects were asked to use the Machover Draw-a-Person Test in order to identify adult survivors of sexual abuse. Four common indicators in the drawings that help in diagnosis of childhood sexual abuse were found: (1) a double chin or cheek, either empty or shaded; (2) shaded, hollow, dot, or omitted eyes; (3) a barrier between the upper and lower body; and (4) clinging, cut-off, detached, or omitted hands and arms. According to the results, "the well-known systems that characterize sexually abused survivors—sexual difficulties, anxiety, depression, feelings of helplessness, poor self-identity, poor self-image, and poor interpersonal relationships—seem to be symbolized by the four indicators."

Luster, Stephen A., & Small, Tom. (1997). Sexual Abuse History and Number of Sex Partners among Female Adolescents. *Family Planning Perspectives, 29* (5), pp. 207–211.

The researchers found that adult survivors of sexual abuse are more likely to engage in sex with many different partners than adults who had not been sexually violated. They also noted that a disproportionate number of teenage mothers have been victims of sexual abuse. Luster and Small hypothesize that adolescents who are currently being abused may seek other sexual partners as a way of coping with the pain of the experience.

Palmer, Sally E., Brown, Ralph A., Rae-Grant, Naomi I., & Loughlin, M. Joanne. (1999, March-April). Responding to Children's Disclosure of Familial Abuse: What Survivors Tell Us. *Child Welfare, 78* (2), pp. 259–283.

Adult survivors of physical, emotional, or sexual abuse in childhood were interviewed, and 92% were pleased that they had revealed the abuse. Problems emerged when the child disclosed abuse but the abuse did not end, when the child offered partial or incomplete disclosure, and when children denied abuse because of manipulation by the abuser. Children who told the truth about their abuse found it difficult to disclose because "of the fear of the consequences, self-blame, lack of awareness, and difficulty in talking about the abuse." Telling the truth, however, helped them understand the abuse was not their fault. Because believing children is so important and because children are often not forthcoming with the truth, this study illustrates the need for parents and child welfare workers to recognize signs of abuse.

Ray, Susan L. (2001, April/June). Male Survivors' Perspectives of Incest/Sexual Abuse. *Perspectives in Psychiatric Care, 37* (2), pp. 49–61.

Most research on sexual abuse has been done on females, not males. This report investigated 25 males, all of whom had been sexually abused as children, who participated in an interview to determine the effects of childhood and adolescent sexual abuse on their lives. Most of the abuse occurred when subjects were six years old or younger, and most of the perpetrators were male. Respondents reported having feelings of isolation, anger, and depression; suicidal tendencies; addictions; a low sense of self; and distant relationships. The report concludes that psychologists ought to explore the possibility of previous sexual abuse among men who seek treatment for any of the above issues.

Snyder, Howard N., & Sickmund, Melissa. (2000). *Juvenile Offenders and Victims: 1999 National Report.* Washington, DC: Office of Juvenile Justice and Delinquency Prevention.

Age 14 is a young woman's year of greatest risk of sexual assault.

Sobsey, Dick, & Varnhagen, Connie. (1991). Sexual Abuse, Assault and Exploitation of Individuals with Disabilities. In C. Bagley & R.J. Thomlinson (Eds.), *Child Sexual Abuse: Critical Perspectives on Prevention, Intervention and Treatment.* Toronto: Wall and Emerson, pp. 203–216.

Children with disabilities are particularly at risk for sexual abuse. Researchers evaluating the findings of several incidence studies suggest that the risk of sexual abuse is at least 50% higher for children with disabilities than for nondisabled children of similar age and gender.

Stone, Robin D. (2001, August). Silent No More: Coping with Sexual Abuse. *Essence Magazine, 32* (4), pp. 122–133.

This informative and encouraging article by the editor-in-chief of *Essence Magazine,* a survivor of sexual abuse, is directed toward the actual victims of sexual abuse rather than those who may be counseling or supporting them. The article summarizes the cases of four girls who had been abused as children, offers information about the prevalence and causation of sexual abuse of children, and offers victims practical advice for recovering from sexual abuse. "Because sexual violence...is fueled by the abuser's need for power and control, those who have less power, such as children, are often more vulnerable" (p. 123). "For survivors of sexual abuse, there is no one formula for recovery, but every path to healing ultimately requires that we speak out about the ways in which we have been violated" (p. 124). Several notable suggestions are offered for victims in recovery.

- Avoid asking yourself why. Asking why deepens the wound and feeds the feelings of shame and guilt. An unanswered why improperly places the responsibility on the victim.
- Keep your body moving. Dancing, swimming, yoga, or any physical activity can help you rebuild and regain a healthy relationship with your body.
- Talk to yourself. Learn to love yourself by creating powerful, loving affirmations that support and encourage you.
- Rehearse the confrontation. Write out what you would say to your abuser, and write the response you believe the abuser would have. Keep writing both sides of the story until you experience peace. Repeat this exercise as many times as necessary.
- Create a safe place. When you go to your safe place, sit quietly, pray, meditate, or just hold loving thoughts about yourself.
- Get professional help or support.

Tudiver, Dari, McClure, Lynn, Heinonen, Tuula, Kreklewitz, Christine, & Scurfield, Carol. (2000). Remembrance of Things Past: The Legacy of Childhood Sexual Abuse in Midlife Women. *A Friend Indeed, 115* (4), pp. 1–6.

Sexual abuse survivors may not seek preventative medical care because invasive tests or procedures may cause memories or unresolved anxieties to surface. The authors explain that "Pap smear tests, use of vaginal probes in ultrasound examinations, touching and compressing of the breast in mammograms, or dental care can evoke feelings of powerlessness and depersonalization reminiscent of previous abuse" (p. 2). Health-care professionals need to be sensitive to those patients who exhibit severe anxiety or display "uncooperative" behaviors when being examined.

Widom, Cathy Spatz, & Ames, M. Ashley. (1994). Criminal Consequences of Childhood Sexual Victimization. *Child Abuse and Neglect, 18,* pp. 303–318.

In her research, Widom seeks to find out whether subjects who were sexually abused were more likely to engage in later delinquent and criminal acts. Widom found that there is a widespread belief that those who suffer childhood sexual abuse are more likely to commit criminal acts, but that the belief is incorrect. Most people who suffer this type of abuse in childhood are depressed, sexually disturbed, and suicidal. Although her findings indicate that sexual abuse sufferers are not more likely to commit crimes, they are more likely, when the crimes are broken down into categories, to commit sexual crimes.

Williams, Linda M. (1994). Recall of Childhood Trauma: A Prospective Study of Women's Memories of Child Sexual Abuse. *Journal of Consulting and Clinical Psychology, 6,* pp. 1167–1176.

Williams reports that as many as one in three incidents of child sexual abuse is not remembered by the adults who experienced them. Further, the younger the child was at the time of the abuse and the closer the relationship to the abuser, the more likely the adult is not to remember.

CHAPTER 8

Winning the Battle for Self after the Big Lie in Chris Crutcher's *Chinese Handcuffs*

Joan F. Kaywell and Sue Street

INTRODUCTION

Chris Crutcher is not an author who shies away from difficult subject matter. In *Chinese Handcuffs,* Crutcher takes on one of the toughest and most sensitive issues—sexual abuse. He does not stop there. In one of his bravest story lines, Crutcher also deals with divorce, drug addiction, gang mentality, teenage pregnancy, and suicide. The story has a heavy, dark feel to it—as it should—but Crutcher is adept and qualified to handle such issues; he is a family therapist by trade. What makes him such an effective storyteller, however, is how he imbues the theme and plots of this story with a special undercurrent of spirituality, humor, and hope.

SYNOPSIS OF *CHINESE HANDCUFFS* BY CHRIS CRUTCHER

The point of view in the story alternates between third-person and first-person, as Dillon, the novel's protagonist, writes to his dead brother Preston. Through Dillon's journal entries, readers glean insight into the painful experience of Preston's life, his drug addiction, his gang involvement, and his physical disability. More importantly, after witnessing Preston's suicide, Dillon writes to gain some understanding of his brother's senseless act, the aftermath, the breakup of his family, and his own familial issues. In one of his letters, for example, Dillon recalls the time he and Preston tortured a cat: "I accept Charlie the Cat as a major saint; he's the one who taught me not to judge. Since the day he died, I can't look at the horror in *anyone* without looking at the horror in myself" (Crutcher, p. 15). This experience gives Dillon strength and self-knowledge that helps him throughout his story. From this early entry on, Dillon faces the sober reality that people—all people—experience both good and bad things in life. The choices we make in response to what happens to us, or what is done to us, determine our own characters. After witnessing one suicide, Dillon will be damned before witnessing another. This is where Jennifer Lawless, the school's top basketball player, comes into the story.

Jennifer's stepfather, T.B. Martin, has sexually violated her for years. It has become her big Secret, the big lie she's learned to live with. Because of her stepfather's prominent position as an attorney, specializing in family law, Jennifer sees no way out but has made a livable plan for herself. She will do well in school and then run away with her little sister Dawn. Suicide, however, seems like her only option when she tells Dillon,

> "I had convinced Dawn to leave with me," Jen said. "I finally figured out I have to leave Mom there. If she wants out, she'll have to do it herself. But now she's pregnant. And it's a girl. She waited for the ultrasound to tell us, wanted to be sure the baby was okay. It's a girl. It's okay. It's okay until the minute it gets here. Then it gets *my* life. I can't do it, Dillon. I can get Dawn out, but now there's a baby. A baby girl. I can't beat him, Dillon. He'll kill it. He'll kill its heart, just like he did mine." (p. 183)

The story Crutcher tells of Jennifer, first when she is touched by her father and later, when she is raped by her stepfather, is painful to read. Having been sexually abused by her biological father when she was six, Jennifer had already been in therapy for what had happened then, but her mother stopped taking her when the therapy was no longer required. When Jennifer tried to tell on T.B. when she was eleven, she learned that "Child Protective Services isn't for rich people, and it isn't for smart people" (p. 128). T.B. is a loathsome character who is as smart as he is abusive; he spends his time "grooming" Jennifer. T.B., being wealthier and smarter than Jennifer's real father, explains to CPS that Jennifer is using that experience as a way to work out her resentment of him taking over his role as "father." Further, "he tied [her] dog to the back bumper and ran over her" (p. 129) the day that Jennifer told, and he has always kept his wife submissive by secretly beating her. Dillon becomes better equipped as the novel progresses to help Jennifer get the help she needs when he learns what has been done to her.

In recalling Charlie the cat, Dillon knows that he cannot name the horror in others and overlook the horror in himself; he knows he needs adult counsel for this monster. Even as society condemns the physical and sexual abuser, we cannot overlook the cycle of abuse that creates abusers. This passage is the only insight into T.B.'s mind we get as readers:

> Women were so stupid!...For years he had to beat [his wife], had to get into a rage just to deal with her.... Just knowing his rage kept her in line. And Jennifer. If it hadn't been for that dog, he might have had more trouble with her, but once he'd crushed his stupid cute little skull into the pavement, well, that was that. He hadn't spent his childhood locked in closets and tied to his bed doing nothing. He'd thought. In utter darkness he had figured out the world. (p. 194)

His voice is harsh and sardonic. He mentions his bitch of a mother who had an unfortunate "accident" because of failed brakes; his sickness is evident. What is scary is the success of the social mask that has kept T.B. unrecognizable to the general public, in fact, kept him wealthy and respected as a family lawyer.

In a story about sexual abuse, "things get misnamed" (p. 84), and understanding this is the key to understanding abuse. There is so much we call love, for example, that is not love. Jennifer recalls a very important lesson from a therapy session about her mother's inaction: "[K]ids have an inalienable right to unconditional care, and parents who don't give it are breaking a spiritual law" (p. 153). Abuse, in any form, depends on perverting definitions. Jennifer realizes that nothing is what it seems, and for teenagers—especially abuse victims—this is an important lesson to learn. One of the first steps to recovery is realizing that what we have been told is "love" and the things done to us or not done for us in the name of "love" are or were bogus.

Chinese Handcuffs shows the reader that life is a tangled web of many experiences, some of which are very unpleasant. Crutcher refers to these unpleasant things that we must learn from as keeping us in "Chinese handcuffs." When we learn what we need to learn from the experience, we find out that the only way to get out of its control is to let go. Crutcher's metaphor illustrates a powerful truth. Jennifer's control keeps her in T.B.'s grasp, and T.B.'s control keeps the family as his prisoners. By the novel's end, Dillon has learned the lesson: "Well, bro, I guess that about wraps it.... I've got better things to do with my life than spend it...writing to a man who never reads his mail. My struggle with you is finished. I'm going to let you go, push my finger in and release us from these crazy Chinese handcuffs" (p. 215). Only by giving up control do the people in this novel begin to be free—to stop fighting and start choosing.

MOVING BEYOND THE TEXT

This next section explores how teachers anonymously responded to the novel and then shows how a teacher might have suspected the abuse and referred Jennifer for professional help had Dillon not gotten involved. Finally, a mock counseling session is offered on how Jennifer might have addressed these issues prior to her suicide attempt.

TEACHERS RESPOND TO THE TEXT

At the very beginning of *Chinese Handcuffs,* I thought the novel was just going to be about an athlete, which is definitely not a strong identification for me. Then, as Dillon Hemingway writes in one of the letters to his dead brother, Preston, about humor and intensity (pp. 7–9), it occurred to me that Crutcher's athletes display but one form of intensity in their athletic discipline. There are other forms. Most successful people are intense in some way, driven by financial, humanitarian, or intellectual goals, for example. But what makes us human and allows us to cope with our failures and difficulties is our sense of humor. Without it, we would be robots. Laughter helps us to cope with disasters as large as war, or the massive death and destruction of the September 11 attacks on the World Trade Center and the Pentagon, or things as personal as the loss of the life of a loved one. Without a sense of humor, we would be lost, as Dillon says Preston was.

Jen's description of abuse by her own father (p. 42) made me cringe. I believe that reading *Chinese Handcuffs* has affected me so deeply because I have played the part of Dillon in my own life. When I was a young teenager, my best friend confided in me about a date rape. She was on vacation with her family and another friend. They met some seemingly nice guys who invited them to a movie. My best friend was held at knifepoint on the movie theater floor and raped. It was cathartic for her to tell me about her feelings of guilt. I would just listen. She would cry and talk. I knew that I could not fix her pain but that I could just be there to listen. I finally convinced her to see a counselor. She was so afraid of her parents knowing of her rape because she felt that they might view her as a promiscuous young girl who was "asking for it." Her therapist helped her through these feelings and probably saved her from years of emotional turmoil.

I have played the part of Dillon at another time for another friend whose father abused her from when she was very young until his death when she was only nine. My friend suppressed the memory for almost 40 years, until after her mother died and there was no one left to confirm her horrible memories. She has worked with a therapist, and I have had endless discussions with her about her memories and what we heard our parents and neighbors whisper when they thought we weren't listening. We have no doubts that the abuse was real. On page 70, speaking about her mom and stepfather, Jen says, "I really don't like to talk about them, okay? I made a decision a long time ago that if I pretend they don't exist, I don't have to deal with them." This is the way my friend seems to have dealt with her father. I first met her 43 years ago, when she was twelve. Before her memories surfaced, I don't think I heard her speak about her father more than a handful of times, and she never spoke with love or tenderness. Even as a child everything she said about him seemed cold and factual to me. I was uncomfortable with that but at the time had no idea what it might mean.

In chapter 4, the description of Preston's involvement in the gang rape of a young woman and his suicide riveted me. I was both revolted and fascinated. I can understand why a drug-dependent person would see no way out, but I so wanted to tell him not to pull the trigger on himself. One big benefit of aging is that you do learn that sufficient time changes the way you see things. Forty years ago, divorce, abortion, unmarried motherhood, and even changing your hair color were considered scandalous behavior. Had he waited and been willing to put in the effort, Preston might have served a jail term, received some psychiatric help, and continued his life. Suicide is far too permanent a solution.

When Dillon writes to Preston that Stacy "left for about six months shortly after your funeral, to stay with some relatives in South Dakota; her parents said she needed to heal" (p. 90), I was immediately suspicious. In the next paragraph, Dillon says four months after Stacy left, her parents adopted a baby boy. I figured it out immediately and was surprised that Dillon didn't, but things were different in my day. This novel keeps bringing me back to the 1950s. It was common practice then, if a girl became pregnant, to ship her off to "an aunt." This usually meant a home for unwed mothers. The family then made some excuse why the girl was staying with this fictitious aunt for several months. When the baby was born, it was usually put up for adoption, and the girl came home to resume school and her normal life. Pregnant girls were not permitted to go to school with the rest of the population. I never did figure out that one. Did they think the rest of the girls might learn too much about sex from the pregnant one? I think seeing what the "unwed mother" (the term of shame) had to go through could have been the biggest deterrent to sexual involvement. In those days it was a humiliating embarrassment.

I also admire the courage and commonsense approach that Stacy displays when she decides to tell the truth about her baby and his father. She says, "If it was a mistake, it's mine, and I may as well start living with it." The narration goes on to say, "[S]he realized what was missing in her life.... It was humor. It was laughter.... You can't laugh when you lie because lies signify shame, and there is no laughter in shame" (p. 159). The shame of her baby had muffled the joy. When our minds are occupied with covering up a mistake and maintaining a lie, there is little room for real improvement. In fact, the lie often increases in size and does proportionate damage to us in the long run. Look at many prominent politicians for examples. Stacy shows a healthy instinct for putting her life back on the right track. She will probably get herself in trouble for making the announcement over the P.A. system, but it saved her the slow, whispering pace of gossip and long stares in the hallways if she told only a few friends first.

Jen's mother really disturbs me! I hate her and pity her at the same time. She is obviously a victim, too, but I can't forgive her for not protecting her own child. Surely if a woman knows a man will beat her, she should fear for the physical safety of her children, even if she's unable to fathom the possibility of sexual abuse. Even after marriage to a proven sexual abuser of Jen—his own child—this woman's choice of men continues to place Jen in danger, and Mom seems clueless.

Crutcher's idea that CPS is for poor kids but not rich kids really hit me. So many girls in my past 18 years as a high-school teacher flash through my mind. Betty was the gorgeous class president, but the rumor mill said that she was slapped around by her boyfriend. I had both Betty and the boyfriend in my class. He was a mousy nothing, while she was the real brains of the operation. I did not believe the rumors, but now wonder whether I should have. And then there was Amanda, who was homecoming queen and calendar cover girl. She was in another one of my classes where she continuously called attention to herself (even though she seemed to get enough attention as it was). When she came back a year after graduation to crown the new queen, she was so thin as to elicit concern from the school. There was talk of anorexia. I wonder whether the call for attention in my class was a call for help. When girls are pretty, popular, smart, and well dressed, it is difficult for teachers to see what they may be hiding. Am I so obtuse that I need a black eye or a tearful appeal before I can see that a child needs help?

I have a girl in my extended day language arts class who looks as though she is 40 years old. She is overweight. She doesn't smile. She wears her hair in one thick braid running down her back. She's quiet and nervous. She can't focus, and she can't read. This week I went into the SED (Severely

Emotionally Disturbed) building at my school and was surprised to see that girl sitting in the first row. Her teacher told me that Clarisse has a lot of problems, especially since her mother had a kidney transplant and Clarisse had been put into the role of caretaker. She said there were still lots of mysteries concerning Clarisse; she suspected that Clarisse had secrets that needed to be told. Clarisse kept running through my mind as I read Crutcher's description of T.B.'s rape of Jennifer. The irony, of course, is that Jennifer is beautiful, talented, smart, and rich. Dumpy, plain Clarisse sits in a class with a trained SED teacher, a paraprofessional, and a psychologist helping her work through the shame and fear in her life. With hard work and good luck, Clarisse's support base will give her life.

Chris Crutcher's final prophetic statement on Jen, her mom, Stacy, and Dillon is revealed in Dillon's words on page 220. "I guess some things just can't be fixed." He is speaking to the senile Mrs. Crummet about the murder of her hostile cat years ago. The damage will always be there, but if it's acknowledged, if you admit it, then you can deal with it and get on with the rest of your life. What a great piece of advice for everyone!

A COUNSELOR TALKS WITH JENNIFER

Most professionals agree that a child who voluntarily discloses abuse to someone has taken the first step toward taking control of her life and is ready to begin the healing process. For many adolescents, a caring and concerned teacher or counselor is the first step in the disclosure. Let's add a chapter to Jennifer's life, making her a 15-year-old girl attending 10th grade.

Jennifer lived with her mother and stepfather in a middle- to upper-class neighborhood. T.B. has been her stepfather since she was six and began coming into her bedroom at night when she was about nine. Her mother worked late frequently and had gained a great deal of weight since her little sister was born. T.B. had initiated sexual intercourse by the time Jennifer was eleven. It was disgusting to her, but she was also disgusted with herself as she often found herself responding sexually to his advances. She hated him, but the sexual part (as it had been with her biological father) often felt pleasurable.

She felt immense guilt for her pleasure and had a vague feeling she was responsible for this relationship. It was this guilt that kept her from initially telling anyone or from saying "No!" to T.B. when he came into her bedroom. Yet there were times when she found herself very angry and wanting everything to end, no matter what, even in spite of his threats to murder her dog. She wanted her mother to do something and wondered how her mother could not know or not do something in response to what had been going on right in her own home for years! But Jennifer never said anything. And other than her mother, Jennifer did not know who to trust or who to tell or who would believe her. She did not know where to begin. Jennifer felt trapped and did not know where to turn or what to do.

Her only outlet was her writing. Jennifer wrote in a diary that she carefully hid under her piles of boxes and junk in her closet. Nobody ever went in there. She wrote in code terms anyway. But she also loved to do school-work that involved writing, and English and journalism were her favorite subjects. Jennifer had started writing poetry in her diary, and she found it was a wonderful way to express her feelings. She thought of herself as someday being a writer, but she did not know how that would be possible. Her mother had not gone to college; in fact, she had dropped out of high school when she became pregnant with Jennifer. Her mother had never suggested that Jennifer go to college. Still, Jennifer tried very hard to do well in school because it was the only place she experienced any success, any pleasure or sense of accomplishment.

Jennifer was the last student in her English class to turn in her paper. Ms. Smith had noticed that Jennifer had seemed particularly low lately. She did well on tests and homework but never raised her hand to comment or respond in class. Yet she knew the answer when called upon. She spoke quietly and chose her words carefully when she spoke.

"How are you doing, Jennifer?" asked Ms. Smith as Jennifer turned in her paper.

Jennifer did not answer, but only shrugged with a weak smile. The truth was, she was discouraged when she came to school that morning and was further discouraged because she had not studied enough to do well on the test that day. T.B. had come into her room last night when she was sitting down to study for the test, and somehow she'd not gotten much studying done. She was afraid if she said anything, she might start crying. And so she simply shrugged without speaking.

"Things piling up these days?" asked Ms. Smith, with genuine care in her voice.

"Yeah, sorta." Jennifer's voice was low, and she could feel her throat swelling and tears coming up, tears she was unable to stop. She knew she could not say a word without crying.

"Life has a way of doing that sometimes. Anything you want to talk about?"

Jennifer could only stand there with tears in her eyes, not trusting herself to speak. She finally shook her head no, which she knew was really ridiculous because clearly there was something she needed to talk about.

She handed Ms. Smith a collection of her poems and left hurriedly. These
are the five poems that Ms. Smith read.

"Love"

I saw you in my dreams that night.
You came up to me so gentle and loving.
As you held me in your arms,
You said I could trust you with my life.
You bought me things and
Treated me like I was your special little girl.
You came into my room that night.
You slid your hands around my small, fragile body.
You whispered softly in my ear,
    "I love you."
As you caressed my body,
    my mind started wandering—
or maybe I just started dreaming.
The last thing I remember is a deep, sharp pain
    and a gush of warmth.
My mind hasn't been quite right
    since that night you showed me
    how much you loved me.

"Who's There?"

She's just a little girl frozen in time,
Walking down the dark, dirt road,
Letting the rain wash the blood from her body.
Someone whispers her name.
She runs as fast as her little legs can go.
Her heart beats faster and faster.
The rain has begun to fall harder.
The blood continues to flow.
Again she hears the voice.
She stops in her tracks
And looks up at the sky—
God?

"Mother"

I found myself wandering the streets,
    too afraid to go home,
    knowing in the back of my mind

something was going to happen.
I found myself in the bathroom at school
   a razor blade at my wrist,
   tears rolling down my cheeks.
I found myself looking at you.
   You were looking at me lying there in the casket,
   this time with tears rolling down your cheeks,
   asking me, "Why?"
I found myself saying to you,
   "You let him hurt me.
   You didn't protect me,
   so I had to protect myself."
I found myself asking God to forgive me
   for being dirty and naughty.
God forgave me and said,
   "It was not your fault, my child.
   Your soul is pure and clean."

"In the Shadows of the Night"

In the shadows of the night,
I find myself embracing my blanket tightly, weeping softly, not to
wake anyone.
In the shadows of the night,
if I listen carefully, I can hear the screams of all the little ones as
they cry out each and every night in pain.
In the shadows of the night,
I roll over, my hands over my ears trying to drown out the footsteps
that are coming nearer.
In the shadows of the night,
I lie quietly, dying inside my own body, the pain too much to bear.
Wishing I was in someone else's body.
In the shadows of the night,
I lay bleeding, helpless, cold, dirty, and scared.
In the shadows of the night,
I reach up and touch your face, so soft. You glide across the room,
in a bright light, taking my hand, lifting me up into the cool, brisk
midnight air.
In the shadows of the night,
I look down upon the body from which my soul has just been taken,
With others standing around asking what they could have done.
"Protect your little ones," they hear someone whisper.

"I Wish"

> I see the hurt in your eyes.
> I feel the pain in your heart.
> I feel the anger boiling in your veins.
> You were hurt too.
> I can feel your breath on my body,
> the roughness of your hands,
> the beating of your heart,
> the sweat that drips from your brow,
> the brute strength that pushes you to force me,
> the overpowering of your mind,
> the knife as I stab you.
> I can hear your cries, but you never heard mine.

Immediately Ms. Smith went to the school's guidance counselor, Ms. Casey, a woman she respected for her great rapport with the students. Ms. Casey asked Ms. Smith to try to convince Jennifer to come to her of her own volition. Ms. Smith was not entirely sure whether Jennifer would go on her own, so she tried to show interest in Jennifer's problem, but she did not want to push her either. "Jennifer, I read your poems," said Ms. Smith. "You know Ms. Casey, the 10th-grade counselor, is a great person to talk to. Have you ever talked to her?" Jennifer shook her head no, still not trusting herself to speak. "Some of the other girls have told me she is very good to talk to. Maybe you could go see her. I wish I had the knowledge and skills necessary to help you, if what I think is true is true, but you really need to talk to someone with more experience than I have. I trust Ms. Casey, and I will stick by you every step of the way. Just so you know, there are a lot of people around here who really care about you, myself included, so please come see one of us if you need to."

Jennifer left, averting her eyes with a barely audible, "Thank you."

Jennifer thought hard about what Ms. Smith said. Were there really people at school who cared about her? What would they think of her if they knew the Secret? They surely would not care about her then. They would think she was awful. Child Protection Services didn't believe her when she told, so what could a counselor at school do? But she thought and thought, and finally decided to make an appointment to talk to Ms. Casey. After all, she didn't have to tell her anything. She would talk to her about colleges, and how she could get money to go to college. Then later on, if she wanted to talk to her, she would at least know her. Maybe she would even like her.

Jennifer went in to talk to Ms. Casey. Ms. Casey was a good counselor who really cared about her students. She took an immediate liking to this shy, quiet girl. Ms. Casey knew that if Jennifer was a sexual abuse survivor, and she suspected that she was because of the intensity of Jennifer's poetry, this first meeting would have to establish a collaborative and empowering counselor/student relationship built on an atmosphere of trust and safety. If Jennifer chose to disclose her abuse, then Ms. Casey would need to gain understanding of how the abuse was affecting her.

Ms. Casey: Hi, Jennifer, how are you today?

Jennifer: Fine. (Jennifer is only vaguely aware that her voice is tight and her body constricted so much that she appears quite stiff. She is very aware, however, of her need to be very careful about saying something she does not want to say or giving away the secret unless it seems okay to do so. At the moment, Jennifer is quite sure she can not begin to tell Ms. Casey the awful story, the Secret.)

Ms. Casey: I don't think you and I have talked before. But you left a request that you wanted to talk with a counselor about your plans after graduation. I would be glad to help you with these if I can. I think first I would like to know how your classes are going at this time and where you see yourself going after graduation.

Jennifer: Umm, everything is fine in my classes, and I think I want to go to college. (Jennifer is not sure how to respond, and she is busy on one level in her mind sizing up Ms. Casey as a counselor, as a person she could trust.)

Ms. Casey: Have you thought about the community college? Or the state university? If you continue doing so well on the basketball court, you may even get a basketball scholarship. Have you talked with your parents about this? What do they say?

Jennifer: (Jennifer is not sure where to go with this one. Talk to her parents about college? Ha! That was a real laugh!) Well, I'm not sure. (pause) I guess I need more information. (pause) I think I also need help paying for it, so the scholarship idea is what I want, or a loan, or something like that.

Ms. Casey: Have you thought about your major? Is there a field of study that really excites you?

Jennifer:	Well, I like to write, sometimes, but no, I haven't thought much about what my major would be. (Ms. Casey knows that many times students come to talk to her pretending they had come for one thing but really wanting to talk about something far more personal and serious. In observing Jennifer, she notices that she appears only minimally interested in college; she is distracted. Jennifer is not offering much information but also isn't in a hurry to leave. Ms. Casey decides to shift the subject to learn something about Jennifer's social life and interests.)
Ms. Casey:	I hear a lot of the kids are going to the American Idol concert this weekend. Are you headed that way?
Jennifer:	No. (Her eyes down, Jennifer thinks about how much she would like to have friends to go to that concert with. She could go with Dillon, but she does not have close girlfriends because she would have to bring them home sometime, and this would mean bringing them way too close to the Secret. Ms. Casey tries switching to a different area to learn more about Jennifer.)
Ms. Casey:	What do you and your parents do for entertainment on the weekends?
Jennifer (noticeably swallowing):	I'm sorry, but I need to get back to class. (She is not ready to say anything at all about her family. She is afraid of what might come out.)
Ms. Casey:	Okay, but you know you are welcome to come back and talk anytime. Let me show you where the college catalogues are in the guidance office, so you can begin to read those to get some ideas.

It was a long and slow process, but on her third visit, Jennifer finally told Ms. Casey what had been going on her world for the past six years. Ms. Casey, of course, was obligated to report the situation to her state's sexual abuse hotline, and the local social services agency was at the house within 24 hours to investigate.

It was an ugly mess, but it also felt very empowering. Jennifer was free! She had made the decision to tell! She had taken a step on her own behalf! Jennifer had a good feeling about herself, but the aftermath with her family was really ugly. Her stepfather denied her whole story, claimed she was doing it only to get attention; after all, she had a history. When the nurse examiner reported that she indeed had engaged in sexual intercourse, T.B. claimed she was promiscuous with young men, older men, men of all ages. The worst part was that her mother did not defend or support her, and in fact was inclined to agree that Jennifer had made up the whole thing for attention. She seemed unclear about what she believed, however, and vacillated from a grudging belief in her daughter to a righteous indignant denial that her T.B. could ever have done such a thing. She was very angry with Jennifer—that much was clear—for she was the sole supporter of the family now that T.B. had been removed from the home and been incarcerated.

The good part was that both Ms. Casey and Ms. Smith stood by her the whole way. And even though it was hard to get out of class to come see her, Ms. Casey made efforts to see Jennifer even during her lunch hour or after school; she was a real friend and support to Jennifer. The movement into a new phase of her life was very difficult. Jennifer had to learn that the whole business was not her fault, and she had to learn a completely new way of looking at herself and evaluating herself. Building self-esteem from ground zero was hard. Ms. Casey helped, but she made it clear to Jennifer that the real work would have to take place inside Jennifer's own head. Initially, Jennifer also struggled with a great deal of guilt.

Ms. Casey:	Hi, how are you doing today? What a pretty shirt you have on! Is that new?
Jennifer:	Yes. It was the first thing I bought with my money now that I have a job.
Ms. Casey:	Good for you. Taking control of your own life is a wonderful thing! It's scary sometimes, but it's also very empowering to be "mistress of your own destiny!"
Jennifer:	I guess so. (Jennifer doesn't sound quite sure.) I think today is one of those days that is scary, or hopeless even. (Jennifer's voice trails off.)
Ms. Casey:	So tell me what's going on today that your world looks so dark?
Jennifer:	I just feel so awful. My mom will never forgive me. She's never stopped being mad at me. I've made a real mess of the family. My little sister even calls me names, and (pause) it's just awful at home.
Ms. Casey:	So you're really feeling like you've ruined everyone's life? (Ms. Casey's voice conveys a clear mocking tone.)

You feel like everybody around you would be much better off if you had just kept your secret and not told anyone about the ugliness that filled your life?

Jennifer
(protesting):

Well, maybe it wasn't so bad with T.B. and all. Maybe I should have thought of other people's lives that are now ruined, and it's all my fault.

Ms. Casey:

So you think you should have sacrificed your own life so the rest of the family could go on pretending nothing was wrong? That's very noble, but I think you have things a little mixed up. Your family was not normal. A healthy family does not tiptoe around a secret. Was it good for your parents to allow this to continue? Was it good for T.B. to continue to sexually abuse you? Was it good for your mother to continue to turn a blind eye to the whole thing? Was it fair to your mother that your stepfather was conducting a sexual relationship with you? What does that say about his relationship with her? So you ruined that very committed and devoted relationship. Big deal! Personally, even though I am certain your mother would not agree with me at this point, I think any woman is better off without a man who is being unfaithful to her, especially a man who is being unfaithful to her with her young teenage daughter. (pause) Now wouldn't you agree? (More silence. They both know Ms. Casey is right.)

Jennifer
(slowly):

Yes. I do think that's true. But Mom doesn't see it that way.

Ms. Casey:

Maybe she does sometimes see it that way. But it might be very hard for her to admit it. That would mean she would have to accept some responsibility for her part in her marriage and in your abuse. It's always easier to blame others for your problems. (More silence.) Life is much harder for a single mother who has to make ends meet. Things are easier when there is an additional income and a man to take care of the cars and the house. I do hope that someday she will see that she deserves a man who loves her, cares for her, and is a responsible husband and parent. She deserves that, and so do you.

Jennifer:

Oh, I don't know if I will ever find that. I don't even know if I deserve that.

Ms. Casey: Oh really!? (Ms. Casey's voice takes on that mocking tone she uses so often with Jennifer.) Tell me about that. I think you do deserve to be loved and respected and treated well by a man. If you would treat your love with respect and consideration and generosity—and I know you would—then don't you deserve the same thing from the relationship?

Jennifer: I never thought of it quite like that. I know things don't happen like in the movies, but I don't know how to begin. I mean, I used to dream about a guy coming along and taking me out of my home and away from T.B., but I know nobody would actually do that. I would never tell any guy about what...T.B. and I...what happened to me with T.B.... I couldn't. I would die before I'd tell a guy.

Ms. Casey: Well, I agree that you don't need to run up to people in the halls at school and tell them all the details of your life. And maybe you don't want to tell guys you date. But someday you will find a guy who loves you very much, and then you may want him to know all those significant experiences that went on in your life. These are the things that have made you who you are, for better and for worse. If he loves you, he won't desert you. He will love you for who you are—a warm, caring and very special person.

Jennifer: I guess so. Sometimes I think that, but today is not a great day.

Ms. Casey: We have talked and talked about how the things that have happened to us, even the things we have done, the mistakes we have made, are not who we are. They have contributed to us becoming who we are, but they are not us. We can change whenever we want to and become whatever we want to. It is not always easy, but it can be done. You're changing how you feel about yourself. You're learning that what happened to you was not your responsibility. You were too young, too vulnerable to fight an adult. You didn't have the tools, or resources, or knowledge to understand how to fight that.

Jennifer: I know! I know! Cooperation is not consent! I say that to myself a million times a day!

Ms. Casey: And, as for your belief that your sexual response made you a willing participant, remember that sexual response is a normal, natural thing. Many people respond to sexual advances, even when they don't want to. Many girls respond sexually to unwanted, unwelcome advances. The guilt over that is probably why many girls don't disclose. They think it's their fault. It's the responsibility of the adult who is in control, not the child who has no choices! Everything you did, you did to protect and take care of yourself and your little sister. You did the only thing you could. You can't be blamed for that. Remember, you were a child; he was the adult.

Jennifer: I am trying to remember that. I tell myself that sometimes when I start feeling down. It's hard, though.

Ms. Casey: There are many people who will help you. Many of those people you don't even know, but if you ask for help they will help you. Nobody else blames you. The most important thing is that you stop blaming yourself and start making plans to get on with your life. Remember, your focus should be on your future, not your past. We cannot change the past, only the way we feel about the past. Your life can be healthy from now on. No more secrets! You are now free to be the beautiful, wonderful person you really are inside. Take the time to get in touch with that lovely lady, and you will blossom.

Jennifer (smiling a contented smile):   Someday.

Ms. Casey: You are a beautiful child and are greatly loved. When you begin to love yourself, the universe will open to you in a magnificent way. Trust me.

Jennifer (hugging Ms. Casey):   I do.

CONCLUSION

The effects of sexual abuse on young girls can be devastating. It can direct their lives onto paths that they otherwise would not have considered. High-risk sexual behavior with multiple partners, alcohol and drug abuse, connecting with peer groups whose activities and goals are nonproductive, and dropping out of school are frequent responses to the low self-esteem, even self-loathing, that results from sexual abuse. These girls grow up confused about their relationships, confused about reality, and seriously confused about right and wrong. It is imperative that we prevent sexual abuse where we can, and that we encourage young people to come forward and put an end to the abuse that may be occurring in their own lives.

Today we know that thousands of women have been sexually abused as children and young women, and we know this abuse is ongoing. Many girls and young women continue to be sexually abused today, emphasizing the need for us to educate our society about the problem and to encourage girls and young women to speak out about the abuse. The more awareness that is created around this subject, the more difficult it will be to keep secrets about it and the harder it will be for abusers to continue to perpetuate suffering on vulnerable girls and on young boys.

Final Thoughts from a Teacher

I have a boy named Nathan in my first-period class. He wears ripped clothing, and he tends to be a behavior problem, yelling, and engaging in typical acting-out, attention-seeking behavior on a daily basis. But I have also noticed that he is very needy. He craves a handshake and thrives on interaction with me. He lingers around the soccer field while I run practice; he stays after school and talks with me. I do not know whether he is abused or neglected, as I suspect. I do not pretend to understand his life or what it is like to be him. I have learned that I cannot solve my students' problems. I cannot control what happens in their lives. I can't make decisions for them. I can't magically change their situations.

> What I can do is listen.
> What I can do is treat them with love.
> What I can do is offer them hope.
> What I can do is show them a better way to live.

Whether we like it or not, children of abuse will likely become part of the cycle and be the future abusers of children. Learned behavior is difficult to uproot. The Dillons, Jennifers, and Stacys of the world are destined to repeat the mistakes of their pasts, to become victims of dysfunction unless they get professional help. I hate the feeling of helplessness, and now that I'm grown and *can* do something about the world around me, I must decide how I am to respond. That is the message I give Nathan and my other students. They *can* do something, no matter what has happened to them. They can choose how to respond. They can break free of their "Chinese handcuffs" by getting closer to people rather than pulling away all the time.

REFERENCE

Crutcher, Chris. (1989). *Chinese handcuffs*. New York: Greenwillow Books.

CHAPTER 9

Voices of Healing: How Creative Expression Therapies Help Us Heal, Using Laurie Halse Anderson's Novel *Speak* as a Springboard for Discussion

Diane Ressler and Stan Giannet

INTRODUCTION

In today's society, many creative expression therapies exist: art therapy, music therapy, poetry therapy, and journal therapy. These are all ways to help someone who has experienced a traumatic event to heal, to regain his or her voice. Dr. Louise DeSalvo in *Writing as a Way of Healing: How Telling Our Stories Transforms Our Lives* says, "As a teacher of writing, I regularly witness the physical and emotional transformation of my students. I see how they change physically and psychically when they work on writing projects—diary, memoir, fiction, poetry, biographical essays— that grow from a deep, authentic place, when they confront their pain in their work" (DeSalvo, 1999, p. 11).

Suzette Henke in "Literary Life-Writing in the 20th Century" says, "I suspect that most individuals in contemporary society have, at some time, experienced a traumatic or defining moment that marks the personality for a lifetime" (Henke, 2001, p. 41). The truth of this statement hit home for America on September 11, 2001. People are still struggling to go on after such unbelievable evil. Many jumped into action, wanting to do something to feel like they were a part of the solution; however, much emotional pain remains. How do we cope? "We receive consolation and hope from reading authors 'who, while offering no answers to life's questions, have the courage to articulate the situation of their lives in all honesty and direct-ness.... Their courage to enter so deeply into human suffering and to become present to their own pain gave them the power to speak healing words'" (DeSalvo, 1999, p. 54).

One such young adult (YA) novel, *Speak,* by Laurie Halse Anderson, shows the power of a creative expression therapy—art. Art is what leads Melinda through the pain of a rape into finding her own voice. Laurie Anderson in an article written for *The Alan Review* said that "in the writing of *Speak,* I found my own voice, and the courage to follow my own nightmares" (Anderson, 2000, p. 26). Anderson's own bravery enabled her to show us Melinda's courage to enter her pain through her art and thereby to begin her healing. We teachers and counselors do not want to see children abused; however, we see the effects of abuse almost daily in our classrooms. For us and for all who read it, *Speak* is a book of hope.

ORGANIZATION

After presenting the protagonist's self-healing work through her art and personal written expressions, four authentic writing samples are given; these are honest writings from real traumas. Included with the examples are therapist responses from Dr. Stan Giannet, a clinical psychologist. Dr. Giannet's responses are conversational in tone, sounding as he would sound in a therapy session with a patient. As you read, consider the benefits of using such creative expression therapies to help people, especially troubled or abused adolescents, find their own speaking voices and use them to begin healing.

SYNOPSIS OF *SPEAK* BY LAURIE HALSE ANDERSON

Laurie Halse Anderson's *Speak* is written in four distinct sections, each a marking period of Melinda's freshman year at Merryweather High School. Anderson comments, "I knew what had happened to Melinda from the beginning, but she wasn't ready to talk about it. By the end of the first marking period, I jotted a few notes to myself, imagining what her report card would look like. As soon as I did, the structure of the book clicked into place: four marking periods, four report cards, a school year from the first day to the last" (Anderson, 2000, p. 25).

First Marking Period, Pages 1–46

First marking period starts with Melinda's first day of her freshman year. She is an outcast. Readers are introduced to Melinda through her own descriptions and thoughts. She brings us, as readers, to school with her, to all of her classrooms to meet all of her teachers, to the lunchroom where she is the victim of the first set of flying potatoes, to the deserted janitor's closet she finds and claims for herself. Most importantly, she brings us into her feelings, especially into her feeling of sanctuary in her art class as Mr. Freeman gives her a project, to turn a "tree" into a piece of art.

Reader Response #1

This beginning reminded me of a student from a composition class I taught a few years ago at a nearby community college. This student had put off Composition I until almost the end of her studies. She thought she'd have to take prerequisites, but she passed the placement test and was right up front in my classroom on the first night. Like most teachers, I try to make my students feel at home from the very beginning. I introduce myself, the structure of the class—especially the journals and the essays—and the required writing the students will do. Finally, I ask the students to write a narrative essay about themselves, one that is funny or sad or anywhere in between but that must be true. I read them some examples, my favorite entitled "With a Gun at My Head," written by a colleague and friend of mine, Gabriel Horn. He wrote this when we were selected to attend a summer workshop together.

When "Bev" started writing, she had a few notes scribbled down. I looked up a few times to see her in tears. She was definitely having a difficult time with whatever story she was telling. When she finally "gave up" and brought the paper to my desk, I marked the edge so that I could identify her work when I did my grading. If writing it had made her cry, I knew reading it would probably make me cry, too. And I was right. Although I saw lots of fragments, I saw real power in her words—real pain, too. After reading my comments and working long hours on revising, she handed in the final copy of the essay. Her words still bring tears to my eyes and hers. Bev obviously used written expression to "get out" what was eating her inside. Her words touched me because I, too, had suffered the death of someone dear to me. I wrote that and more on her rough draft. As a consequence, we connected and have been friends ever since.

What is Love? by Beverly Wilson: (in memory of Harold Kendall, 6/13/30–8/4/94)

Ten years ago, I ended a two-year, live-in relationship. Unfortunately, eviction proceedings filled the same span of time. These two devastating events propelled me into a beautifully uplifting and love-filled experience.

I now needed a place to live. The rental ads in the local paper revealed a phone number for an affordable room. I nervously made the call and an appointment with the resonant voiced stranger. The owner of the room and the voice also had magnetic eyes into which I could hardly stop looking. I became instantly drawn to his strength. The rental lasted eight months.

My giving notice of intent to move changed the relationship from landlord and tenant to friendship. That friendship evolved into a love affair that lasted six years. He demonstrated his love by checking my car without being asked. He remodeled the bathroom because I hated green. He asked for, and listened to, and usually agreed with my opinions.

I reveled in our quiet unspoken commitment. I felt as if I had been embraced by the arms of a solid oak tree. The sun shone through the branches. A gentle breeze rustled the leaves. I had been given a gift of spirit that would last beyond his passage to the other side, beyond passage into the light.

He picked flowers for me while he was working in the yard. He showed his feelings for me for 2190 days. I thought I had more time to enjoy him, but reality lifted its dark head. I got up, made a joke with him while I was dressing, and went to work. During the middle of the day, the center of my existence took one last exploding heartbeat. My heart stopped beating with his until his legacy of strength, honesty, and hope caused love to bloom again in my memory. (Wilson, 1997)

Therapist's Response to #1

Two things have been linked with healing in traumatic situations: disclosure and support. Disclosure is absolutely important. When people experience a traumatic event, it is vital that they speak about it, discuss it, and relate with people about it in order to share their feelings and even their memories about it. The worst thing a person can do is to suppress the trauma. Eventually something's going to give if a person keeps a trauma bottled up; it's going to fester and will sooner or later take its toll on an individual. Projective projects such as art therapy and journaling are very helpful in helping patients to disclose and release their traumas.

The second factor associated with healing is to make certain we give the person an overwhelming degree of social support. It is essential for trauma victims to regain a sense of connectedness with other people—people who are there for them unconditionally, who regard them without judgment. Someone who's experienced trauma needs to find an environment where he or she is in a position of trust. A support group can help the bereaved to know that they are cared about, that the group is with them and will accept them no matter how bizarre their experiences, and that they are appreciated for who they are. In contemporary society, we have lost that connectedness. We shield ourselves because our current system (incorrectly, I might add) teaches us to erect boundaries and walls.

One of the risks for suicide among adolescents is lack of social support, their feeling socially isolated, alone, and empty. Melinda, for example, didn't have that support. In her loneliness and isolation, she attempted to find meaning. She tried to transform the loneliness into a reflective solitude by finding that janitor's closet and making it her safety zone, her little niche where she could reflect and feel safe. I admired the art teacher. By being open about his feelings, he created a very therapeutic environment—a holding environment—for Melinda. His class also gave her safety and a moment to look forward to; you did the same for Bev. One of the most important ingredients in being an effective healer is to be able to show your emotions with people, to connect with those with whom you work.

Second Marking Period, Pages 47-92

Melinda's second marking period begins after she realizes that the "IT" who raped her, the "Beast," is actually a student at Merryweather. Rather than confronting him, Melinda tries to make the janitor's closet—her escape—more homey. She tells the readers that "I want to confess everything, hand over the guilt and mistake and anger to someone else. There is a beast in my gut. I can hear it scraping away at the inside of my ribs. Even if I dump the memory, it will stay with me, staining me. My closet is a good thing, a quiet place that helps me hold these thoughts inside my head where no one can hear them" (Anderson, 1999, p. 51). Readers see the beginning of the stirrings to find her voice, to speak about her pain. Although her tree project in art isn't going very well, she brings turkey bones from her dysfunctional family's Thanksgiving holiday. Using the bones and the head of a Barbie doll, Melinda creates a sculpture out of it and is impressed with her creation. Mr. Freeman tells her, "This has meaning. Pain" (p. 65).

Reader Response #2

When I read about Melinda's turkey-bone sculpture that she did in art class instead of doing her tree project, I was reminded of a time in my own life when a personal experience I wrote about for a class called "Writing the Story of My Life" became my own struggle to speak my pain—a struggle that created many turkey-bone writings before I finally wrote my healing narrative. The course was taught by my colleague and friend, Gabriel Horn, whom I hadn't seen in quite a while. I knew his wife had been close to death from breast cancer, but I hadn't heard more than that. For myself, I had just had a dear, dear friend die in my arms as a result of a massive heart attack.

So when I heard Gabe was teaching this class, I wanted to take it in order to see a friendly face, to write, and to keep myself too busy to think. I didn't want to or expect to write about Gerry's death. As I walked out of the first class with Gabe, we talked about the loss of his wife, Simone, and about what had just happened to me. Then he gave me my assignment—to write about Gerry. For Gabe, I knew I had to try, but for me, I wasn't sure I could do it. Twelve revisions and a second section of the class later, I had a finished chapter in the story of my life, a chapter that had meaning. Pain.

Below is an excerpt from that chapter of my life. Gabe said that I was writing the piece for him because he was grieving and couldn't write. He and Simone had been extensions of each other. For me, Gerry had been a miracle in my life, but I'd known him only eight months. At the very beginning, he and I both knew his time was short. My rough drafts had been a "turkey-bone sculpture" instead of a "tree," but I had used a creative expression therapy to allow my heart to speak its pain. By the end of the first section of the class, I started healing and Gabe started writing again. I could not have written the story nor relived my pain without Gabe's strength, his belief in me. He knew the pain I felt; he was there, too. In some way I know that the writing of my experience contributed to his being able to write again for himself.

Perfect Love by Diane Ressler

Gerry had died in my arms, his arms, his body encircling mine. Now my arms, my body, my soul ached for what they would never have again, for what we'd now never share. Now I sat with Lisa, his daughter, in a cramped room in a local ER. Her long dark hair hid her face, sculpting itself around her hands as they covered her eyes. As she cried, the doctor's words repeated in my head. He'd walked in and said, "I'm sorry. He didn't make it. You know his heart stopped at the house and we just couldn't get it back." Lisa collapsed in grief, screaming, "No! I want my daddy back!" The doctor left, and I just sat, guilt-ladened and terrified.

His heart had stopped at my house. He was 45 years old and he was dead.

The ER nurse interrupted my thoughts as she motioned me outside of the room. Lisa was still crying, her friend, Kim, trying to comfort her. She kept saying, "Where is he? I want to see my daddy." As I closed the door behind me, the nurse said, "She really doesn't want to see him." But I did. I needed to. She led me to the treatment area and drew a curtain to give me privacy. Gerry lay there, tubes still protruding from his mouth. His feet were purple—I used to like that color—his arms, splotched red. I'd never seen a dead body before a funeral home had done what I now knew to be its magic.

She left me. I walked over and took his hand in mine. Less than an hour ago that hand had been warm, had been mine as it had played with my hair and caressed my face. Now it lay cold, dead. Less than an hour ago Gerry had been alive, had held me in his arms as we'd talked about losses and love. Now he was gone, my worst fear realized. "Less than an hour ago." Those words repeated in my head; if only I could awake from this nightmare. I talked out loud. I had to believe that he was there, somewhere, listening. "I love you, Gerry," I said as tears cascaded down my cheeks. Why couldn't I have said those words an hour before when he asked? Instead I said I couldn't, that I didn't know. "But I know, Blue Eyes," he said. "I can see. Your eyes can't lie." Now I stood, silent, his hand still clasped in mine. Death had yet again stolen someone I loved and I was terribly alone.

I reached down past the tubes to kiss his forehead, and then I walked away. Lisa needed me. She was facing death with all its questions and confusions, but I didn't have any answers for her. I wasn't sure I had any for myself.

Somehow I found my way back to her. So many decisions had to be made by a 20-year-old in her grief. "We'll need to have a funeral home decision. We can't keep the body overnight," the nurse explained. Someone would even be calling from the organ donor system about his eyes. After giving his doctor's name for the death certificate, Lisa followed me to my car. She sat, stunned. I drove. I tried to talk, to tell her she wouldn't go through this alone! All the while all I wanted to do was find a place to hide!

We found his briefcase in the trunk of his car still parked next to mine in my driveway. Lisa sat inside by my front door, a picture in slow motion as she searched for papers, for an uncle she didn't know, an uncle her dad hadn't really talked to since her grandmother had died. And for the second time in less than an hour, I was on the phone delivering the news. With Lisa, I only knew what I had seen first hand. I knew the attack had been bad. I had heard the gurgle, seen his eyes, but as the paramedics drove away, my mind didn't want to believe he would die. I prayed out loud as I rushed to his house to try to find Lisa's new phone number. Then, sitting on his bed, I dialed. When Kim, who was spending the night, put her on, I could barely form the words, "Lisa? This is Diane. Your dad had a heart attack. I'll meet you in emergency."

But Robert, he didn't even know me! Here was some strange woman telling him his brother was dead. Again the grief, the hysterics I couldn't allow for myself erupted in my ear. Once he was composed, I handed the phone to Lisa so they could talk. He would drive down; he promised. And I made a silent promise to Gerry that I would be there for her, that she wouldn't be alone.

As the TV droned on, still taping what had begun with Gerry making fun of my inability to redo wiring so that I could preprogram, I wasn't sure, however, how I would ever keep that promise. My brain was on overload; my heart was numb. I could survive no other way. Even my house wasn't mine. Furniture still sat where it'd been thrown by me or by the paramedics, and somehow all I could smell was the cold, odd air of a funeral home. Lisa talked and cried; I just stood there in disbelief. How could such a perfect day have turned so horrible?

Reality knocked as another of Lisa's friends arrived to take her home. Kim and I ran errands to Gerry's, to the hospital, then met Lisa back at her house. I couldn't stay there. I can't handle cigarette smoke, and her nerves told her she needed to smoke. I knew she wasn't alone; I promised I'd be back in the morning. But that left me alone with my grief and it exploded! Tears sprang from depths I'd never known—or had always managed to hide—through all of my losses. I couldn't hide those tears now! Gerry had died in my arms, his arms, his body encircling mine! How long would my arms, my body, my soul ache for what they would never have again, for what we'd now never share?

We'd never made love, not really, because I'd been too afraid. He had wanted to, but I hadn't wanted him to die in my arms. I had told him about a "Golden Girl" episode where just such a thing had happened to Betty White's character. He'd laughed, and we'd verbally played out such a scenario. I didn't change my mind, and he never gave up trying. I guess we'd been lovers, nonetheless. He was one of the most romantic, passionate men I'd ever met. Now his electric kiss and gentle caress would be only memories.

I couldn't believe he was dead. I couldn't stop crying. For seven hours my dogs kept trying to lick away my tears, to give me squeaky toys to make me better. What a gift of love they've been to me. But all I could see was how they rushed to Gerry's side, tails between their legs, ears down. They'd known! I don't know how I ever survived that night. His last words had been to me, an intimate desire not for himself but for me. No one had ever put me first; Gerry had died putting me first. I kept crying. I can't believe a human body can physically cry for that long. Finally, the night was over.

The Pastor gave a service at the very end as Lisa had wanted. Afterward, people left. I wasn't sure what to do. I wasn't family and usually only family stayed. But Lisa pulled me up with her. Together we stood to say goodbye. Robert came up behind us then walked away. Lisa reached out her hand and ran it through her father's hair. "I love you, Daddy," she cried, then she moved over. She was honoring my love for him by allowing me there, allowing me time.

I touched his hand. I reached over and kissed Gerry's forehead. I knew he was watching, that he knew the kiss was for him. As I backed away, releasing his hand, my eyes filled with tears and Lisa's words from the hospital echoed in my head. I wanted her daddy back, too. I had loved him! I knew my love hadn't been perfect, hadn't dispersed my fears. Instead, those fears had cost us precious time we'd now never have. Gerry had understood those fears and had loved me anyway. In fact, in eight short months he'd given me more love than most people experience in a lifetime. He'd even died in my arms, loving me. (Ressler, 1996)

Therapist's Response to #2

Melinda, the protagonist of *Speak,* showed some psychological problems and some aspects of being physically sick. "My throat is always sore, my lips raw...my jaws are clenched so tight I have a headache.... What's wrong with me? It's like I have some kind of spastic laryngitis" (Anderson, 1999, pp. 49–50). She talked about these physical symptoms, and she deliberately tried to block the event of the rape so that she could function. Research has shown that the more an individual tries to suppress something, the more difficulty a person will have doing so, and the more pronounced it will become. Melinda was constantly grappling with just that.

It was so difficult for Melinda after experiencing a rape and after being doubted and ostracized by the people who were most important to her to be able to trust again, to be able to come out and express herself in ways that might have been shocking, that might have been controversial or novel or bizarre. Finding that person to trust—that solace—can be such a healing, curative factor. Melinda found that one person, her art teacher, who, through his ability to see some beauty about her and see the fact that she was fragile, was able to bring out that healing expression. Mr. Freeman unconditionally accepted her and her sculpture, seeing how wounded she was, and we do that as faculty members, as teachers. Students bond with us and connect with us and we're able to help them, not only intellectually and academically but personally as well. Having the ability to empathize is vital in being an effective instructor.

I was crying when I read your emergency room scene. I noticed that your writing and Bev's writing (from marking period one) share such commonalities with each other and with the way Anderson deals with Melinda's trauma. Like Mr. Freeman's assignation of the art project, I'm sure you helped Bev when you gave her the opportunity to disclose through her writing. We need someone to guide us with compassion and love and to show, that no matter what it is, he or she will accept what is written or drawn. You provided that—"I'll be there for you"—for Bev.

People cannot deny that there is a powerful transferential process and a counter-transferential process. Students can affect their teachers in remarkable ways, eliciting and prompting them to feel certain things and to express their own sentiments, pain, and experiences through the prism of their students' experiences. Not only were you there for Bev and her healing process, but Bev also elicited from you experiences and feelings about what you went through when you experienced that remarkable loss of Gerry.

Third Marking Period, Pages 93–137

The third marking period for Melinda is a time of being "frozen" like her tree. Even though she thinks of speaking out, she sees the results of other students speaking out in class and decides on silence. In both her English and art classes, she learns about going past the surface meaning of things. "Hairwoman" has the class studying the symbolism of Hawthorne, and Mr. Freeman has Melinda researching Picasso. Mr. Freeman tells her, "When people don't express themselves, they die one piece at a time. You'd be shocked at how many adults are really dead inside—walking through their days with no idea who they are, just waiting for a heart attack or cancer or a Mack truck to come along and finish the job. It's the saddest thing I know" (Anderson, 1999, p. 122). And although Melinda says, "Hawthorne wanted snow to symbolize cold," she also says that "once the snow covers the ground, it hushes as still as my heart" (p. 130). She wonders whether "Hester tried to say no. She's kind of quiet. We would get along. I can see us living in the woods, her wearing that A, me with an S maybe, S for silent, for stupid, for scared. S for silly. For shame" (p. 101). The marking period ends with Melinda reliving in her thoughts the night of the rape. Readers know that Melinda will not be under the snow much longer.

Reader Response #3

Melinda's third marking period reminded me of the writing given to me by a ninth-grader a couple of years ago. I had overheard Joey talking with his group about an event that had happened to his family when he was in the fifth grade. His group asked him a few questions and I simply listened. I didn't want to interrupt their interaction, especially because he was actually talking about the death of his sister. Besides, the year was nearing its end, and I just wanted him to feel comfortable talking. I thought, then, about an assignment that I could develop that would allow students—Joey included—to write about a traumatic event in their lives. I knew that as a class they felt safe with me. I just had to find the perfect model exercise.

Once again I found the resource I needed in a book by Gabriel Horn (1992), *The Native American Book of Change.* In his work, Gabe describes his experience teaching middle-school students how words can both hurt and heal. First, he shows his students how wrong stereotypical words can be, and he leads them to see personally how much those words can hurt. Then he has them draw Native American–like shields to show the stereotype for what it is—a lie. Finally, Gabe has the students write about their experiences doing this before introducing a unit of study on Native Americans and all the hurtful words and events they've experienced. By having students write about how they used to respond to hurtful words and by comparing that way with the new way presented, teachers like Gabe hope that some may choose this more constructive outlet for their pain.

By modifying that lesson somewhat, I asked my students to create a shield that reflected the person I knew them to be and then to go a step further by writing about a time when someone said or did something to hurt them. I wasn't sure that Joey would write about what he'd told his group, and I wasn't going to push the issue. A part of me was hoping, though, that this assignment would allow him to write—to become "thawed" and receptive to the healing that could be gained from the written expression of the event. He did write of the death of his sister. His words, written almost four years after the event, still ring with the pain the family suffered. I believe his sharing with the group and his writing of the story have benefited his life. This year, Joey is much more outgoing, a young man who smiles and talks and even gets in trouble in class.

The Summer of Fifth Grade by Joey Baughman, 5-18-01

One morning I woke up because my mom was crying, so I walked out into the living room and there were two detectives standing by the front door. They told my mom that my 25-year-old sister had died late that night.

The detectives said that her boyfriend told them that they were fighting. Her boyfriend said that if she broke off their engagement, he would kill her. So she said, "Yeah right," then threw the ring at him. They started arguing some more, so he grabbed his gun and shot her in the back left side of her head. Then he called the police. The police went over to my sister's house. Her boyfriend told the police that she had committed suicide.

So the police told my mom that my sister committed suicide, but my mom and I didn't think she did because she was right-handed so why would she shoot herself in the left side of her head? Her boyfriend was left handed, almost like he pinned her down and shot her in the back of the head. This all happened at the end of summer after 5th grade.

My mom and I were hurt by the words we knew were lies. We were hurt to know that our legal system allowed my sister to be killed and have a killer to tell lies and go free. (Baughman, 2001)

Therapist's Response to #3

In this third marking period, I was impressed by Melinda's ability to find meaning for herself in her friend, David Petrakis, the "genius" student who is the underdog fighting the system. David genuinely accepts Melinda as a friend and shows some degree of compassion. At the beginning of the novel only her pain was talking, and I was concerned that she was experiencing that pain alone. With David's help, she began to trust again, making her more apt to confront the memory and let it go. Gradually she allowed people such as David to come into her life, which showed her attempt to find meaning in her pain and to let go.

When she relived the night of the rape in her thoughts, she used words such as "hurt me" and "pain." Therapeutically, that's something that's healthy. We say in traumatic situations that one of the first steps to healing is being able to relive the pain and to find meaning in that pain. Often when people experience pronounced pain or pervasive adversity, they try to suppress or deny it by going about their daily lives totally oblivious as to how their lives have been inalterably changed. Instead, it is much more healthy to realize when something makes an indelible mark and be able to say, "I have changed because of this!"

Your student, Joey, did the reliving of the pain in his writing. It is important to memorialize, to always be mindful of a defining memory and of the meaning that a particular person or event played in one's life. People die only when we no longer remember them. It is okay to feel anger, loss, pain, and even outrage, but we must also find meaning in the pain, in the death. I recently lost my grandmother. She was my life for 32 years, my second mother. She was so instrumental in who I am today, and her loss is something that I have to grapple with every day. Society doesn't prepare us for death. As we often do with human sexuality, we deny and suppress it. Who reaches out to the bereaved? The abused? If people would show more care, if people could feel what it is like to treat others gently with compassion, and if people would help others to find meaning for their lives, I think society would change dramatically for the positive. Unfortunately, I don't see that happening.

Fourth Marking Period, Pages 138–198

Melinda finds her voice during the fourth marking period. Andy, a.k.a. IT, is dating her ex-best friend, Rachel. Melinda worries about Rachel and doesn't want her to be hurt. Finally, Melinda begins to find her voice and writes to Rachel in study hall about what had actually happened at the party. Even within the note, she draws as she writes; she "carve(s) out the words" (Anderson, 1999, p. 183). Rachel reads and responds, their friendship blossoming again until Melinda answers the question, "who." Rachel cannot face that truth. She screams hurtful words at Melinda and gets a pass to see the nurse.

Now that Melinda has warned her friend, Rachel is able to see Andy's lecherous character and spends the rest of prom night with her exchange-student friends. Andy rages. Melinda finds her voice when she again becomes his prey. Locked in her escape closet with him, she fights back. "She claimed it (her voice), claimed herself as worthy and strong enough to fight back. She screamed the house down and saved herself, scarred, bloody, and alive" (Anderson, 1999, p. 26).

Reader Response #4

This last section of the book reminded me of a poem written by Kayla Rigney. She is a woman writer who has suffered much in her lifetime yet continues to enjoy words by writing and by inspiring new writers. Last year, she individually e-mailed all of my creative writing students and answered all of their writing questions. She sent my class a poem entitled, "The Last Closet" which was published in the 2000–2001 edition of my school's literary magazine. Her words really do show that work of art, that "tree" of Melinda's.

The Last Closet by Kayla Rigney

She stood in front of the Last Closet, almost afraid to open the door. It wasn't as if what lay beyond was any great mystery (it was, after all, *her* closet); but it contained bits and pieces of a life lived.

There were people she knew who didn't bother to live, and as a result, their closets were never full.

She knew, to the exact dust bunny, what was inside that Last Closet. She also knew what she *wanted* to be there. She had a list:

> *Children of Paradise*, restored, on DVD.
> The gray matter ripped from her brain by a drunk driver nineteen years, five months four days and two hours ago.
> The Loew's Delman.
> That diamond ring she accidentally flushed down the toilet.
> Abby, the Scottie Dog who taught her to love ghost railroads.
> All of Harry Nilsson's unreleased music.
> Guilty Pleasures—like *Buckaroo Banzai* and *Lathe of Heaven*.
> Tulsa, Oklahoma.
> The Honky Dreds.
> "Far Beyond the Stars."
> That one perfect performance of "A Christmas Carol."
> And finally, although she already had a copy, a First Edition of Jack Finney's *Time and Again* simply because … It's not really a novel.

Other people set great store in the Last Closet; but she knew the truth.

The Last Closet inevitably holds those once-treasured pieces of life that get left by the wayside to make room for reality. (Rigney, 2001)

Therapist's Response to #4

By the book's end, Melinda speaks of something that happens so often in our society—date rape. Unfortunately, we continue to reinforce silence in children and adolescents who have experienced this kind of trauma. The book is a powerful exposé of what happens when a child is raped, but it also is a good indicator of what goes on in the family dynamics, in the sociocultural aspects of being an adolescent, and in the psychology of adolescence. Anderson includes everything from conforming to peer pressure to pain, to isolation, and to loneliness. Additionally, readers acquire information on defense mechanisms, methods of escape, the role that parents play, and the ability of parents to understand and to become intricately involved in their adolescents' lives in order to be in touch with and support them.

How important it is to find meaning in our everyday experience. Our society reinforces living for yesterday or living for tomorrow, not appreciating the 24 hours a day that we have, not appreciating just the things that appear to be inconsequential or trivial but can have an inordinate amount of meaning, a great degree of purpose, and give us a reason to live. It's a sad fact that most of us don't appreciate those moments until we lose them and then, retrospectively, we reflect and find the meaning. The memories make us who we are, being mindful and appreciative of those who have affected us. The people who truly become interpersonally and intrapersonally successful in life not only find purpose in the joy, but also find great meaning in the struggles and in the pain they experience. They see struggle as a beautiful launching pad for growth. The metaphor of the wounded zebra is not an uncommon portrayal of adolescent life today. At the end of isolation, self-deprecation, self-effacement, and pain, one can still grow and change. We are fortunate to have creative expression therapies to help our "wounded zebras" heal.

One More Personal Experience Piece

A colleague of mine, a high school English teacher and a consultant with the Tampa Bay Area Writing Project (TBAWP), shared a personal experience piece she wrote at the 2001 TBAWP Summer Invitational. She read of the abuse she suffered during her first marriage, finally speaking of her healing using very powerful words. She ended her piece with what I feel is the next step in our healing: sharing the healing to help someone else.

"A Bruised Butterfly" by April Templeton

Now, four years after the abuse and two years after leaving him, I can finally write about my experience as a victim of domestic violence. For too long the memories have kept me prisoner, a haunting reminder of what I faced. I still can't admit the abuse to my family, but I can acknowledge it to myself. I was a victim. I was abused physically, mentally, and verbally. Years after the fact, I'm beginning to heal because I'm allowing myself to write about it. Thanks to the power of words, I'm healing from wounds inflicted what seems a lifetime ago. And thanks to the strength gained through feminism and a bit of growing up, I am armed with self-confidence, courage, and independence to never allow such horrific actions to happen to me again.

My next step is to speak out. Only a handful of people know about the abuse (no one in my family), and it's one of those topics that when broached, is quickly talked about and then dropped, as if no one wants "to go there." Even my own husband, the first person I confided in about the abuse years ago, twice refused to read this piece, saying he could not bear to hear about something that hurt me so terribly. The third time I asked, he agreed. His acknowledgment of my abuse after years of silence proved yet another affirmation that I was a victim.

I need to find my voice. I need to learn to speak of the abuse, and more importantly, my recovery. For how many women are out there who are still suffering abuse, or are closed in their cocoons, unable or ashamed to admit the horrific actions they have endured? Though I have traveled miles on the road to recovery, I am not completely free. Only when I am able to speak openly about the abuse and not treat it as a "don't go there" issue will I be completely free from the clutches of this monster I should not bury, but instead expose to those who need to hear my story. (Templeton, 2001)

CONCLUSION

Speak is a book of hope, a book of metaphors for speaking out and growing through the trials of life. Melinda was blessed to have Mr. Freeman and the "art therapy" assignment after the trauma of her rape. Her year, her work on her "tree," her attempt to finally find her voice exemplify the healing engendered by creative expressions. The writers included in this chapter used words; others use music, dance, art, or some other healthy outlet. The idea is to acknowledge the inner hurt and in that acknowledgment give the pain strength to speak. The writers in this chapter spoke through their words, Melinda spoke through her art and her words, and Laura Halse Anderson spoke through her words in this novel. We as a people have a great history of masterpieces created by human beings just like us. Their lives weren't perfect, but like Melinda, they "turned an object into a piece of art" and made it "say something, express an emotion, [and] speak to every person who looks at it" (Anderson, 1999, p. 12).

The writers in this chapter showed extreme courage to "write their healings." Melinda's strength of character provides a model for all who have struggled to find their voices. We can only hope that with such novels, with writers like Laurie Halse Anderson developing plots around such topics as sexual abuse, more children will be spared such horrors in their own lives. We hope these young adult novels, these personal experience pieces, these "trees" will be our connections to others who are experiencing the same hurts, connections that will offer consolation and the beginnings of the courage to heal. Laurie Halse Anderson, I thank you for such a wonderful book; it shows students that they can find the courage to speak their pain, that they must to acknowledge their own voices, and that creative expression therapies are powerful tools to use in the healing process.

EPILOGUE

As a closing to this chapter, I present reader response comments from my creative writing high school students and my Composition I and II community-college students. I used the book as a read-aloud in order to see how Melinda spoke to them.

High School Responses

Jessica, a Senior

This book is almost high school through my eyes but to a lesser extent. I didn't lose friends. I just never had any. Emotional problems scarred me rather than a rape. I also turned to art to express myself. Imperfections in art show imperfections of life. A butterfly with sagging wings showed an extremely depressing time; I truthfully can see myself through Melinda's eyes.

Jenna, a Senior

People are harsh, and friends can be among the harshest. I believe that there is no truth if you do not speak. I believe that if you don't take the step to protect yourself, you will get walked on, pushed around, and used just to be thrown away. You have to be careful who you confide in, but you have to confide in someone. There are honest, brave people out there who want to help you. You just have to find them. But you have to put caution tape around your heart and protect every part of who you are.

Scott, a Senior

Transitions are often hard when you're a number. By the end of the third summer, your illusions about the world and school around you are gone. You don't think the same; you don't act the same. In essence, you become a new person. Melinda went through the first transformation, the first year of high school. For me, it built my inner strength. Once I had that, I was ready to branch out. Entire worlds open to her like a great shining heavenly gate slowly opening, showing her shades of perfect light. Perceptions will eventually reach perfection, and Melinda and I will emerge from our original cocooned world of naiveté as picture-perfect butterflies.

Eryn, a Senior

I've read this book before. It's very good! I think this is all very true. Everything Melinda goes through could happen. She's just the opposite of me, though. If that happened to me, I would have told my friends and spoken loudly and clearly about everything wrong he did. Something similar happened to me. I really liked this guy who went to school here last year and we were just acquaintances. I was interested in having him as a boyfriend, but he just wanted to be friends. We stayed close last summer until he left for college; he would come over every day and we would just chill. I really missed him when he was gone, so I called him. That turned into a routine. I'd call him every night. One day he said he was going to come down and visit his family for fall break and that he would love to see me. He called me the night he got in and said he wanted to see me and he'd call me later. He called me at 2:30 in the morning for me to come over. When I got there, he was drunk and smelled like beer. The first thing he said to me was something like how I should give him oral sex. I said no and he was pushing me to do it. I left because I was so scared. He was three times my size, and I really thought he would hurt me. When I left, he said he never wanted to talk to me again. I feel really bad about it, like I should talk to him since he was drunk, but still that's no excuse. I'm over it now.

Tracy, a Junior

Melinda went through a tough time and year. Tragic memories and nightmares enveloped her mind, spinning and spiraling thoughts of what happened to her that hideous night with Andy at the party. All of her friends made fun of her, ignoring her for the entire year because they thought she was a "narc." No one knew why she called the cops. Being raped, she was ashamed of what happened. Days went by and the year was almost over. Soon everyone knew the truth about the horrible night, and again IT tried to rape her in the janitor's closet. Now everyone is ashamed of how they treated her and start talking to her again. Rachel, who was her friend throughout middle school and ignored her the entire year, crawled back for forgiveness.

My world relates and nightmares spiral through my mind every night, rewinding in my mind. Shedding my tears, I feel ashamed. High school being a happy time became an abomination to me. I was made an outcast by friends I thought I had made. I was left out. Shielding my heart from the world, I became a zombie. I couldn't change anything so I decided to become stronger. I want to peel my shame away to find a beautiful spirit, a normal human being. Instead, I lock up the memories and throw them away.

Takiesha, a Freshman

I read another book about a girl named Rachael who was raped by her dad's friend and that made her kind of miserable. In my elementary years, when I was in the fourth or fifth grade, my friend got raped by our janitor. She was hurt and I felt sorry for her. I really don't wanna talk about it because it really hurts me to see something wrong with one of my friends. She's never told anybody.

Community College Students

Karla

I was able to relate to this story because it reminds me of some of the things I have heard from my stepdaughter. She did not experience a rape; however, she always felt like an outsider in high school. She frequently came home to tell about this or that clique; how senseless it all seems and how cruel they all are. The most disturbing behavior that I observed about her interactions at school was that she never revealed her true self to anyone, not even to a close friend. When I tried to advise her to actually tell someone exactly what she thought, I could see a wall go up. She felt that I must be really stupid to think that revealing anything to any of her peers would help her. Unlike the character Melinda, she never resolved any issues and left high school with very poor memories.

I think that *Speak* might be very helpful for any high school student to read. Most adolescents don't want to get advice from an adult because they don't feel that an adult can relate. In a well-written book, the adult writer can make a protagonist into a teenage role model. There is nothing more cathartic than reading about someone going through the same experiences that you are. As you begin to relate to that character and see how she resolves the problem, you may be more likely to follow that positive example.

Leslie

Melinda is on the bus facing her first day of high school. No one will speak to her, but she faces this with a sense of humor. She tries to make light of all that frightens her. Melinda has been through a terrifying ordeal, yet she keeps this to herself, choosing to not tell anyone until much later in the school year. For Melinda, art becomes a way to express herself even though she fears the expression. Melinda sticks her hand into the broken globe and pulls out her destiny, a tree. This is a wonderful symbol for Melinda, even though the tree assignment is initially scary to her. Once she fights off Andy and the students realize what really happened to her, the tree becomes symbolic of her young life. The dead branch, the rape that is now over; the initials, the boy who violated her; and the new growth represent the new and healing Melinda. This is a wonderful story of how a young girl is able to come to terms with a very bad experience and emotionally heals. Melinda comes to realize that what has happened is not her fault.

Michael

Me.
Now you see that I am like the tree, stout and tall. I will never fall.
My limbs are numb, my leaves are gone. Still I continue to grow.
Deep inside you see my blood boils like lava flowing into the sea.
The bark on the outside shows some wear and tear.
I continue to grow even though no one knows I'm here.
The end of the season is near.
My leaves come back and I am finally free—free of the fear that
    comes with being alone.
Now I am surrounded by people under my shade who finally know
    I'm here.

Anesta

The beginning of high school is traumatic without all of the added stress Melinda faced. As an outcast, who could she speak to? Even if the words would come out, who would listen? I liked the bird she added to the tree in the end. As the words surfaced, she must have felt that her words were like that bird—finally taking flight, leaving behind the dying shell of her soul. That half-dead limb has to come off, lest her soul die completely.

Mark

As I think back to my own high school days, I start to wonder about certain people who were kind of outcasts from the rest of the students. Why were they outcasts? Did they have a traumatic experience? I have to admit that I was always one of those bully types of people who picked on the "not-so-popular" kids. I feel bad for what I did and wish the bullying had never happened.

REFERENCES

Anderson, Laurie Halse. (1999). *Speak.* New York: Puffin.

Anderson, Laurie Halse. (Spring 2000). Speaking out. *The ALAN Review, 27* (3), 25–26.

Baughman, Joey. (2001). The summer of fifth grade. Unpublished story.

DeSalvo, Louise. (1999). *Writing as a way of healing: How telling our stories transforms our lives.* New York: HarperCollins.

Henke, Suzette. (2001, May/June). Literary life-writing in the 20th century. *Poets & Writers, 29,* 40–43.

Horn, Gabriel (White Deer of Autumn). (1992). *The Native American book of change. Native ways series, Volume III* (pp. 47–81). Hillsboro, OR: Beyond Words Publishing.

Horn, Gabriel (White Deer of Autumn). (1993). With a gun at my head. In Gabriel Horn, *Native Heart: An American Indian Odyssey* (pp. 13–15). San Rafael, CA: New World Library.

Ressler, Diane. (1996). Perfect love. Unpublished story.

Rigney, Kayla. (2001). The last closet. *The Cauldron: Untitled: No Boundaries, 32,* 59.

Templeton, April. (2001). A bruised butterfly. Unpublished story.

Wilson, Beverly. (1997). What is love? Unpublished story.

CHAPTER 10

Finding Strength in Friendship in Jacqueline Woodson's *I Hadn't Meant to Tell You This*

Leslie Hibbs and Tom McDevitt

INTRODUCTION

Secrets revealed one rainy, August day in 1999 ruined my family. My father-in-law, a trusted, involved step-grandparent, sexually molested his six-year-old step-granddaughter. He exposed himself to her and her young friend and tried to get these children to perform sexual acts on him. When his step-granddaughter told her mother, he laughed it off and said she was lying. I was certain he was the victim of a terrible mistake. Long after the rest of the family knew the truth, I remained his most vociferous defender. He continued to claim his innocence until his own attorney questioned him. How surprised I was, four months after the incident, to discover that he was guilty.

As a sexual predator with the financial resources to hire expensive and skilled counsel, he was sentenced to two years of house arrest. He may go anywhere he needs to go: He may attend church, get a haircut, and shop at the grocery store. He has lost his computer and all computer equipment because investigations proved that he frequently logged onto child pornography sites. He is allowed to keep his digital cable access, however, and his truck and his boat. His wife, the victim's step-grandmother, decided to save their marriage and emotionally supported him. He spent a total of one night in jail.

His victims have been in therapy. His step-granddaughter is confused. Police officers and detectives interrogated her. Her step-grandfather, a person she trusted, called her a liar. Her step-grandmother still visits the child, but the visits are strained. The child has lost a step-grandfather who was involved with her. Her best buddy who took her to movies, football games, swim dates, and video arcades is gone. Holidays and birthdays are strange. Pieces of the family are missing.

The predator, sentenced to house arrest, may experience some inconvenience and some embarrassment, but he still maintains many of his privileges. Even after committing this act that left his step-granddaughter traumatized, his life remains remarkably unchanged. He is often allowed to visit with his family, volunteer at the church, and enjoy the comforts of his home. When a child is abused by a close family member, both she and the family members have to deal with the shame of being the relative of a sexual predator. I remember my own confusion in trying to deal with the truth of my father-in-law's guilt. I still have trouble reconciling in my mind that a man who has lived a caring, loving life can expose himself and request sexual favors from six-year-olds.

The hero of the story is the victim's mother. Immediately upon the disclosure, she knew the truth. She acted at that moment. This mother questioned the predator, and, when she realized what had really happened to her baby, cut him out of her life. This man, whom she had known and trusted for 25 years, is a monster. She will not forgive him. She will never see him again. She once loved him; now she only waits for his death. She is her daughter's hero.

SYNOPSIS OF *I HADN'T MEANT TO TELL YOU THIS* BY JACQUELINE WOODSON

Lena, the sexually abused child in Jacqueline Woodson's novel *I Hadn't Meant to Tell You This,* has no such hero. This is the story of two motherless girls. One girl, 12-year-old Marie, has a father who doesn't touch her; the other, 13-year-old Lena, has a father who sexually abuses her. Marie and Lena notice their differences immediately. Marie is popular; Lena is the new kid. Marie is black and attractive; Lena is white and unkempt. Marie is wealthy, and Lena is poor. In a town where African Americans hold the power and wealth and the whites are the minorities living on the fringe, Lena is an outcast. Looking beyond Lena's oily hair, dirty hands, and wrinkled clothes, Marie accepts Lena as a friend. Through this friendship, the author explores themes of grief, loss, secrets, and incest without traumatizing the reader.

ORGANIZATION

Using Woodson's novel as a springboard for discussion, a behavioral specialist and a media specialist offer various lessons learned in response to a girl's sexual abuse and another's neglect, including lessons on grief, loss, secrets, incest, and blame. In the end, heroes are made, but their scars remain forever.

Lessons on Grief

Before she walked away from the family home, Marie's mother often hid in the bathroom, ran the water, and cried. After Marie's mother left home, the water in the bathroom still ran, and Marie listened as her father cried. These are the lessons Marie learns about grief. Grief is to be suffered alone and hidden away. Marie longs for her father to pull her close and hold her, but he hasn't touched her in years. She doesn't know whether his hands are smooth or callused or how the skin on his face feels. Marie's father ensures that she has clothes, a safe home, and food to eat, but he neglects to give her what she really needs—appropriate physical touch. Instead, she has a father who is afraid to touch her. As Marie watches a television commercial in which "at one point this father took his daughter in his arms and gave her this big hug, and they both looked so happy and comfortable" (Woodson, 1996, p. 31), she wonders how her father's hug would feel. With no mother or siblings in the home, Marie has little physical contact. The lack of physical affection in her life causes Marie to be interested in and nearly jealous of Lena's situation. "What does it feel like, Lena?" (p. 57) she asks, wondering how a father's touch, or anyone's touch, would feel. Lena's friendship offers Marie something Marie desperately needs. Lena gives Marie someone to touch. Lena puts her head on Marie's shoulder. Marie can touch Lena's wrist. Marie and Lena can hold hands. Woodson uses Marie's plight to illustrate that children who experience no physical affection suffer almost as much as those who suffer the wrong kind of affection.

Research shows that touch and massage can be very effective in improving attention, diminishing depression, decreasing stress hormones, and enhancing immune function (Field, 1998). Other studies seem to confirm that children need physical signs of affection from their parents to maintain healthy attitudes. Parents who openly express their love help their children develop healthy self-esteem and an optimistic outlook on life. Such attitudes lower risk factors for stress-related diseases in adulthood. Loving parents may also promote a host of healthy habits, from proper nutrition to choosing supportive friends. The Touch Research Institute in Miami, Florida, has been studying the effects of massage on children. "For 15 to 20 minutes, twice a week, children at two Miami preschools are given therapeutic massage by volunteer senior citizens in the community who massage each child's face, neck, arms, legs, and back just before the children's nap time. So far, the results have been very positive. The school's director reports that the children eat and sleep better, have calmer dispositions, and are generally happier" (Touch Research Institute, 2001).

Lessons on Loss

Lena and Marie find that the loss of their mothers marked the end of happiness for each. The loss of their mothers is also what initially brings them together as friends. When Marie's mother left two years before, Marie had hoped that she would eventually return. Marie realizes now that her mother will never return. The only contact she has with her mother are the postcards her mother sends from places far away. The loss of her mother means the end of physical affection for Marie. Marie is left with a distant, angry, silent parent who blames the ills of the world on white people. Marie's loss is all the more poignant because she knows that her mother made a conscious decision to leave. Marie's dream is to leave home to find her mother, send for her father, and be a family again. She knows, however, that her mother is happier away from their family.

The death of Lena's mother marks the beginning of Lena's sexual abuse. Lena knows that the sexual abuse brings her more loss. Her innocence, her safety, and the father that she trusted are gone. In spite of the abuse, she still loves her father because, as she explains to Marie, "If I don't that only leaves me and [my little sister]" (Woodson, 1996, p. 78). Statistics confirm that Lena's abuse by her father follows the numbers. According to the Anti Child Porn Organization, 95% of sexual abuse victims know their perpetrator (Anti Child Porn Organization, n.d.). Victim accounts reflect the confusion children often feel; they love their abuser but hate the abuse. In Lena's abusive relationship she attempts to end the abuse by purposely making herself unattractive through poor hygiene. Marie describes Lena when she first sees her as a girl whose "hair was oily, and the shirt she was wearing had ring-around-the-collar" (Woodson, 1996, p. 15). Poor hygiene is one of the indicators of sexual abuse, according to the Child Abuse Prevention Council of Sacramento (n.d.). Lena wants to escape the house before her abuser wakes. She chops her hair short to help speed her morning escape. Lena tells Marie that she doesn't have the privacy Marie enjoys and cannot be in her bathroom or close the door to her bedroom. Poor hygiene is a defense mechanism for sexually abused girls in much the same way as putting on weight or becoming anorexic.

Lessons on Secrets

Marie wants to know why Lena never told. She wonders why Lena didn't "call the cops" (Woodson, 1996, p. 76). Lena explains to Marie that she refuses to tell because telling means separation from her little sister Dion; she needs her sister more than she needs to end the abuse. This response is very common. "[I]n some cases where the support system is available, the child may choose not to tell for fear of the consequences" (http://www. calib.com/naic/pubs/f_abused.htm#signs). Lena explains to Marie that a social worker visited Lena's home soon after the death of Lena's mother, suspecting abuse. The social worker sent Lena to one foster home and Dion to another; but Lena, having just lost her mother to cancer, could not conceive of life without her sister. Lena felt as though she had to run away, find Dion, and move back in with their abusive father. Since then, their father has been vigilant. "[H]e's been moving us every time somebody starts sniffing around," Lena tells Marie (Woodson, 1996, p. 77).

A central focus of the story is Lena's hopeless situation. Her father, her abuser, is also the person in whom she must trust to keep the family together. Lena operates, then, with a distorted sense of trust. Lena is smart enough to understand that her father is committing a heinous offense, but she also knows he is the only one who will take care of both her and her sister. A child's trust in his or her primary caretaker is central to their relationship, and when abuse occurs in this context, the betrayal is intensified. Lena's betrayal is complete and layered: Her mother left her by dying, the social services system tried to separate her from her sister, and her father continues to use her as a replacement for her dead mother. Because Lena ran away from foster care to reunite the family, her father is assured of her silence; Lena can take no more betrayal.

Although the reader may want Marie to tell a responsible adult, her silence is essential to Lena. Ironically, Marie's silence helps restore Lena's faith in people. A child like Lena, who cannot tell her secrets without losing her family, often feels unsure about ever sharing her secrets. Marie's silence shows Lena that she can trust some people even if she cannot trust her father. One characteristic victims share is an inability to trust. Marie proves herself to be trustworthy, and that will help Lena heal. Marie wrestles with the right course of action to best help Lena and decides that her friendship demands her to respect Lena's secret.

Lessons on Incest

Because incest is the issue, because Lena has no other parent or responsible adult in her life, and because Lena is an outcast in her community, the reader clearly feels the hopelessness of her situation. Lena explains that she can't hate her father; instead, she feels sorry for him in spite of what he does to her. She understands that he is old, close to 50. He is a "pale, older man, who looked like he could have been [her] grandfather" (Woodson, 1996, p. 80). Lena seems to know that he is pathetic: "[H]e wants to be a real daddy and do stuff with us," she tells Marie. "He tries" (p. 83). Through Lena's disclosure to Marie, the reader is able to discern much about the nature of her abuse. Lena explains that the abuse started just after her mother's death: "[H]e was wanting me to sleep in his bed all the time where Mama used to sleep" (p. 77). The reader also understands that her abuse includes no vaginal penetration because she is not afraid of getting pregnant. "He doesn't do that," she explains to Marie (p. 79).

Lessons on Blame

Most importantly, Lena understands that the abuse is not about her. Lena pleads with Marie to not hate her for something that isn't her fault. Children often blame themselves or believe the abuse is punishment for being "bad." Lena's belief that she is blameless would certainly be a wonderful reminder for any child reading this novel. Children going through a similar situation need to be told repeatedly that the blame always lies with the adult. Marie, too, in a particularly mature manner, views Lena's father with pity. Her own father, with his inability to show affection, has given her insight. Marie realizes that Lena's father is a pathetic, twisted man, and she "couldn't get mad at him" (p. 82).

This humanization of Lena's father gives the reader a sense of near understanding of the sexual predator. The predator isn't the stereotypical stranger parked in a dark alley; he is usually a loved neighbor, grandfather, or uncle. Many predators do not consciously choose their victims. Ninety-nine percent of the things they do for a child are genuine acts done with good intention and with proper behavior. That one percent of inappropriate predator behavior, sitting back in their minds somewhere, is usually triggered by a personal, emotional crisis. Lena's father lost his wife, and while that fact does not excuse his behavior, the significance of the loss seems consistent with the profile.

I Hadn't Meant to Tell You This shows that it is okay for an abused child to acknowledge that the person committing the abuse is not a monster. The child can understand that the person committing the abuse may even have positive qualities. Woodson makes it clear, though, that the sexual predator is wrong, destructive, and sick. Woodson never absolves the abuser, but she allows Lena to feel loathing and love, and that makes it okay for the reader, too.

CONCLUSION

Sexual abuse leaves scars. Even after the truth is told, the attorney is paid, and the therapy is complete, a family rarely totally heals. In my own situation, anger, humiliation, blame, and sadness fester under the surface of our family gatherings. I have made sense of nothing but am trying to forgive myself for continuing to support and love a man who has torn our family apart and destroyed the innocence of two little girls. Memories of abuse will cause a little girl to cry at night. And the mommy's job, the hero's job, is to hold the little girl tight and keep her safe.

In Woodson's novel, Lena takes Dion and they leave. Lena's father has started abusing Dion, and Lena won't let that happen. That makes Lena her own hero. Marie keeps Lena's secret, and that makes her a hero, too. No kindly teacher, no brave coach intervenes to save Lena and her sister Dion. A neater, happier ending might have pleased the reader. Leaving Lena and Dion alone, on the road, certainly makes it more difficult for the reader to sleep at night. And maybe that's exactly what Woodson intended.

REFERENCES

Anti Child Porn Organization. n.d. Retrieved May 3, 2004 from http://www.antichildporn.org.

Child Abuse Prevention Council of Sacramento. n.d. Retrieved May 3, 2004 from http://www.capcsac.org.

Field, Tiffany. (1998, December). Touch therapy effects on development. *International Journal of Behavioral Development, 22* (4), 777.

Touch Research Institutes. (2001, October 19). University of Miami School of Medicine. Retrieved from http://www.miami.edu/touch-research/home.html.

Woodson, Jacqueline. (1996). *I hadn't meant to tell you this.* New York: Delacourt Press.

CHAPTER 11

A Therapeutic Teacher's Reader Response to Beatrice Sparks's *Treacherous Love*

Terry Burkard Plaia and Judith M. Bailey

INTRODUCTION

Every day, students enter my classroom with problems that I hear about.
Mary didn't do her homework because she was at the hospital with a sick
grandparent, or Johnny had to work last night and study for two tests in
other classes, so his essay—assigned last week—isn't complete. Sometimes the situations are valid excuses for an extended deadline, and sometimes they are not. In either case, I deal with the situation promptly and, I
hope, with mercy when it is warranted. Such things are the reality of working with teenagers today, and like other teachers, I take them in stride.

What disturbs me is the students with problems that I don't hear about.
They rarely say anything, but over time you learn to spot some of the troubled ones. The student who enters the room with a chip on his shoulder,
ready to pick a fight, or the one who sleeps through class repeatedly
because he isn't sleeping at home, for instance, has bigger problems than
today's lesson. And some of the problems can't be so easily seen. Sufferers of emotional and sexual abuse are among the hidden ones. Sexual
abuse of a child has been defined as occurring "when a child is exploited
for the sexual gratification of an older person. This abuse may be in the
form of fondling, penetration, or exposing sexual body parts," and is far
more common than most people realize. After 30 years of research investigating hundreds of studies and making statistical adjustments for what is
known about additional factors, Lloyd deMause (1998) concludes that the

sexual abuse rate for America is most probably 60% for girls and 45% for boys; about half of these are directly incestuous.

I have seen some abused students and tried, in some small measure, to lead them toward help. Knowing that this abuse is so common and yet hidden, I feel I must find some way to address it in my classes or at least make my room a haven where students may find some help in the power of literature and words. I have always enjoyed discussing novels in class but only recently became truly aware of the therapeutic possibilities of those discussions. *Treacherous Love,* edited by Beatrice Sparks, is very real, very possible, and is a novel that I make sure is available to my students.

SYNOPSIS OF *TREACHEROUS LOVE* EDITED BY BEATRICE SPARKS

Treacherous Love graphically shows how a young girl may become prey for a molester and could be recommended as a "how not to" book for adolescent girls. Fourteen-year-old Jennie's life is falling apart. Her parents' marriage is in trouble, and they pay little attention to her. Dad is most often not there, and Mom takes too many pills trying to deal with her own problems. Jennie also feels like she has lost her two best friends: Marcie moves away, and Bridget now spends all her time with her new boyfriend. Jennie knows why no boys are interested in her; she hates being short and flat-chested, looking like a baby. The only true friend she has is her diary, where she records the loneliness of her life.

At the lowest point in her self-esteem, she meets Jonathon Johnstone, a substitute math teacher who is full of praise for her academic abilities. Soon he asks whether she can be his student aide, helping him grade papers because he has suffered an eye injury. She develops a crush on Mr. Johnstone and is surprised and delighted when "J.J." reveals his feelings for her; they begin a relationship. Over time, though, her loneliness returns, and she begins to feel trapped in the lie she's been telling her mom and friends about her involvement with this teacher. In the end, it is Jennie's innocent trust—in saving J.J.'s notes to her and her diary—that put the molester behind bars.

ORGANIZATION

During the summer of 2001, I attended workshop training in "Read 180, Target on Reading" where, among other skills, I learned how to use "reader's response" to increase students' reading comprehension. The first part of a reader's response is simply thinking aloud and making mental connections to the reading material. According to Harvey and Goudvis (2000), the connections we make as readers fall into three categories:

- Text-to-Self: Connections that readers make between the text and their past experiences or background knowledge;
- Text-to-Text: Connections that readers make between the text they are reading and another text, including books, poems, scripts, songs, or anything that is written; and
- Text-to-World: Connections that readers make between the text and the bigger issues, events, or concerns of society and the world at large. (p. 21)

In an attempt to model the use of reader's response and to show the power of words and literature as a part of the healing process, I chose to respond to *Treacherous Love* and engage in a discussion about the novel with Judy Bailey, a licensed clinical social worker. The novel reminded me of all the hidden problems that some of my students might be facing and our responsibility as teachers to help our students avoid entrapment by such molesters. The questions I attempt to address in our reader-response discussion include the following: What can teachers do to help these students? How can we avoid placing abusers in the classroom? How can we make our children strong enough to avoid entanglement with those who may use any position of power for evil purposes?

A TEACHER CONVERSES WITH A THERAPIST ABOUT THE NOVEL

The dates at the beginning of my response are the dates of Jennie's diary entries to which I am responding. Each response on my part will be labeled to identify the type of connection I am making to the text.

Teacher's Reader Response # 1 (September 9–11), Text-to-Self and -World

Early in the novel, the author establishes the fact that Jennie is having trouble dealing with her home life. Her parents constantly argue but never discuss their situation with Jennie. In front of her, they pretend that everything is fine, but Jennie fears they will divorce. Occasionally my students come to school and are unable to concentrate, or even stay awake, because similar situations have kept them up all night. They might tell me that they were unable to do an assignment because of "problems at home." Like Jennie, they are alienated from discussion of the problem and feel helpless. They are also still young and egocentric enough to see themselves as the core of the family and the source of the problem. They think that the stress they put on their parents' relationship is causing the friction between the adults. I try to be sympathetic. At this time they probably are embarrassed by the situation and have few adults they can confide in. I rely on instinct in selecting my next options. In addition to being more flexible with assignment deadlines, I also ask whether they would like to speak to a guidance counselor or social worker. At their request, I will make arrangements with the social worker. There have been instances when the social worker confided in me later that the student revealed serious abuse that initiated court action and the prosecution of the perpetrator.

Therapist's Response to #1

It sounds as if you have been around adolescents enough in the classroom to observe warning signs. You seem to respond with sympathy and understanding and make efforts to have the students evaluated. That's a good thing!

Teacher's Reader Response #2 (September 15), Text-to-Self

Jennie and Bridget discuss the fact that some boys will hit only on girls with "big boobs." Jennie writes, "It seems like now only the nerds give me a second look, and only the scumballs hit on Bridget. That's probably because she's got big boobs. I wish I had big boobs—or any boobs at all" (Sparks, 2000, p. 10). At some time in her life, every woman alive has probably felt this way. I remember it clearly. Society rewards women with ample breasts and slim bodies. We recognize this fact very early, usually about the time that we become aware of our own lack of pulchritude. If we're lucky, we discover that we do have other qualities that are more important than our cup size. Also, there's nothing wrong with nerds! I was one. Those teenagers who use their brains and work hard will generally get more education and earn better incomes than the ones whose main goal in high school is to be "cool." They will, therefore, be in a position to provide well for their dependants. Teens need to be reminded of this fact from time to time, and I try to do that with my students. It helps them realize that they need to plan their future based on something more substantial than looks.

Therapist's Response to #2

One of the most important things to a teen is appearance. You are right. They do need to be reminded of the bigger picture. However, it is difficult for teens to see that far ahead.

Teacher's Reader Response #3 (November 2), Text-to-World

Jennie writes, "I'm the dumb kid who has probably caused most of my parents' stress. I don't clean my room, I whine, and pout, and zillions of other things that I'm not going to do again after this very minute. My changing will probably help Mom and Dad have harmony in their marriage more than anything" (p. 17). Like many teens, Jennie accepts a large part of the blame for her parents' marital difficulties. Besides being unrealistic in her case, this is simply too great a burden for any child to bear. The worst part of it is that the parents in this situation are so preoccupied with their problems that they often don't pay much attention to their children, much less discuss private emotions with them. Being ignored by a parent is often interpreted as disapproval, thus confirming the child's misplaced sense of guilt.

Therapist's Response to #3

You mention two dynamics here. One is the parents' lack of attention and communication with their daughter. Parents are focused on their own issues and often think they are protecting their child by not talking about the marital problems. The second dynamic is the child's perception of how the world revolves around him or her. Reading about situations like Jennie's may help some students see that their real-life home and school situations are not rare circumstances. I can see this as one of the benefits of reader's response.

Teacher's Reader Response #4 (November 25), Text-to-Self

Jennie, Bridget, and Marcie's friendship reminds me of my friendship with Marcy and Penny, a friendship that began when I was about the same age as Jennie. The three of us were always together, and we discussed *everything*. We managed to get into and out of trouble together. More than 40 years later, though we're spread from Florida to Maine, we still keep in touch. We still share our joys and sorrows and try to help one another find solutions to life's difficulties. While many people find solace in writing in journals, my solace has always been in long talks with these two friends. Unfortunately, Jennie does not talk to her friends because of her promise of secrecy. Perhaps they would have been able to talk her out of involvement with J.J., which is exactly why he demands the promise in the first place.

Therapist's Response to #4

There is no way to know how you might have dealt with a situation similar to Jennie's. You were lucky to have two very close friends with whom you shared everything. The power of a manipulative sex offender can be very strong, and it is not surprising that Jennie did not tell her best friends.

Teacher's Reader Response #5 (January 24), Text-to-Self

Jennie once again reveals her insecurities when she writes, "What's wrong with me that no guys like me?...and I wish I wasn't so skinny and short. I look like a baby" (pp. 33–34). Wow! Do I remember that feeling! I was always the shortest one in my class, was very skinny, and looked very young. My mother's assurances that I would be thankful years later for my youthful appearance did nothing to help my frustration at the time. *At 14, girls want to attract boys!* The fact that I didn't, temporarily damaged some of my self-esteem. The same must be true for Jennie, and without much of a support system, this adds to her vulnerability.

Therapist's Response to #5

Your comment here is a perfect example of how important it is for teens to have love, support, and reassurance from parents and/or guardians. Perhaps if Jennie had been communicating better with her mother, she would not have become so vulnerable to a sexual predator. This is where teachers can be offering healthy support, but it is also why J.J. was successful at seducing Jennie. Jennie was naturally drawn to his supportive comments about her academic abilities. From a healthy teacher, those kinds of supportive comments are helpful to a child whose home life is falling apart. Flattering comments from a sexual predator, however, are lethal; their words are like a narcotic for their prey.

Teacher's Reader Response #6 (January 27), Text-to-World and -Self

In addition to all these normal adolescent struggles, Jennie's mom adds one adult-sized problem. Dad left without even saying goodbye, and Mom breaks down while trying to tell Jennie. Jennie feels that she must take charge. That evening she writes, "Mom looked like a frightened, frozen, lost little child, and I scrunched down and took her in my arms, wiping away her tears and telling her that everything would be all right, that together we could work it out. I could feel myself becoming the mother figure and wondered how that could possibly be" (p. 35). The report of the situation continues in Jennie's January 30 diary entry: "Mom is taking pills that the doctor prescribed.... We still haven't mentioned Dad.... I wonder why he doesn't phone or write something. I wonder why he hates me.... [I want to] plead with him to forgive me for whatever it is" (p. 37).

It can't be healthy for 14-year-olds to have this much pressure. Half the time they are the ones who need to be cuddled and soothed. Surely Jennie needs to be told that she is not the reason that her dad left. Teens still need someone to make rules for them. At this point in the novel, Jennie is too embarrassed to talk to her friends, and her mom is a wreck because she isn't getting any real help. The pills enable her to avoid the situation when she needs to confront it. Jennie, too, is overburdened and has no support system. She thinks she is in control but desperately needs someone to talk to. This makes her highly vulnerable. Loading all this guilt and responsibility on a child comes close to being child abuse itself.

Therapist's Response to #6

By not finding a support system for herself, Jennie's mother did herself and her daughter no good. When parents are substance abusing to the point where they are neglecting the needs of their child, it is abuse and should be reported. In a sense, Jennie went from having two parents to having no parents. Jennie's father left without saying anything because that was easier for him. He did not think about what would have been best for his daughter. When children are left to find their own supports, they often pick the wrong people. They turn to people who are available and willing to give them attention, often as a means of getting their own needs met. This is why we see teens get involved in "bad crowds." In Jennie's case, she turned to another adult who was able to meet her needs on some level while capitalizing on her vulnerability.

Teacher's Reader Response #7 (February 10), Text-to-Self and -World

"I don't know when I've ever felt this good and nourished and appreciated in my whole life," writes Jennie (p. 40). At her lowest emotional point, Mr. Johnstone, a substitute teacher, picks her to be his aide because of "her superior ability and positive attitude" (p. 42). After gaining approval from her mother, Jennie works as Johnstone's aide until the principal forbids her continuation of that after-school role, saying it simply was not "prudent" (p. 55). Jennie feels, like many students, that rules are created only to make life difficult for students. In their naïveté, students tend to be very trusting and think adults are, if not trustworthy, at least honorable. Mr. Doney, the principal, on the other hand, has been entrusted with the safety of all the students in the school. He is aware of the danger of a teacher being too close to a student and advises Johnstone not to risk even the appearance of impropriety. Male teachers in my high school don't even keep a female student for detention unless their classroom door and the one across the hall are both open so that another teacher can see them and witness their behavior. It's a good rule for teachers because we never know what might be said by a troubled student to compromise our reputations.

Therapist's Response to #7

Mr. Doney made the right decision, and your school has a good policy for very good reasons.

Teacher's Reader Response #8 (April 22–May 7), Text-to-Self and -World

Jennie's diary entries mention Mr. Johnstone's change of verbal strokes to physical ones. She writes about his stroking her hair, touching her neck, massaging her shoulders, and secretly sending her notes and giving her small gifts. Late in the school year, he comes to school wearing an eye patch and again requests Jennie's help as his aide. He says he has permission from the principal and insists Jennie get an okay from her mother.

I can accept the fact that she has a crush on her teacher and that she's flattered by all the attention he gives her, but shouldn't some alarm be ringing inside her head at each of these advances? I can remember that when I was 10 years old, back when no one talked about such things, the man who ran a local gas station asked me to do some clerical work for which he would pay me. He was a person I had spoken to briefly for years. He knew my family, and I trusted him. When he gave me the money, he stroked my hair and asked me to sit on his lap so he could hold me. I left as fast as I could and avoided that side of the street for months. I also remember that a friend had previously done the same work for this man and suddenly refused to continue. She moved away without ever saying anything to me, and I felt betrayed by her. I warned my younger sister to stay away from the man but told no one else. Part of me didn't think anyone would believe such a thing, and another part was afraid of what my father—a normally peaceful person—might do to the man if he found out. Even though nothing had actually happened, I remember feeling dirty. In fact, I have always avoided thinking about it, and this is the first time I have ever revealed this secret to anyone other than my sister. I can't imagine how someone who is actually abused must feel.

At this third request for a specific student as an aide, after advising against it before, shouldn't the principal be concerned? What about Mom? She should at least think it curious that the principal has once again changed his mind. If either of them had done something about their doubts, Jennie might have been saved a lot of pain.

Therapist's Response to #8

To answer your first question, "Shouldn't an alarm be going off in her head?" No, not for Jennie, because of her vulnerable situation and her desperate need for love and attention. I wonder whether Mr. Johnstone lied about having permission from the principal. Mom gives her permission primarily for two reasons: She, like most people, trusts teachers; and she has no idea what kinds of feelings her daughter is having for Mr. Johnstone. He probably was a victim of sexual abuse himself, in that sexually deviant behavior patterns are established in childhood. The mean age for sex offenders is between 26 and 32, and fewer than average are married, but they do not necessarily fit the stereotype of "isolated degenerates, sexually frustrated and totally unable to find appropriate outlets" (Schwartz, 1988, p. 16). Mr. Johnstone, however, appears to be the type of offender that has exclusive sexual interest in children. This type of seducer prefers victims who cooperate and is usually dissuaded if the child resists. He is usually able to identify those children who will not divulge the sexual behavior and is skilled in courting and grooming them. Mr. Johnstone, believe it or not, is pursuing love and affection as well as physical contact, and that's why he says he is "in love" with his victim (Schwartz, 1988, pp. 20–21).

Teacher's Reader Response #9 (June 8), Text-to-World and -Self

Jennie, worried about her mom and sorry that she sometimes behaves disrespectfully toward her, writes, "I don't know how she stands me...and obviously Dad couldn't! Well, to hell with that! I don't need him and he doesn't need me, So what? Who cares?" She decides to forget about Dad because both Mom and Mr. J. said to "forget about unimportant things" (Sparks, 2000, pp. 102–103). She obviously isn't going to forget her dad. She is so full of pain caused by his complete absence and guilt because she thinks she is responsible for her parents' split that her self-esteem is extremely low. She has nowhere to turn for help except, she thinks, to Mr. J.

How many kids in our classes also blame themselves for their parents' divorces and have no one to talk to about how they feel? Years ago I worked at an elementary school where the guidance counselor created a "Divorced Kid Club." If a student's parents were divorced or separated, the student could get a weekly pass to attend the "secret" meeting. No other students knew the nature of the meeting, and members of the group were free to discuss their feelings, knowing their words would be kept confidential. Do such groups still exist in elementary schools? What about middle schools? I don't see this happening at my high school, but then, I don't think many high school students would reveal their vulnerabilities to a relative stranger. Most high school kids see their counselors only once or twice a year, usually in a large group setting. The closest thing I have seen as far as meetings like that is our Straight and Gay Alliance (SAGA) meetings, where kids confide all sorts of family difficulties and help one another cope. Sometimes knowing others care makes the difference between coping and attempting suicide.

Therapist's Response to #9

As a high school social worker and a clinician in private practice, I think there is a growing trend for schools to provide more services to students during the school day. At this point in time, every school in every district across the country operates independently of one another. It has been frustrating to come into this position as a school social worker and have no guidelines or clear expectations for the job's duties and responsibilities. School social workers are a fairly new idea above and beyond guidance counselors and substance-abuse counselors. The newest research shows that a child's affective presentation directly affects his/her ability to learn and perform. That, coupled with tragedies such as Columbine, have demanded the presence of professional counselors in the schools. I think we need to pay more attention to our younger children and provide more services from kindergarten through eighth grade than we do now. Often, by the time the child reaches high school, it's much more difficult to make positive change, but it's not impossible.

Teacher's Reader Response #10 (June 18), Text-to-World

Jennie thinks J.J. is becoming her boyfriend now that he gives her quick hugs or kisses the top of her head when no one is looking. J.J. makes it clear that if she tells anyone about their special friendship, he'll lose his job and have to move away. The implication is that it would be her fault if he loses his job and, as a result, she would lose his love. She writes, "He asked me to carefully destroy the notes he writes me, too—*but I cannot do that!* They are too precious to me. I keep them locked away in my treasure chest. He will be glad someday I did!" (p. 108). Of course she won't tell! She is so desperate to be worthy of someone's love, she'd do almost anything. It's beautifully ironic that acting out of love, she defies his one request and saves his notes, sure that one day his notes and her diary will provide romantic memories for the two of them.

Therapist's Response to #10

Well, they sure do provide memories for the two of them, however, not romantic ones. The innocent, trusting love of a 14-year-old girl shows that even the best con artists dig their own graves. J.J. really had confidence that she would do anything he asked of her.

Teacher's Reader Response #11 (July 7–15), Text-to-World

J.J. asks Jennie to lie to her mom in order to spend time with him. Once the lies and the secret meetings begin, the relationship escalates. She meets with J.J. at his home, where he gives her wine and pot, telling her that it is safe as long as he is there to protect her. At the same time, he tells her about his "terrible shyness," which makes her want to help and protect him. Jen is so trusting and innocent that she has no idea that she is being manipulated. She is dreaming of the day when she can introduce J.J. to her mom, and she just knows that her mom will have no objections to her mar-rying this wonderful older man.

In the privacy of his home, J.J. also begins photographing Jennie. This quickly leads to nude photos of Jennie so that in their old age they can remember how beautiful she was. Jen is hesitant but poses to please J.J. The first hint of doubt is revealed when Jen writes, "Sometimes I wonder about the...photography stuff...but I know J.J. would never do anything, well...you know...that was wrong (Sparks, 2000, p. 136). Jennie is defi-nitely being controlled. Deep down, she knows it but is trying not to admit it even to herself. Jennie feels guilty for having a boy her age as a friend because J.J. doesn't like it. She can't have any friends because J.J. thinks they're too immature. She can't get a part-time job to help her mom because her time must be free for J.J. Although this relationship with J.J. seems to be the only source of acceptance for her, Jennie is beginning to feel restricted by him.

Therapist's Response to #11

I have seen many adult women allow themselves to be controlled in a relationship. This tends to happen when one does not have a strong sense of self. The need to please their partner outweighs their need to be honest with themselves. When you understand that dynamic, it is easy to under-stand how a teenage girl full of self-doubt would fall victim to such a con-trolling person.

Teacher's Reader Response #12 (August 2), Text-to-World

For whatever reason, J.J. suddenly starts making excuses why Jen cannot visit or call as often. She complains that they never go anywhere or do any-thing, and in addition to the wine and pot, he now gives her uppers and downers. J.J. soothes her fears, and they talk about their plans to run away and marry when she turns 15 in October. She will be the perfect wife because J.J. will mold her. Somehow she manages to forget that she doesn't like this molding process or how restricted she feels. Perhaps she feels so unworthy that she thinks obedience is the price she must pay for love.

Therapist's Response to #12

Perhaps, but I tend to think it's more of a good manipulator at work than it is Jennie thinking she is unworthy. Having worked with sex offenders in a maximum-security prison, I have learned what smooth operators they are. They actually make their victims believe that the positives will outweigh the negatives. In addition to that, they isolate the victim from others so that the victim feels the predator is the only one for him or her and the only one who can understand and provide for his or her needs, ultimately minimizing the sacrifices.

Teacher's Reader Response #13 (August 5), Text-to-World

Jennie, feeling guilty about her bad attitude, uses a hidden key to let herself into J.J.'s home in order to leave him a surprise bouquet of flowers. While she is in the kitchen, the phone rings and the answering machine clicks on. A man's voice says, "I thought you'd learned your lesson about getting involved with chickie littles.... I'll help you get a job in California... and YOU'RE RIGHT! YOU GOTTA DUMP THAT JAIL-JELL and NOW! Bring all the yummy pictures you took and start runnin' as soon and as fast as you can before she talks to someone" (p. 145). What a horrible way to find out you've been betrayed! Jennie had done absolutely everything she could to please him and finds out that he doesn't even love her. Feeling completely worthless, she writes, "I'm caught in his sticky, evil, obscene web, and I'll never through my life, be able to get out of it. Oh, please, please, God, let me die. I feel so guilty! So dirty, so used!" (p. 146).

Jennie thinks she can't tell her mom because it would destroy any love her mom might feel for her. Even after realizing the betrayal, Jennie still feels partly responsible. Often when we know we've done something our parents would not approve of, we fear losing their love. Fortunately, that's not the way it works. In spite of the problems she is having, Jennie's mom does love her. Caring, loving parents don't ever stop loving their children, no matter what their differences. Parents understand that, but Jennie does not have the benefit of that experience. When Jennie refuses to leave her bed and cries all day long, her mom realizes that someone must have done something terrible to cause Jennie such emotional anguish. Jennie initially refuses to talk, but her mother remembers her initial suspicion of Mr. Johnstone and asks Jennie whether he is the one who hurt her. Mom convinces Jennie to see a rape counselor, and Jennie finally sees the need to prevent Johnstone from doing this to others. I loved the way her mom comes to the rescue and supports Jennie. She had been all wrapped up in her own problems, but now she spends all her time talking with Jennie and helping her. She also calls Jen's dad, and when he arrives, the three of them talk together. Jennie learns that her mother's anger prevented her father from contacting her, but they now realize how wrong and unfair that is to Jen. I see students every day with one angry parent interfering with the other parent's relationship with their children. I can't understand why the parents can't see the damage they cause their children.

Therapist's Response to #13

To comment on your first point, I think Jen's not wanting to tell her mother has less to do with doing the right thing and more to do with fear of what may be a reality. To comment on your last point, we all know it is easy to see things from an objective point of view and difficult to make sense of a situation when we are in the middle of it. Combine that with adults who are having marital difficulty and who are lacking in parenting skills, and we can see why parents would not see the damage they are causing their children.

Teacher's Reader Response #14 (September 28), Text-to-Text and -World

Jennie is prepared for the trial, where the defense attorney claims she is making untrue charges to ruin Mr. Johnstone's career. When that accusation is made, Jennie produces all the notes that J.J. wrote to her and proves her abuser's guilt. Both she and her mother get help in recovering from their emotional trauma, and, at least for a while, the world is safe from J.J. Johnstone. When Jennie first says she is saving the notes, I knew they would play an important role in the plot. I expected Jennie's diary to be important in the trial but then realized that a diary might be presented by the defense lawyer as fantasy, not proof. Isn't it wonderful that something Jennie does out of pure love saves her and possibly others from future abuse? I wish evidence as strong could decide more abuse cases.

Therapist's Response to #14

You made a good point about the diary, and I was glad the notes provided the evidence needed to convict J.J. It was also nice that Jennie's parents realized they needed to unite to support their daughter in spite of their divorce. Even though Jennie's father marries someone else and moves to another city, it is good that he continues to be in Jennie's life to support her. J.J. needs to take responsibility for his actions, understand their inappropriateness, express empathy for Jennie, and then work on learning new behavior. Unfortunately, sex offenders just released from prison are at high risk to reoffend within two years.

CONCLUSION

Throughout most of this novel, Jennie clearly suffers from a lack of attention, affection, and interest from her parents. Like many parents today who are absorbed in their own problems, they fail to see that Jennie not only knows of their arguments but also blames herself for their differences. Thinking she is at fault and unworthy of being loved are what make Jennie so vulnerable. Could it have been avoided? Perhaps. If Jennie's parents had taken time to include her in some of the discussions about the future of the family, she might have understood that she was not to blame and that she was loved by both of them. It's a shame the divorce process doesn't include more counseling for both parents and children. It seems the elementary school "Divorced Kid Club" might be much more important now than years ago when most families lived closer and there was an extended family as a support group.

Schools and school systems are not perfect. Obviously, some predators still make it into our school systems, despite screening processes. Still, we must be vigilant in completing the processes, without bypasses or shortcuts that are sometimes taken to avert teacher shortages. We must also pay attention to the practices and attitudes of the teachers who are already in our classrooms. Encouraging teachers to use reader response strategies might help students connect with literary characters in situations similar to their own and help them find solutions. Administrators should be aware of any teacher or coach who spends a great deal of time "after hours" with students, and perhaps teachers should be advised to avoid one-on-one contact with a student when possible. This would protect the teacher as well as the student from unfounded rumors.

Parents also should be aware of any adult who spends frequent time alone with their child. Most importantly, though, parents should give enough time, attention, and caring to produce a child who feels loved and competent and possesses self-confidence. Unfortunately, with more and more single-parent families and less time for families to be together, this becomes a daunting task. Much of the parenting that some children now receive comes from schools, especially at the elementary level. Many high schools have added courses such as "Family Living" and "Parenting" in recent years to better prepare students for these roles in their lives. As we see fewer nuclear families with built-in support systems, the schools of the future might well utilize more teachers and social workers to continue producing emotionally healthy adults with more than adequate parenting skills. This idea is supported in "The History of Child Abuse," by Lloyd deMause (1998), when he says,

We cannot be content to only continue to do endless repair work on damaged adults, with our therapies and jails and political movements. Our task now must in addition be to create an entirely new profession of 'child helpers' who can reach out to every new child born on earth and help its parents give it love and independence.... To those who object to the cost of helping all parents, we can only reply: Can we afford to teach parenting? What more important task can we devote our resources to? (p. 235)

As far as "doing endless repair work" in the classroom, we also cannot afford to stop. Many students are damaged long before they enter our classrooms. In addition to our emotional support, they need to be exposed to some literature that tells them they are not alone; others have survived what they're going through now. Reader response gives us another option for therapy, one even the silent students can use. It teaches them the power of thoughtful connections and the power of words. Literacy can help students to cope with a sometimes hostile world and to come to grips with and solve some of their own particular problems.

REFERENCES

deMause, Lloyd. (1998, Winter). The history of child abuse. *The Journal of Psychohistory, 25* (3), 216–236.

Harvey, Stephanie, & Goudvis, Anne. (2000). *Strategies that work: Teaching comprehension to enhance understanding.* York, ME: Stenhouse Publishers.

Schwartz, B.T. (1988). *A practitioner's guide to treating the incarcerated male sex offender.* Washington DC: U.S. Government Printing Office.

Sparks, Beatrice. Ed. (2000). *Treacherous love: The diary of an anonymous teenager.* New York: Avon Books.

Index

AA programs, 142
Abandon(ed), 5, 40, 73, 106, 112, 134–35
Abandoning mode, 8
Abandonment, 1–3, 27, 154
Abortion, 111–12, 169
Absence(s), 33, 96, 224
Absent, 33, 96, 134, 160
Absenteeism, 34
Abuse, 1–11, 29, 32, 35, 40, 44–52, 54–58, 62–70, 77–81, 85–88, 91–95, 97–101, 103–9, 114, 121, 125, 127, 129, 133–37, 139, 145, 147–48, 150, 152–53, 156, 158, 160–64, 167–69, 171, 176, 179, 182, 186, 197, 199–200, 208, 210–13, 215–16, 218, 221, 223, 228; Adolescents, 128; Animal, 97; Child, 5, 7, 10, 65, 80, 91–94, 98–99, 105–7, 109, 127, 128; Drug, 43, 93–94, 98, 160, 181; Elder, 97; Emotional, 6–7, 9, 43–47, 49–53, 55, 57, 69–70, 73, 77–81, 84, 86–88, 92, 101–6, 111, 137, 150, 155, 161–62, 215; Laws, 10; Mentally, 200; Pet, 97; Physical, 2, 9, 28, 44–45, 47, 49–50, 51, 80, 86–88, 91–99, 101–9, 111, 114, 127, 128, 150, 161–62, 200; Psychologically, 137; Sexual, 1, 7, 9, 47, 49, 86–88, 92, 94, 106, 108, 145–47, 149–65, 166, 167, 170, 177, 179, 181–82, 201, 208, 209–10, 213, 215–16, 223; Substance, 40; Survivor, 67, 147, 163, 176; Verbal, 9, 69, 137, 200; Victims, 167; Youth, 88
Abuse and Neglect, 41
"Abused Boys, Battered Mothers, and Male Involvement in Teen Pregnancy," 106
Abuser(s), 8–9, 45, 50, 53, 93, 102, 104, 128, 141, 148, 152, 162–64, 167, 170, 182, 210–11, 217, 228
Abusive, 47, 51, 103, 150, 166; Adults, 99, 108; Boyfriend, 100, 104; Caretakers, 94; Dad, 114; Family, 135; Father, 101, 211; Incident, 103; Man, 100; Mother, 106; Parents, 94–95, 98; Relationship(s), 87, 104, 210; Scene, 80; Situation, 29, 84; Stepfather, 46; Stepmother, 82; Stepparent, 102; Tactics, 133; Teacher, 137; Treatment, 91
Academic: Ability, 87; Achievement, 33; Failure, 40
Acceptance, 40, 50, 152, 226
Accident(s), 83, 96, 167; Prone, 96

Ackard, Diann M., 6
Acting out, 45, 135, 182
Act out, 49, 97
Adaptive strategies, 15
Addiction(s), 34, 36, 68, 73, 162, 165
Addictive patterns, 31
ADHD, 96
Adjunctive strategy, 85
Administration for Children and Families, 2
Administrators, 229
Adolescence, 20, 59, 68
Adolescent literature, 40, 77–78, 80
Adopted, 78, 128–30, 135, 169
Adoption, 71, 129, 169; Open, 130
Adoptive: Children, 130; Families, 130, 142; Parents, 129, 135; Records, 130
Adultery, 10
Advice, 51, 163, 204
Advocate, 75
Advocates for Youth, 147
Affection, 69, 74, 105, 146, 212, 223, 229
Affective: Development, 69; Presentation, 224
Affirmation(s), 163, 200
Aggression and Violent Behavior, 107
Aggressive, 45, 87–88, 95–97, 98, 99, 106, 108, 149, 159
AIDS, 73
ALA Best Book for Young Adults, 5, 102–3, 151
ALA *Booklist* Editors' Choice, 103
ALA Notable Book, 100–101
ALA Quick Pick, 151
ALA Top Ten Best Books for 2000, 151
ALAN Review, The, 6, 10, 48, 186, 205
Alcohol, 3, 30, 33, 50, 71–72, 94–95, 97–98, 112, 136, 181
Alcoholism, 5, 32, 34, 38, 103–5
All We Know of Heaven, 10
Alone, 189, 191–92, 196, 204, 209, 213, 229–30
Alpert, Judith L., 157
Alter-ego, 134
Ambivalent mode, 8
American Academy of Child and Adolescent Psychiatry, 91, 97–98, 149

American Academy of Pediatrics, 44, 52, 93–94
"American Academy of Pediatrics Report," 44
American Family Physician, 108
American Humane Association, 1–2, 43
American Journal of Family Therapy, The, 8, 106
American Journal of Public Health, 158
American Journal of Art Therapy, 161
American Psychological Association, 99, 157
American School Board Journal, 160
Ames, M. Ashley, 164
Amnesia, 70
Anda, Robert F., 106
Anderson, Laurie Halse, 151, 185–86, 189, 193–95, 197, 199, 201, 205
Anderson, Stephen A., 106
Angelica, Jade Christine, 157
Anger, 27, 40, 46, 50–54, 56–59, 61–65, 91, 103–4, 109, 112, 114, 121, 131, 153, 155, 162, 175, 189, 197, 213, 227; Cues, 58; Issues, 58; Management, 50–52, 58, 64–65
Animal cruelty, 109
Animals, 97, 109
Anorexia, 170
Anorexic, 153, 210
Anti Child Porn Organization, 210, 213
Antisocial, 95, 99
Anxiety, 53, 98, 107, 150, 161, 164
Argument(s), 91, 102, 112, 229
Armstrong, Leah, 29–30
Arrest(ed), 5, 71, 109; House, 207–8
Art, 151, 186–87, 189, 194, 198, 201, 204; Teacher, 189, 194; Therapy, 27, 185, 188, 200; Work, 78
Assault, 93, 99; Aggravated, 109; Sexual, 148, 162
Assaulted, 98
Assignment, 195, 200
Athletic(s), 50–51, 57, 131–32, 168
Atkins, Catherine, 151
At-risk: Child, 20; Group, 160; Youth, 79
Attachment(s), 9, 45, 69, 75
Attention, 74, 146, 170, 182, 209, 216, 219, 221, 223, 229; Span, 96

Attitude(s), 120, 147, 209, 222, 227
Australia's Book of the Year Award, 103
Authority, 93, 105, 127, 132; Figures, 53, 55–56, 58
Autobiography, 4
Awareness, 62, 85, 162, 182

Baron, Mary, 6
Babysitter, 134
Bad Beginning: A Series of Unfortunate Events, The, 47
"Bad Girls: Violence among Young Women Keeps Rising, and Interventions Designed for Boys Just Don't Cut It," 109
Bailey, Judy Plummer, 215, 217
Band director, 102
Baseball, 151
Basketball, 166, 176
Battered: Child syndrome, 109; Mothers, 106; Wife syndrome, 19
Battery, 91, 93
Baughman, Joey, 196, 205
Bauman, Karl E., 158
BCCB Blue Ribbon Book, 151
Beat, 104, 117, 167, 170
Beaten, 40
Beating(s), 101, 139, 166
Becvar, D., 16, 28
Becvar, R., 16, 28
Bed-wetting, 44
Behavioral: Conduct, 48; Indicators, 96, 98, 149; Modification, 61; Problems, 40, 45, 159; Specialist, 208
Beineke, Rachel, 48
Belief(s), 93, 99, 122, 124, 133, 139, 157, 164, 178, 181, 212
Belittle(d), 40, 44, 104
Bernet, William, 69, 73, 78
Betrayal, 211, 227
Betrayed, 227
Bibliotherapy, 85
Bigotry, 52
Binge and purge, 6
"Binge and Purge Behavior among Adolescents: Associations with Sexual and Physical Abuse in a Nationally Representative Sample," 6

Bisexual, 98
Bite marks, 96
Blackbird, 153
Black eyes, 96
Blame(s), 44, 55, 86, 94, 139, 179, 181, 209–10, 212–13, 219, 224, 229
Blaming, 139, 181
Block, Francesca Lia, 152–53
Body of Christopher Creed, The, 47
Booklist Editors' Choice, 101
Booklist Top Ten First Novel, 151
Borderline: Pathology, 9; Personality, 19; Syndromes, 150
Born Blue, 4, 69–70, 78
Borrego, Joaquin, Jr., 107
Boundaries, 16, 20
Brain: Damage, 98; Swelling, 98
Brave New Girl, 153
Breathing Underwater, 101
Bridgers, Sue Ellen, 10
Brown, Jocelyn, 158
Brown, Laura, 157
Brown, Ralph A., 161
Bruise(s), 91, 95–98, 100, 104, 109, 113
"Bruised Butterfly, A," 200, 205
Brute(s), 131–32
Bullies, 105, 122, 129
Bully, 112, 117, 124, 129, 205
Bullying, 88, 95, 105, 205
Burned, 40, 111, 124
Burns, 96, 109, 114
Byars, Betsy, 100

California Consortium to Prevent Child Abuse, 105
Cancer, 133, 195, 211
Case(s), 86, 91–92, 94, 97, 105, 109, 145, 159, 163, 211, 219, 228; Scenarios, 10; Study, 107
Cathartic, 67, 168, 204
The Cauldron: Untitled: No Boundaries, 205
Causation, 163
Causes, 69, 97
Center for Disease Control, 146
Chapman, Daniel P., 106
Chemical: Dependency treatment, 149; Imbalance, 15, 19

Child Abuse & Neglect, 6, 10, 48, 164
Childhood Abuse and Neglect: Specificity of Effects on Adolescent and Young Adult Depression and Suicidality," 158
Child Abuse and Trauma Scale, 44
Child Abuse Evaluation and Response Center, 148
Child Abuse Ministry, The, 157
Child Abuse Prevention Center, 94
Child Abuse Prevention Council of Sacramento, 210, 213
Child Abuse Prevention Services, 3, 44, 94
"Child Abuse Reporting: Teachers' Perceived Deterrents," 10
Child Abuse: The Hidden Bruises, 97
"Child and Adolescent Abuse and Neglect Research: A Review of the Past 10 Years. Part I: Physical and Emotional Abuse and Neglect," 9, 68
Child Called "It," A, 4, 104
"Childhood Sexual Abuse and Revictimization in Adolescence and Adulthood," 160
Child Maltreatment, 107, 159
Child Neglect: Injuries of Omission," 7
Child Protective Services, 10, 158, 166, 170, 175
Child Protective System (CPS), 141–42
Child rearing modes, 8
Children's Defense Fund, 2
Child Safety Institute, 3
"Child Sexual Abuse and Emotional and Behavioral Problems in Adolescence: Gender Differences," 159
Child Sexual Abuse: Critical Perspectives on Prevention, Intervention and Treatment, 162
Child Welfare, 161
Chinese Handcuffs, 165, 167–68, 183
Choice(s), 50, 118, 136, 143, 166, 170, 181
Christopher Award, 103
Chronicles of Narnia, 31
Church, 68, 207–8
Cigarettes, 31
Clearing House, 89

Client-Centered Therapy: Its Practice, Implications and Theory, 28
Clinical, 80, 84, 87, 108, 217
"Clinical Assessment of Child Victims and Adult Survivors of Child Maltreatment," 7
Clinicians, 85
Coach(es), 51, 53, 68, 101, 112, 129, 131, 213, 229
Coalition for Children, 96–98
Cognitive, 28, 45; Capacity, 121; Dissonance, 53–54, 57
Cohen Ivker, Naomi A., 159
Columbine, 105, 225
Coman, Carolyn, 100
Comfort, 143; Zone, 75–76
Comic Creators' Guild Award, 155
Commission on Violence and Youth, 99
Communication, 16, 106, 130, 219
Community, 107, 127, 159, 209, 211; Medical, 108
Compassion, 104, 129, 194, 196–97
Con artists, 225
Concentrate, 97, 140, 217
Concentration camps, 132
Conduct: Disorder, 96, 98; Problems, 149
Confide, 202, 218, 224
Confidence, 64, 113–14, 128, 132–33, 150, 225
Conflict(s), 27, 50–51, 57–60, 78, 156; Resolution, 58
Confrontation(s), 128, 163
Confusion(s), 191, 208, 210
Connectedness, 188–89
Connections, 201, 217, 230
Consequences, 76, 143, 154, 159, 162, 211
Contraception, 106
Control, 33, 36, 46, 53, 55, 58–60, 62–63, 94–95, 100–101, 112–13, 128, 131–32, 134–36, 140–41, 148, 163, 167–68, 171, 178, 181–82, 221
Controlling person, 226
Controversial, 129, 194
Convict, 228
Conviction, 92, 148
Cope, 100, 112, 168, 224, 230

Coping, 161, 224; Mechanisms, 88;
    Strategies, 103, 157
Coping with Family Violence, 108
Coretta Scott King Genesis Award, 46
Corporal punishment, 91
Counseling, 10, 14–15, 17, 19–21, 27–28,
    40, 55, 93, 135, 163, 229; Approaches,
    15; Goals, 20–21, 55; Objectives, 55;
    Session, 168; Techniques, 128
Counselor(s), 11, 15–17, 19–26, 52–60,
    74–77, 111, 114–24, 139, 141, 143,
    168, 171, 175–76, 186, 224–25, 227;
    Guidance, 51, 70, 74, 175, 218, 224;
    Substance abuse, 224
Counter-transferential process, 194
Courage, 47, 60, 117–18, 123, 133,
    135–36, 151, 154, 170, 185–86,
    200–201
Court(s), 104, 109, 159, 218
Courtois, Christine A., 157
Covey, Steven R., 134, 143
Cowdry, R. W., 146
Cowen, Perle Slavik, 7
Cracker Jackson, 100
Cramer-Benhamin, Darci B., 106
Creative Expression, 185–86, 190,
    199–201
Crime(s), 91, 136, 147–48
Criminal(s), 137, 164; Behavior(s), 43,
    99, 159
"Criminal Consequences of Childhood
    Sexual Victimization," 164
Crisis, 14–15, 39, 156
Croft, Janet B., 106
Cross Creek Counseling Center, 146
Cruelty, 88, 97, 109
Cruise, T., 7
Crutcher, Chris, 49–51, 61, 63–64, 67–68,
    101, 111–12, 125, 128, 143, 165–67,
    170–71, 183
Cry, 66, 96, 98, 111, 168, 193, 213
Crying, 92, 100, 172, 191, 193–94, 196
Cultural: Situation, 138; Values, 3
Cultures, 130
Custody, 8, 73
Cut, 46
Cuts, 96

Cutting, 46
Cycle, 101, 114, 125, 136, 182
"Cycle of Violence Often Begins with
    Violence towards Animals, The," 109

Damage, 98, 170, 228
Dance, 201
Dancing, 163
Danger, 14, 104, 170
Dangerous, 112
Date rape, 101, 147, 149, 159, 168, 199
Death(s), 2, 72–73, 92, 98, 103, 136, 138,
    141, 153, 168, 187, 190–91, 195–97,
    208, 211–12
Decisions, 191, 210
Deem, James, 79, 82, 87–89
Defense(s), 20–21, 117, 120; Attorney,
    228; Mechanism(s), 199, 210
Defensive, 45
Defensiveness, 93
Defiance, 88
Definition(s), 1, 6, 43, 80, 91, 145, 160,
    167
Deikstra, Rene F. W., 159
Delacorte Press Prize for a First Young
    Adult Novel, 5
Delayed recall, 157
Delays, 96, 98
Delinquency, 149
Delinquent(s), 96, 99, 164
deMause, Lloyd, 8, 146, 215, 230
Denial, 40, 178
Dental care, 164
Dependent(s), 45, 136, 218
Depressed, 30, 134, 164
Depression, 9, 45–46, 96, 98, 107,
    149–50, 158, 161–62, 209; Maternal,
    107
Deprivation, 135
Dersch, Charlotte Alyse, 158
DeSalvo, Louise, 185–86, 205
Desert Flower: The Waris Dirie Story,
    147
Destruction, 88, 125, 168
Destructiveness, 96
Detachment, 46
Detention, 33, 35, 68, 222

Detox facility, 38–39
Developmental: Delays, 98; Tasks, 1–16, 20, 94; Trajectory, 28
Developmentally delayed, 137
Diagnosis, 109, 161
Diagnostic impression, 84
Diary, 155, 172, 185, 216–17, 221–22, 225, 228
Dietz, Patricia M., 106
"Differentiating between Parental Alienation Syndrome and Bona Fide Abuse-Neglect," 8
Disabilities, 162
Disability, 103, 165
Disaster(s), 112, 168
Discipline, 49, 51, 66, 92, 95, 127, 136, 168
Disclosure, 162, 171, 188, 208, 212
Disease(s), 31, 209
Disengagement, 18
Dissociation, 99
Dissociative, 157
Disorder(s), 74, 85, 96, 98, 158
Distress, 73, 85, 97
Division of Youth and Family Services, 109
Divorce(s), 9, 30, 40, 102, 165, 169, 217, 224, 228–29
Documentation, 109
Domestic violence, 9–10, 69, 93, 97, 106–7, 136, 139, 200
Don't You Dare Read This, Mrs. Dunphrey, 13, 28
Door Near Here, A, 5, 29–30, 40–41
Dosh, Shannon D., 127
Draper, Sharon, 45–46
Drawings, 149
Dream(s), 51–53, 82–83, 124, 173, 210
Drinking, 75, 94, 112, 133
Drown(ing), 70, 73
Drug(s), 3, 43, 46, 50, 71, 74–76, 93–95, 97–98, 127, 130, 134, 136, 138, 142, 149, 153, 160, 165, 169, 181
Drunk, 33, 202; Driver, 198
Dynamics, 16, 219
Dysfunctional, 5, 13, 17, 19, 31–32, 40, 47, 56, 63, 99, 157, 182, 189

Eastern: Philosophies, 130; Religions, 124
Eating disorder(s), 47–48
ECPA Gold Medallion Winner, 105
Edgar Allen Poe Award Finalist, 151
Education, 76, 218
Educational: Achievement, 45; Neglect, 29
Educator(s), 11, 49, 69, 80, 87–88, 128
"Educator's Role in Reporting the Emotional Abuse of Children, The," 89
"Effects of Parental Verbal Aggression on Children's Self Esteem and School Marks," 48
Ego, 133, 136
Egocentric, 218
Eisner Award, 155
Emotion(s), 82, 108, 128, 132, 135–36, 139, 153, 219
Emotional, 6–7, 28, 46, 146; Abandonment, 154; Abuse, 6–7, 9, 43–45, 47, 49–53, 55, 57, 73, 77–80, 84, 86, 101–6, 111, 137, 150, 161–62, 215; Abuser(s), 45, 53; Anguish, 227; Arousal, 157; Bond, 45, 136; Crisis, 212; Damage, 98; Deficits, 40; Development, 43, 45, 73; Difficulties, 69; Distress, 73; Harm, 73; Health, 37; Maturity, 59; Neglect, 2–3, 9, 29, 69; Numbing, 85; Nurturance, 43, 74; Ordeal, 157; Outburst, 51; Pain, 70, 114, 185; Point, 222; Problems, 45, 47, 159, 201; Psyche, 113; Questions, 128; Responses, 69; Responsiveness, 73; Significance, 55; Stimulation, 73; Support, 69, 230; Torture, 152; Transformation, 185; Trauma, 78, 228; Turmoil, 168; Vulnerability, 20; Workout, 101
"Emotional Abuse: Destruction of the Spirit and the Sense of Self," 89
"Emotional Child Abuse," 89
Emotionally: Abuse(d), 4, 44, 49–51, 55, 80, 155; Abusive, 46, 51; Charged, 136; Detrimental, 141; Distressed, 78; Heals, 204; Healthy, 52, 230; Supported, 207; Tired, 67; Unable, 129
Empathize, 78, 194

Empathy, 99, 150, 228
Endangerment standard, 9
English, Diana J., 4, 8
English teacher(s), 13, 51, 82–83, 85, 131, 143, 199
Entrapment, 217
"Environment of Child Maltreatment: Contextual Factors and the Development of Psychopathology, The," 107
Escape, 47, 80, 84, 189, 199, 210
Essence Magazine, 163
Ethical, 88, 159
"Ethical Dilemmas in Teaching Problem Novels: The Psychological Impact of Troubling YA Literature on Adolescent Readers in the Classroom," 10
Ethnic: Awareness, 129; Composition, 138; Differences, 10
"Evaluating and Reporting Emotional Abuse in Children: Parent-Based, Action-Based Focus Aids in Clinical Decision-Making," 78
"Evaluation of Physical Abuse in Children," 108
Evidence, 228
Evil, 80, 124, 154, 185, 217, 227
"Evolving Law of Alleged Delayed Memories of Childhood Sexual Abuse, The," 159
Exhibitionism, 145
Expectations, 53, 94, 224
Exploitation, 145
Exploited, 137, 145, 215
Expulsion, 135
"Extent and Consequences of Child Maltreatment, The," 8
External focus, 21
Externalizing, 108

Failing, 102
Failure(s), 51, 168
Faith, 211
Families and Family Therapy, 28
Families of origin, 95, 132
Family: Counseling, 15–17, 27; Counseling approaches, 14; Counselor, 19; Instability, 27; Issues, 16; Life, 33;

Living, 229; Relationships, 49; Situation, 29; Subsystems, 16; System(s), 15, 56, 58; Therapist, 16; Therapy, 15–17; Transaction patterns, 16; Values, 134; Violence, 95, 97, 101
Family of origin, 141
Family Planning Perspectives, 161
Family Therapy: A Systemic Integration, 28
Family Therapy: History, Theory and Practice, 28
Family Therapy Techniques, 28
Fantasies, 102, 149
Fantasy, 85, 152–53, 228
Fatalities, 29, 92
Father of counseling, 21
Fear(s), 51, 58, 67, 83, 96, 100, 102, 112, 132, 150, 162, 170–71, 193, 204, 211, 226, 228
Feeling(s), 40, 51, 61, 66, 75, 78, 80, 85–87, 102–4, 108, 112, 114, 121–22, 132–33, 135, 152, 154–56, 161–63, 168, 171–72, 177, 181–82, 187–89, 216, 220, 223–24
Feldman, Ronald, 9
Felitti, Vincent J., 106
Felony, 147
Female genital mutilation (FGM), 148
Feminism, 200
Field, Tiffany, 209, 213
Fight, 114, 197
Fighting, 45, 56
Findings, 157, 159, 162
Fiscella, Kevin, 150
Fishman, H., 16, 28
Fitch, Janet, 46
Flashbacks, 150
Flinn, Alex, 101
Fondling, 145–46, 215
Football, 60, 132; Coach, 51; Players, 129, 131
Force, 91, 145
Forged by Fire, 45
Forgive, 104, 170, 174, 178, 208, 213, 221
Forgiveness, 40, 63, 67, 105, 136, 203
Forgiving, 138

Foshee, Vangie A., 158
Foster: Brother, 70; Care, 5, 46, 70, 73,
    211; Home(s), 4, 71, 74, 141, 211;
    Families, 142; Parents, 70, 141
Foxman, The, 104
Fractures, 97, 109
Francoise, Serres, 48
Free services, 135
French, Simone, 6
Friend Indeed, A, 163
Friends, 97
Friendship, 188, 207, 219
Frustrated, 93
Frustration, 51, 91, 220
Future of Child Protection, The, 41
Future of Children, The, 4

Gale Encyclopedia of Psychology,
    94–95
Gang(s), 50, 95, 133, 165, 169
Garbarino, James, 107
Gardner, Richard A., 8
Garneski, Nadia, 159
Gay, 60, 160; Straight Alliance (GSA),
    160
Gender, 6, 10, 50, 134, 147–48, 158, 162
Genitalia, 145, 148, 149
Gerry, 190–94
Giannet, Stan, 185–86
Gladding, S., 16, 28
Goals, 59–60, 70, 74, 137, 168
Goldberg, Glenn A., 105
Golden Kite Award, 151
Gothard, Judge Sol, 159
Goudvis, Anne, 217, 230
Government, 34, 40
Grades, 87
Greene, Wendy F., 158
Gribi, Gerri, 147
Grief, 84–85, 138, 150, 191–92, 208–9
Grieving, 190
Grooming, 146, 166, 223
Growth, 14–15, 19, 55, 88, 151, 199
Guidelines, 141–42, 224
Guide to Crisis Intervention, A, 28
Guilt, 40, 72, 103, 150, 152, 155–56, 163,
    168, 171, 178, 181, 189, 208, 219, 221,
    224, 228

Guilty, 114, 132, 207, 226–27
Gynecological symptoms, 150

Haddix, Margaret Peterson, 13, 28
Haley, J., 16, 28
Hamarman, Stephanie, 69, 73, 78
Handicapped, 132
Hanged Man, The, 153
Hannan, Peter J., 6
Hansen, David J., 107
Happiness, 68, 210
Harassing, 129, 141
Harassment, 154, 160
Hardship(s), 108, 112
Harm standard, 9
Harry Potter and the Sorcerer's Stone, 89
Harvey, Stephanie, 217, 230
Hate(d), 103, 106, 115, 170–71, 211–12
Hate You, 103
Hatred, 129
Heal, 64, 68, 153, 169, 185, 195,
    200–201, 211
Healer, 189
Healing, 64, 67, 81, 84, 95, 105, 155–56,
    163, 171, 185–86, 188, 190, 194,
    196–97, 199–201; Process, 171, 194,
    201, 217; Species Organization, 97
Health, 93, 103, 156
Healthy, 114, 121, 143, 163, 170, 179,
    181, 197, 221; Attitudes, 209; Support,
    220
Heartland Award for Excellence in Young
    Adult Literature, 151
Hecht, Debra B., 107
Heinonen, Tuula, 163
Henke, Suzette, 185, 205
Help, 68, 85, 88, 128, 135, 159, 168, 170,
    181–82, 202, 216, 221, 224
Helpful, 220
Helping mode, 8
Helpless, 7, 95, 174, 218
Helplessness, 87, 161, 182
Hero, 5
Heroin, 4, 70–71, 74
Hibbs, Leslie, 207
High-stress environments, 7
History, 93, 96, 98–99, 104, 106, 133,
    149, 159, 178

"History of Child Abuse, The," 8, 230
Hit, 47, 92, 104, 121
Hobbies, 100
Holiday(s), 61, 208
Holmes, William C., 160
Holton, John K., 44
Home(s), 34, 88, 96, 98–99, 102, 104, 125, 127, 137–39, 151, 153–54, 173, 178, 180, 208–10, 219; For unwed mothers, 169; Life, 33, 217; Visit, 10
Homeless, 6
Homelessness, 100
Homicides, 94
Homosexuality, 60, 68, 98, 152, 160
Honesty, 185, 188, 202, 226
Hope, 5, 28, 46, 54, 60, 66, 75, 99, 143, 151–53, 156, 165, 182, 185–86, 200–201
Hopeless, 178, 211
Hopelessness, 87, 152, 211
Horn, Gabriel, 187, 190, 195, 205
Horn Book Fan Fare Title, 151
Horton, C., 7
Hospital, 103, 192
Hospitalized, 112
Hostility, 44, 52, 88, 107
Howe, James, 101
Human Rights Watch, 98
Humiliation, 104, 137, 213
Humor, 102, 165, 168, 170, 204
Hunt, Irene, 102
Hurt(s), 47, 67, 91, 98, 104, 124, 136, 175, 195–97, 200–202, 227
Hygiene, 210
Hyperactive, 88
Hysterics, 192

"I Am," 19–21, 26
Identity, 156
"I Don't Feel Safe Here Anymore," 160
Ignorance, 153
I Hadn't Meant to Tell You This, 207–8, 212–13
Illusion(s), 127, 202
Immature, 94, 226
"Impact of Couple Violence on Parenting and Children: An Overview and Clinical Implications, The," 106

Impairment, 108
Imperfections, 201
Inadequacy, 45, 87
Incest, 145, 149, 156, 208–9, 211, 216
Indecent exposure, 145–46
Independence, 200, 230
Indicators, 45, 80, 87–88, 93, 95–96, 98, 149, 161, 210
Individuation, 15
Infanticidal mode, 8
Infibulation, 148
Informed consent, 145
Injury, 91, 93–94, 95–98, 109, 147, 155
Injustice, 128
Innocence, 127, 207, 210, 213
Insight(s), 120, 135, 138, 156, 167, 212
Instinct, 135, 170, 218
Integrate(d), 86, 120
Integrity, 60
Intensity, 168, 176
Intent, 73
Intercourse, 145–46, 149, 171, 178
International Journal of Behavioral Development, 213
Internet Comic Award for Best Graphic Novel, 155
Interpersonal: Relationships, 27, 161; Situations, 74; Skills, 106; Violence, 97
Intervention, 93, 141
Interview(s), 107, 158, 162
Intimidating, 88
Intimidation, 154
Intoxication, 30, 35
Intrinsic value, 21
Intrusive mode, 8
IRA-CBC Children's Choice, 100
Ironic, 225
Ironman, 49–51, 67–68
Irony, 171
Irritable bowel syndrome, 44
Isolated degenerates, 223
Isolation, 85, 102, 162, 189, 199
Issues, 15, 19, 27–28, 34, 49–51, 55–56, 58, 77–78, 80, 83, 85–86, 111–13, 127–28, 137, 152, 155, 159, 165, 168, 200, 204, 211, 217, 219
I Was a Teenage Fairy, 152

Jail(s), 71, 137, 169, 207, 230
Jaswant, Guzder, 9
Jones, Rebecca, 160
Journal(s), 13–14, 30, 61, 77, 80–83,
    86–88, 101, 103, 165, 185, 187, 220;
    Reader response, 30
Journal of Child Sexual Abuse, 158
*Journal of Consulting and Clinical Psy-
    chology,* 164
*Journal of Counseling and Develop-
    ment,* 7
Journal of Instructional Psychology, 87,
    89
*Journal of Personal and Interpersonal
    Loss,* 160
Journal of Psychohistory, The, 8, 146, 230
*Journal of the American Academy of
    Child and Adolescent Psychiatry,* 9, 68,
    78, 158–59
*Journal of the American Medical Associa-
    tion, The,* 150, 160
Juvenile: Delinquents, 99; Justice system,
    5, 95; Rehabilitation centers, 137
*Juvenile Offenders and Victims: 1999
    National Report,* 162

Kanel, K., 14–15, 28
Kaplan, Sandra J., 9, 49, 68–69, 74, 78,
    108
Kaywell, Joan F., 13, 49, 111, 143, 165
Keith-Oaks, Judy, 86, 89
Kendall, Harold, 187
Kennedy, Eileen, 79–80
Kenny, Maureen C., 10
Kidnapped, 71, 151
Kill, 72, 92, 102, 104, 166, 196
Killed, 94
Killing, 95
King, Martin Luther, 133
Klass, David, 102
Koch, Gary G., 158
Krahe, Barbara, 160
Kraizer, Sherryll, 96
Kreklewitz, Christine, 163
Kurland, Morton, 108

Labia, 148
Labruna, Victor, 9, 49, 68–69, 74, 78, 108

"Last Closet, The," 198, 205
Lauck, Jennifer, 153
Laughter, 168, 170
Law(s), 91, 116, 128, 139, 142–43,
    166–67; Enforcement, 157
Lawyer, 156, 167
Learned behavior, 182
Learning, 44, 52, 94, 96, 131, 135; Diffi-
    culties, 27; Impairments, 98
Learning to Swim, 155
Legal, 88, 91, 142; Action, 128; Issues,
    159; Ramification, 6; System, 196
Lesbian, 160
Letters, 51, 165, 168
Levi Company, The, 96
Lev-Wiesel, Rachel, 161
Lewis, C. S., 30–31
Liar, 156, 207
Life, 68, 103, 107, 111–13, 115–18, 122,
    124, 130, 133, 136, 151, 155, 168–71,
    173, 179–82, 189–90, 196, 198, 200,
    208–9, 216, 227
Linder, George Flether, 158
Literacy, 52, 230
"Literary Life-Writing in the 20th Cen-
    tury," 185, 205
Literary technique, 61
Loneliness, 153, 155, 189, 199, 216
Los Angeles Times Best Sellers, 153
Loss, 4, 153, 168, 194, 197, 208–10, 212
Lost Boy, The, 4
*Lost Boys: Why Our Sons Turn Violent
    and How We Can Save Them,* 107
Lottery Rose, The, 102
Loughlin, M. Joanne, 161
Love(d), 5, 18–20, 22–26, 32, 34–35, 44,
    46, 62, 64–67, 72, 74, 81, 100–101,
    103, 119, 127, 152, 163, 167, 169, 173,
    180–82, 188, 191–94, 198, 209–10,
    212–13, 220, 223, 225–28, 230;
    Unconditional, 5, 66
Lowenthal, Barbara, 29, 40–41
Luna, Louise, 153
Luster, Stephen A., 161
Lyons, Danielle, 69

MacDougall, James E., 158
Machover Draw-a-Person Test, 161

Madanes, C., 16, 28

Magic(al), 80, 84, 88, 191

Maladaptive: Habits, 75; Peer relationships, 8

"Male Survivors' Perspectives of Incest/Sexual Abuse," 162

"Male Victims of Sexual Abuse: An Analysis of Substantiation of Child Protective Services Reports," 158

Malnourishment, 27

Malnutrition, 29

Maltreated, 94

Maltreatment, 2, 8–9, 29, 40, 69, 84, 92, 145, 158

Mammograms, 164

Mandel, Francine, 108

Manipulate(d), 27, 148, 162, 225

Manipulative: Behavior, 149; Sex offender, 220

Manipulator, 226

Marks, James S., 106

Marsden, John, 103

Massage, 209

Masturbation, 146

Mazer, Norma Fox, 103, 154

McClure, Lynn, 163

McCormick, Patricia, 46

McDevitt, 207

McNamee, Graham, 103

Media, 134; Specialist, 208

Medical: Care, 163; Community, 108; Literature, 109; Neglect, 2

Medication, 19

Meditate, 163

Meditation, 123

Memoir, 185

Memorialize, 197

Memories, 66, 83, 150, 156, 159, 163, 169, 188, 193, 199–200, 203, 213, 225; Repressed, 159

Memory, 150, 156–57, 169, 188–89, 196–97; Delayed, 159

Mental(ly); Abuse, 200; Acuity, 57; Challenged, 129, 131; Disabilities, 147; Health, 7, 65, 135; Illness, 153; Retardation, 98; Torture, 152

Middle Way House, 91

Miklowitz, Gloria D., 104

Miller, Susanne M., 10

Mind, 139; Games, 137

Minnesota Center Against Violence and Abuse, 93, 95

Minuchin, S., 16, 28

Miracle, 190

Misbehave, 114

Misbehaviors, 95

Misconception, 86–87

Misfit(s), 57, 68, 129, 132, 140

Misnamed, 167

Mistreatment, 153

Mock: Counseling session, 22, 113, 168; Family counseling session, 17

Model(s), 95, 99, 134, 201

Modeled, 21, 125

Molestation, 146, 149, 152

Molester(s), 148, 152, 155, 216–17

Monster, 208, 212

Mood swings, 96

Mother Theresa, 133

Multiethnic, 130

Multi-ethnicity, 129

Multiple personality, 150

Multiracial, 128–29

Munsch, Joyce, 158

Murder, 46, 99, 107, 171

Murdered, 47

Muroff, Jessica Pawelkop, 29

Music, 71–72, 77–78, 201

Musician, 104, 147

"My Three Faces: The Writer, the Therapist, and the Man," 143

Narc, 203

Narcotics, 73

Narnia, 30–31, 39

"Narrator Named Julian Drew, A," 89

National: Average, 94; Data, 98; Emergency, 40

National Association of Child Advocates, 2, 44

National Association of Social Workers, 147

National Book Award Finalist, 151

National Center for Child Abuse and Neglect Prevention Research, 44

National Center for Victims of Crime, 150

National Child Abuse and Neglect Data
System, 1, 2
National Clearinghouse on Family Vio-
lence, 45
National Clearinghouse on Neglect and
Child Abuse Information, 3
National Committee to Prevent Child
Abuse, 92, 146
National Council on Child Abuse and
Family Violence, 45
National Exchange Club Foundation, 43,
92
National Foundation for Abused and
Neglected Children, 2
National Incidence Study of Child Abuse
and Neglect (NIS), 147
National Institute of Mental Health, 3,
146
National Network for Child Care, 3
National Victim Center, 146
*Native American Book of Change: Native
Ways Series, Volume III, The,* 195,
205
*Native Heart: An American Indian
Odyssey,* 205
Nazi, 132
Neglect, 1–9, 13, 16, 29, 31–32, 34–35,
38, 40, 69–70, 79–81, 84, 88, 92–93,
94, 99, 105, 107, 134–35, 158, 182,
209; Educational, 29; Emotional, 29,
147; Physical, 1–2, 9, 29
Nemesis, 124, 135
Neumark-Sztainer, Dianne, 6
Neurological imbalance, 15, 19
Newbery Honor Book, 101
New York Public Library Book for the
Teen Age, 5
Nightmare(s), 149, 186, 191, 203
Nolan, Han, 4, 69–70, 78
No More Secrets, 156
Nonfiction, 6, 48, 106, 157
Normalcy, 49, 54
Nude photos, 226
Nudity, 145
Numbing, 157
Nurturing, 27
Nutrition, 1, 7, 9, 35, 37, 209

Obedience, 63, 226
Obsess, 63
Obsession, 101
Obsessive, 19, 50, 80, 112
Odierna, Candace, 69–70, 77–78
Offender(s), 109, 145, 147, 220, 223, 229
Office of Juvenile Justice and
Delinquency Prevention, 162
Oklahoma Book Award, 6
Oppressor, 132
Oral sex, 202
Outburst(s), 135, 156
Outcast(s), 111, 132, 151, 154, 186, 203,
205, 208, 211
Outlet(s), 172, 223
Out of Control, 154
Outrage(s), 135, 197
Overachieve, 97
Overweight, 48, 111, 113–14, 170

Pain, 69, 72–73, 77–78, 83, 96, 101–2,
114, 128, 135, 151, 153, 155, 161, 168,
174–75, 185–87, 189–90, 194–97, 199,
201, 223
Palmer, Sally E., 161
Pap smear, 163
Paradigm(s), 17–18
Paranoia, 85
Parent: Adoptive, 76; Emotionally abu-
sive, 44; First-time, 10; Impoverished,
10; Substance-abusing, 10; Substitute,
9; Teen, 10
Parental: Alienation syndrome, 8; Indica-
tors, 3
"Parent-Child Interaction Therapy with a
Family at High Risk for Physical
Abuse," 107
Parentified, 20
Parenting, 62, 136, 229–30; Classes, 142;
Responsibility, 21; Role, 16–17, 56;
Skills, 8, 20, 228, 230; Strategies, 10
Parents' Choice Award, 100
Parent-teacher conferences, 138
Paris, Joel, 9
Passive, 7, 87, 120
Past Forgiving, 104
Pathological, 31, 157

Patterned Behavior, 45
Paulsen, Gary, 104
Peace, 68, 106, 138, 163
Pediatric Nursing, 7
Pediatrics, 106, 108
Peer: Group, 77; Pressure, 199
Pelcovitz, David, 9, 49, 68–69, 74, 78, 108
Pelzer, David, 4, 104
Penetration, 145, 160, 215
Peretti, Frank, 105
Perfectionism, 50, 57
Perfectionist, 112
"Perfect Love," 190, 205
Perpetrator(s), 67, 93–94, 97, 107, 136, 139, 148, 160, 162, 210, 218
Persona, 117–18, 120
Personality, 185; Traits, 16
Perspective(s), 61, 70, 80, 88, 101, 105, 112, 123, 129, 153
Perspectives in Psychiatric Care, 162
Physical, 6–7; Abuse, 2, 9, 28, 44–45, 47, 49–50, 80, 86–88, 91–98, 101–9, 111, 150, 161–62; Abuser, 167; Activity, 163; Affection, 209–10; Aggression, 48; Appearance, 114; Arousal, 157; Attacks, 100; Boundaries, 146; Complaints, 149; Contact, 98, 209, 223; Disabilities, 147; Disability, 165; Harm, 113; Indicators, 95–96; Injuries, 95; Injury, 91, 93; Neglect, 1–2, 9, 29; Punishment, 99; Safety, 170; Touch, 209; Well-being, 37
Physically: Abused, 49, 51, 94–97, 99, 109, 114, 128, 200; Sick, 193
"Physically Abused Adolescents: Behavior Problems, Functional Impairment, and Comparison of Informants' Reports," 108
Plaia, Terry Burkard, 215
Plastic surgery, 112–13
Playing, 97, 102
Plum-Ucci, Carol, 47
Poem(s), 95, 155, 173, 175, 198, 217
Poetry, 172, 176, 185
Poets & Writers, 205
Point of view, 228

Police, 93, 132, 151, 196, 207
Policy, 222
Poor, 93–94, 208
Pornographers, 148
Pornographic materials, 145–46
Pornography, 207
"Portrayal of Obese Adolescents, The, "48
Positive, 75; Reinforcement, 77, 107; Role models, 99; Social Reinforcement, 107
"Positive Attitudes Solutions and Actions," 92
Post-traumatic stress: Condition, 99; Disorder, 96, 150; Therapy, 157
Potter, Harry, 79–80
Poverty, 3, 7, 27, 94, 105
Power, 50, 53, 55–56, 58–60, 64, 68, 83, 122–23, 133, 137, 163, 186–87, 208, 216–17, 220, 230
Powerlessness, 164
"Practitioner's Guide to Treating the Incarcerated Male Sex Offender, A," 230
Praise, 137, 154
Predator(s), 207–8, 212, 227, 229
Pregnancy, 106, 150, 165
Pregnant, 156, 166, 169, 172, 212
Prejudice, 128
Pressell, David M., 108–9
Prevalence, 163
Prevent Child Abuse America, 4, 44, 86, 89, 92, 97
Prevention: Measures, 10; Programs, 99
"Prevention of Child Abuse," 98
Printz Honor Book, 47, 151
Prison(s), 103, 136–37, 147, 229; Maximum-security, 227
Problem(s), 108, 121, 124, 127, 137, 143, 146, 149, 153, 156–57, 160, 162, 171, 175, 179, 182, 201, 204, 215–19, 221, 227, 229; Adjustment, 27; Psychosocial, 160
Problem-solving, 106
"Prosecuting Child Abuse Cases: Lessons Learned from the San Diego Experience," 92

Prosecutor, The, 109
Prostitutes, 150
Prostitution, 145
Protect, 120, 154, 181, 202, 225, 229
Psychiatric: Disorders, 96; Help, 169;
  Hospital, 103; Problems, 73
Psychiatrists, 9, 98
Psychological, 8, 29, 107; Care, 85; Con-
  dition, 103; Development, 134, 160;
  Diagnosis, 15; Effects, 51; Evaluation,
  32–33; Functioning, 49; Problems, 43;
  Process, 54; Maltreatment, 7; Prob-
  lems, 85, 193; Research, 99; State, 53;
  Therapy, 85; Vulnerability, 95;
  Wounds, 29
Psychologically: Abuse, 137; Mis-
  treated, 8
"Psychological Risk Factors for Border-
  line Pathology in School Age Chil-
  dren," 9
Psychologist(s), 30, 50, 87, 162, 171;
  Clinical, 186
Psychopathologic symptoms, 44
Public: Humiliation, 137; Opinion, 127
Publishers Weekly Best Book of the Year,
  151
Punishment(s), 53, 61–62, 69, 91, 93, 95,
  97–99, 127, 136; Corporal, 91
Push, 6
Put down, 44

Quarles, Heather, 5, 29–30, 41
Questionnaire, 159
Questions, 191

Race, 60
Racial, 128
Racist, 129
Rae-Grant, Naomi I., 161
Rage(s), 103, 114, 121, 135, 138, 150,
  167, 197
Rape(s), 40, 101, 145–49, 151–52,
  153–54, 156, 159, 161, 166, 168–69,
  171, 186, 189, 193–95, 197, 199,
  200–201, 203–4, 227; Acquaintance,
  149; Date, 101, 147, 149, 159, 168,
  199

Rape and Sexual Assault Center, 149
Rasmussen, Rebecca A., 107
Ray, Susan L., 162
Reader response(s), 30, 40, 128, 187, 189,
  195, 198, 201, 216–22, 224–30
Reading, 68, 78–80, 85–87, 114, 124,
  128, 143, 154, 185, 187, 204, 212,
  216–17, 219
Reality, 57, 68, 83–84, 88, 102, 122–23,
  166, 182, 188, 192, 198, 215, 228
*Reason to Hope: A Psychosocial Perspec-
  tive on Violence and Youth Reason to
  Hope,* 99
"Recall of Childhood Trauma: A Prospec-
  tive Study of Women's Memories of
  Child Sexual Abuse," 164
Recognition, 137
Recovery, 151, 153, 163, 167, 200
Reflect, 67, 141, 189, 199
Reframe(d), 21, 57
Reframing(s), 17, 19, 54–56, 123
Regier, D. A., 146
Regression, 103
Rehabilitation, 136–37, 142
Reid, Suzanne, 10
Reinforce, 75, 77
Reinforcement, 107
Rejected, 98, 130
Rejecting, 86
Rejection, 43, 78, 135
Religion(s), 111, 124
"Remembrance of Things Past: The
  Legacy of Childhood Sexual Abuse in
  Midlife Women," 163
Remorse, 136
Remorseful, 139
Report(s), 109, 157–58, 162
Reporting, 6, 10, 80, 87, 94, 141
Procedures, 7, 10
Research, 9, 65, 70, 99, 106–7, 146, 150,
  160–62, 164, 193, 209, 215, 224
Empirical, 16
Researchers, 40, 44, 70, 73, 109, 157–62
Resilience, 28, 99, 137
Resiliency, 5, 40, 99
Resilient, 20–21
Resolution, 86, 150, 158

Resources, 107
"Responding to Children's Disclosure of Familial Abuse: What Survivors Tell Us," 161
Responsibility, 55, 68, 88, 101, 108, 122, 156, 179–81, 221, 224
Ressler, Diane, 185, 193, 205
Results, 108, 159, 161
Retaliation, 97, 132
Retribution, 132
Reunification plan, 142
Revenge, 105, 132, 154
Re-victimization, 150, 161
Reynolds, Marilyn, 154
Rigney, Kayla, 198, 205
Risk(s), 93, 106–8, 132, 138–39, 149–50, 158–59, 162
Rite of passage, 67–68
Ritter, A. William, 109
Ritual(s), 67–68
Rogers, Carl, 21–22, 28
Role(s), 112, 125, 142, 156, 166, 171, 199, 229; Model(s), 68, 99, 125, 134, 204; Playing, 58
Romeo, Felicia F., 86–87, 89
Romeo and Juliet, 10
Rottman, S. L., 5
Rowling, J. K., 80, 89
Royalty, Carolyn T., 127
Rules, 143, 221–22
Rumor(s), 152, 156, 170, 229
Run away, 47, 96, 152, 155, 166, 211

Safe, 78, 85–86, 117, 154, 163, 189, 195, 213, 225, 228
"Safe Dates Program: 1-Year Follow-Up Results, The" 158
Safety, 5, 23, 35, 52, 85, 150, 157, 170, 176, 189, 210, 222
Salzinger, Suzanne, 108
Sand tray, 27
Santelli, John, 106
Sapphire, 6
Sarcastic, 120–21
Scapegoats, 109
Scar(s), 112–14, 146, 148, 153, 209, 213

Scarlet Letter, The, 10
Schaefer-Farrell, Nicole, 79
School(s), 6, 20, 27, 29, 32–37, 39, 45, 48, 87, 93–94, 96–97, 99, 101–5, 107, 111, 127–29, 131–33, 135, 137, 149, 151–54, 156, 166, 169–72, 174–75, 178, 180–81, 186, 201–5, 209, 217–19, 222, 224–25, 229
Schwartz, B. T., 223, 230
Scurfield, Carol, 163
Secret(s), 99, 119, 156, 166, 171, 175–77, 179, 181, 207–11, 213, 223–25
Secret of the Silver Horse, The, 150
Secure, 66, 76
Security, 31, 35, 155
Seducer, 223
Selected, Annotated Bibliography of Child Maltreatment Reporting by Education Professionals, A, 6
Self: Acceptance, 21; Awareness, 15, 19, 21, 61, 135; Blame, 152, 162; Concept, 60; Condemnation, 150; Confidence, 45, 65–66, 87, 200, 229; Control, 131–32, 139; Denial, 87; Deprecating, 88; Deprecation, 199; Destruction, 153; Destructive, 98, 135; Disclosure, 86; Doubt, 156, 226; Effacement, 199; Efficacy, 99; Esteem, 9, 20, 36, 45, 54–55, 64–65, 94, 98–100, 113, 132, 139, 146, 150, 155, 161, 178, 181, 209, 216, 220, 224; Expression, 69, 77–78; Fulfillment, 143; Hate, 152; Hatred, 98; Healing, 186; Hypnosis, 99; Identity, 60, 161; Image(s), 8, 57, 97, 161; Injury, 88; Knowledge, 86, 166; Loathing, 182; Love, 54; Management, 86; Mastery, 132; Medication, 160; Perception(s), 48, 57, 124; Reports, 147; Righteous, 112; Understanding, 85; Value, 54; Worth, 43, 48, 50, 54, 131, 161
Selfishness, 133
September 11, 79, 168, 185
7 Habits of Highly Effective Families, The, 134, 143
Severely Emotionally Disturbed, 171
Sex offenders, 147, 229

Sexual, 6–7, 171; Abuse, 1, 7, 9, 49, 86–88, 92, 108, 145–47, 149–65, 167, 170, 177, 181–82, 201, 209–10, 213, 215–16, 223; Abuser, 167, 170; Abuse survivor(s), 147, 163, 176; Activity, 50, 145, 148; Advances, 139, 154, 181; Aggression, 161; Assault, 148, 162; Behavior, 181, 223; Comments, 146; Contact, 146; Crimes, 164; Difficulties, 161; Encounters, 136; Enjoyment, 148; Fantasies, 140; Favors, 208; Freedom, 127; Gratification, 145, 215; Harassment, 154, 160; Hotline, 177; Indiscretions, 137; Intercourse, 146, 149, 171, 178; Interest, 223; Intimacy, 145; Involvement, 169; Molestation, 9, 149; Offender(s), 147, 220, 223, 226; Orientation, 161; Partners, 161; Predator, 207–8, 212, 220; Preference, 60; Relationship, 179; Response, 181; Victimization, 147, 149; Violence, 163

"Sexual Abuse, Assault and Exploitation of Individuals with Disabilities," 162

"Sexual Abuse History and Number of Sex Partners among Female Adolescents," 161

"Sexual Abuse of Boys: Definition, Prevalence, Correlates, Sequelae, and Management," 160

Sexuality, 65, 197

Sexually: Abuse(d), 47, 49, 106, 146–49, 155, 157, 159, 161–64, 166, 179, 182, 208; Assaults, 154; Deviant, 223; Disturbed, 164; Explicit material, 145; Frustrated, 223; Molested, 207; Victimizes, 149; Violated, 147, 161, 166

Shaken baby syndrome, 92, 98

Shame, 63, 68, 104, 148, 150, 152, 156, 163, 169–71, 195, 203, 208

Shep, Gail B., 160

Sick, 93, 212

Sickmund, Melissa, 162

Sickness, 167

Sign(s), 29, 34–35, 85, 91, 109, 158, 162; Warning, 10, 95, 218

Silence, 112, 116, 119, 145, 152, 194, 199–200, 211

"Silent No More: Coping with Sexual Abuse," 163

Single: Mother, 105, 179; Parent(s), 7, 16, 107–8, 111, 134, 229

Situational tasks, 15

Sleep, 85, 149

SLJ Best Book, 103, 151

Small, Tom, 161

Smoking, 31

Snicket, Lemony, 47

Snow White, 153

Snyder, Howard N., 162

Sobsey, Dick, 162

Soccer, 182

Social, 28, 107; Acceptance, 48; Adjustment, 27; Consciousness, 76; Difficulties, 40; Functioning, 96; Life, 177; Maladjustment, 76; Mask, 167; Maturity, 59; Misfits, 129; Pathologies, 93; Relationships, 161; Sciences, 107; Services, 5, 34, 38, 177, 211; Skills, 9, 45, 99; Stereotypes, 129; Support, 188–89; Welfare agencies, 93; Withdrawal, 85; Worker(s), 9, 69–71, 105, 127–32, 134–42, 211, 217–18, 224, 229

Socializing: Children, 21; Mode, 8

Society, 127–29, 133–34, 167, 185, 188, 197, 199, 217–18

Sociocultural aspects, 199

Socioeconomic, 107, 160

Sodomy, 145

Solomon, C. Ruth, 48

"Songs Related to Domestic Abuse and Sexual Assault," 147

Solution(s), 143, 185, 220, 229

So Much to Tell You, 103

Soul, 72, 113, 134, 151, 174, 190, 192, 205

Spanking, 91, 127

Sparks, Beatrice, 154, 215–16, 218, 224, 226, 230

Spastic colitis, 149–50

Speak, 151, 185–86, 200, 204–5

"Speaking Out," 205

Spirit, 64, 105, 114, 119–20, 124, 188, 203

Spiritual, 64, 107, 113–14, 129–30, 134–35, 167
Spirituality, 67, 165
Sport(s), 64, 129, 131–32, 152
Statistics, 29, 210
Staying Fat for Sarah Byrnes, 111, 125
Stereotype(s), 129, 195, 223
Stereotypical, 195, 212
Stone, Robin D., 163
Story, Mary, 6
Stotan!, 101
Straight and Gay Alliance (SAGA), 224
Strategic approaches, 16
Strategic Family Therapy, 28
"Strategies that Work: Teaching Comprehension to Enhance Understanding," 230
Strategy, 85
Street, Sue, 13, 49, 111, 165
Strength, 188, 200–202, 207
Stress, 30–31, 33, 35–36, 38, 93, 107–8, 205, 209, 218–19; Hormones, 209
Stressor, 157
Stringer, Sharon, 10
Structural: Approach, 16; Counseling, 16; Family counseling, 16
Structure, 27
Struggle(s), 46, 69, 78, 80, 151, 167, 189–90, 199, 221
Studies, 73, 94–95, 108, 146, 160, 162, 209, 215
Study, 6–7, 48, 92, 97–98, 107–9, 148, 158
Substance: Abuse, 40, 74; Abusing, 221
Substitute teacher, 216, 222
Subsystems: Spouse, 16, 19; Parenting, 16–17, 19–20, 27; Sibling, 16–17, 20, 27
Success(es), 46, 75, 167, 172
Suffer(s), 49, 69, 80, 97–98, 134, 158, 164, 185, 209, 229
Suffered, 103–4, 125, 198–99, 209
Suicidal, 164; Behavior, 149; Tendencies, 9, 158, 162
Suicidality, 159
Suicide, 10, 47, 84, 111–12, 138, 156, 159, 165–66, 168–69, 189, 196, 224

"Summer of Fifth Grade, The," 196, 205
Support, 65–66, 68, 76, 85, 99, 106–7, 118–19, 142, 163, 171, 178, 188–89, 199, 213, 220, 227–28; Group(s), 142, 188, 229; System(s), 211, 220–21, 229
Survey, 44, 92, 146–47
Survival, 5, 20, 39, 56, 66, 88; Mode, 38; Skill, 102
Survive, 21, 40, 46–47, 81, 101, 105, 117, 119–20, 122–23, 153, 192, 230
Survivor(s), 67, 69, 147, 150, 157, 161–63, 176
Survivors of Educator Sexual Abuse & Misconduct Emerge: S.E.S.A.M.E., 149
Survivors of Incest Anonymous, 146
Swim coach, 101, 112, 129
Swimmer, 128, 131, 137
Swimming, 101, 131, 138, 163
Sympathy, 133
"Symptomatic Clients and Memories of Child Abuse: What the Trauma and Child Sexual Abuse Literature Tells Us," 157
Symptom(s), 69, 85, 150, 157
Syndrome, 109; Alienation, 8; Battered Child, 109; Battered Wife, 19; Borderline, 150; Irritable bowel, 44; Shaken baby, 92, 98
System(s), 142, 189, 196, 229

Talbot, Bryan, 155
Tale of One Bad Rat, The, 155
Talking, 52, 195
Tampa Bay Area Writing Project (TBAWP), 199
Tantrums, 74, 95
Tapes, 119, 122
Tardiness, 88
Target child, 105
Taylor, Lauren R., 109
Teacher(s), 7, 11, 29, 34–35, 40, 51, 53, 55, 58–59, 66, 78, 80, 85, 99–102, 105, 125, 127–29, 131–43, 155, 157, 168, 170–71, 182, 185–87, 194, 213, 215–17, 220, 222–23, 229
Teacher Magazine, 109

Team, 132, 137, 151
Teased, 48
Teasing, 111
Teen Pregnancy, 106, 165
Television, 95, 134, 142, 209
Telling, 154
Templeton, April, 200, 205
Text-to-Self, 217–22, 224; Text, 217, 228;
   World, 217, 219, 221–22, 224–25,
   227–28
Therapeutic, 77–78; Approaches, 16;
   Conversations, 143; Edge, 63; Environ-
   ment, 189; Goals, 51, 70; Intervention,
   139; Massage, 209; Objectives, 51;
   Possibilities, 216; Setting, 150
Therapist(s), 17, 46, 52, 58, 64, 74, 85,
   135, 139, 156–57, 159, 165, 168–69,
   186, 217–26, 228; Ethnically diverse,
   130; Play, 27
Therapy, 63–64, 85–86, 101, 135–36,
   139, 142, 161, 166–67, 186, 207, 213,
   230; Art, 27, 185, 188, 200; Clinical,
   80; Creative Expression, 185–86, 190,
   199, 201; Group, 47; Journal, 185;
   Music, 185; Parent-child interaction
   (PCIT), 107; Play, 27; Poetry, 185;
   Post traumatic, 157; Psychological, 85;
   Talk, 27
3 NBs of Julian Drew, 79, 88–89
Title IX, 160
Touch, 91, 209
Touch Research Institute, 209–10, 213
"Touch Therapy Effects on Develop-
   ment," 213
Tragedy, 111, 138, 225
Traits, 120
Transferential Process, 194
Transfigured, 124
Transformation, 63, 202
Transformative, 124
Transition(s), 98, 202
Transitional phases, 15
Trauma, 21, 27–28, 67, 77–78, 84, 86, 91,
   113, 138, 150, 161, 186, 188, 194,
   199–200, 228; Narrative, 150
Traumatic, 77, 150, 158, 185, 188, 195,
   197, 205
Traumatized, 86, 208

*Treacherous Love: The Diary of an
   Anonymous Teenager,* 154–55, 215–17,
   230
Treatment, 98, 149–50, 158
Triathlon, 51–52, 60
Trouble, 107, 170, 196, 219
Truancy, 88
True Colors of Caitlynne Jackson, The,
   105
Trust, 74–75, 97, 133, 136, 150, 172–73,
   176, 181, 188, 194, 196, 211, 216
Truth, 112, 138, 151–52, 154, 156, 162,
   167, 170, 172, 185, 197–98, 202–3,
   207–8, 213
Tudiver, Dari, 163
Turner, Ann, 155

Ultrasound, 163, 166
Uncommon Therapy, 28
Unconditional: Love, 5; Positive regard,
   21–22
Underdog(s), 135, 140
Understanding, 50, 218
"Understanding Mental and Emotional or
   Psychological Abuse," 45
University of Miami School of Medicine,
   213
Urquiza, Anthony J., 107
U.S. Advisory Board on Child Abuse and
   Neglect, 40
U.S. Department of Education's Office for
   Civil Rights, 160
U.S. Department of Health and Human
   Services, 2
U.S. Department of Justice, 94, 109
"Use of the Machover Draw-a-Person
   Test in Detecting Adult Survivors of
   Sexual Abuse: A Pilot Study, The,"
   161
*Using Literature to Help Troubled
   Teenagers Cope with Family Issues,
   Volume One,* 143
U.S. Supreme Court Decision *Aurelia
   Davis vs. Monroe County Board of
   Education,* 160

Vaginal, 145; Penetration, 212
Value(s), 14, 20, 60, 121, 123–25, 134

Varnhagen, Connie, 162
Verbal: Abuse, 9, 51, 69, 137, 200; Abu-siveness, 45; Aggression, 48, 74; Assault, 70; Attacks, 7; Challenges, 122; Confrontation, 131; Slings, 105; Strokes, 222; Therapy, 27
Victim(s), 45–47, 49, 51, 69–70, 87, 92–93, 95, 105, 107, 109, 136, 139, 141, 146–48, 152, 156–58, 160–63, 167, 170, 182, 187–88, 200, 207, 210–12, 223, 226–27
Victimization, 147–49
Victimized, 109, 137, 147
Victimizers, 95
Violence, 11, 50, 91, 93, 95, 97, 99, 105–8; Dating, 147, 159; Domestic, 9–10, 69, 93–94, 97, 106–7, 136, 139; Family, 95, 97, 101; Gender-based, 147; Interpersonal, 97; Sexual, 163; Television, 95; Youth, 95
Violence Against Women Online Resources, 147
Violent, 49, 93, 95, 99, 102, 105, 107, 136, 139
Void, 112, 141
Voigt, Cynthia, 155
Vulnerability, 220–21
Vulnerable, 21, 50, 55, 99, 105, 116, 120, 163, 180, 182, 220–21, 223, 229

Waldfogel, Jane, 29, 41
War, 104, 168
Warning signs, 10, 149
Washington Post, The, 93
Watcher, The, 101
We Are Not Alone: A Guidebook for Helping Professionals and Parents Supporting Adolescent Victims of Sexual Abuse, 157
We Are Not Alone: A Teenage Boy's Personal Account of Child Sexual Abuse from Disclosure through Prosecution and Treatment, 157
Weiner, Merrill, 108
Weinstein, Nina, 156
Western: Culture, 130; Thought, 124
Whale Talk, 127–28, 143

What is Love?, 187, 205
What Jamie Saw, 100
"What Social Workers Should Know about Gender-Based Violence and the Health of Adolescent Girls," 147
When Jeff Comes Home, 151
When She Hollers, 155
When She Was Good, 103
White Oleander, 46
"Why I Choose to Teach Sapphire's *Push,*" 6
"Why Sue Ellen Bridgers' *All We Know of Heaven* Should Be Taught in Our High Schools," 10
Widom, Cathy Spatz, 164
Will, 113, 132–33, 153
Williams, Carol Lynch, 105
Williams, Linda M., 164
Williamson, David F., 106
Wilson, Beverly, 187–88, 205
"With a Gun at My Head," 187, 205
Withdrawal, 85, 149
Withdrawn, 7, 96
Withdrew, 114
Woodson, Jacqueline, 207–13
Words, 138–39, 186–87, 193, 195, 197–201, 205, 216–17, 224, 230
Working Group on Investigation of Memories of Childhood Abuse: Final Report, 157
Working out, 114
World Trade Center, 168
Worth, 85
Worthless, 115, 139, 156, 227
Worthlessness, 45, 53, 98
Worthy, 225
Wounded Spirit, The, 105
Wounds, 69, 200
Writing, 51–52, 61–62, 68, 78, 80, 82–86, 95, 101, 103, 122, 128, 143, 163, 167, 172, 185–87, 190, 194–95, 197–98, 220
Writing as a Way of Healing: How Telling Our Stories Transforms Our Lives, 185, 205

Yoga, 163
You Don't Know Me, 102

Young adult: Literature, 11, 48, 79, 88;
    Novel(s), 45, 48, 100, 151, 186, 201
Yukon Jack, 63

Zebell, Nancy, 107
Zelkowitz, Phyllis, 9
Zenith event, 136

About the Editor and Contributors

DR. JOAN F. KAYWELL is Interim Department Chair of the Department of Secondary Education and Professor of English Education at the University of South Florida. She is passionate about assisting preservice and practicing teachers in discovering ways to improve literacy. She donates her time extensively to the National Council of Teachers of English (NCTE) and its Florida affiliate (FCTE), and is Past-President of the Assembly on Literature for Adolescents (ALAN) and Past-President of FCTE. She is a regular reviewer for *English Journal* and *The New Advocate.* She is published in several journals, regularly reviews young adult novels for *The ALAN Review,* and has written several textbooks: *Adolescent Literature as a Complement to the Classics, Volumes One, Two, Three, & Four* (1993, 1995, 1997, 2000, Christopher-Gordon) and *Adolescents At Risk: A Guide to Fiction and Nonfiction for Young Adults, Parents, and Professionals* (1993, Greenwood Press). She is the series adviser for the Greenwood Press's *Using Literature to Help Troubled Teenagers* series. This sixth book on *Abuse Issues* completes the series.

LEAH ARMSTRONG holds an M.S. and Ed.S. in Counseling and Human Systems from Florida State University. Currently, she is pursuing a doctorate at the University of Sarasota in Counseling Psychology. Mrs. Armstrong is employed by Hillsborough County School District as a school psychologist.

JUDITH M. BAILEY, LCSW, ACSW, is a licensed clinical social worker in the state of Maine and holds national recognition as part of the Academy of Certified Social Workers. She has an M.S.W. from Rhode Island College in Providence. Some of her past experience includes individual and group counseling with the blind and visually impaired, crisis work as an Emergency Service Clinician in the Providence area ERs, psychotherapy with people who have chronic mental illness, and counseling and crisis intervention with maximum security inmates at the Maine State Prison and Maine Correctional Institute. Currently, Judy has a full-time private practice in Hallowell, Maine.

SHANNON D. DOSH graduated from of the University of South Florida with a Master's degree in English Education. She is a third-year teacher presently employed at Belleview High School teaching English III.

DR. STAN GIANNET is currently the Associate Dean of Arts, Letters and Sciences at Pasco Hernando Community College in New Port Richey, Florida. Dr. Giannet has his Ph.D. in Clinical Psychology and spent nine years practicing both individual psychotherapy and family therapy. Along with his duties as Associate Dean, he teaches child and adolescent psychology classes. Having worked with young adults as both a therapist and a professor, he has always valued projective tasks such as journaling and art therapy.

LESLIE HIBBS is a media specialist at Ridgewood High School where she has taught English, journalism, and television production. In 2001, she was recognized as Ridgewood High School's Teacher of the Year.

DR. EILEEN KENNEDY is a licensed psychologist, practicing pediatric psychology at the Cleveland Clinic Foundation. She also teaches in the Division of Developmental Pediatrics at Children's Hospital Medical Center of Akron, Ohio.

DANIELLE LYONS graduated from the University of South Florida with an M.A. in English Education. She is an English teacher and forensic coach at Alonso High School in Tampa, Florida.

TOM MCDEVITT is a behavioral specialist with a Master's degree in Human Service Administration. He currently works in Florida for the Pasco County School District, counseling emotionally handicapped and sexually abused teenagers.

CANDACE ODIERNA holds a Master's degree in Guidance and an Educational Specialist degree in Educational Leadership. She currently works as an Administrative Resource Teacher in Adult and Community Education in Tampa, Florida. She is dedicated to promoting the emotional well-being of adolescent students and is a proponent of using adolescent literature to help troubled teenagers.

JESSICA PAWELKOP-MUROFF is the In-school Education Specialist for the Southwest Florida Water Management District. She graduated from the University of South Florida with a B.A. in Public Relations and an M.A. in English Education.

TERRY BURKARD PLAIA teaches English at Dunedin High School in Florida. She holds an M.Ed. from the University of South Florida. She is a member of the Dunedin High School Literacy Cadre and continues to update her training in literacy instruction and Read 180 training.

DIANE RESSLER, a teacher with 20 years of experience, is a teacher consultant with the Tampa Bay Area Writing Project (TBAWP) and teaches full time at Dunedin High School. She has also been an adjunct professor at Pasco Hernando Community College since 1989. Ms. Ressler has her M.A.T. from Fairleigh Dickinson University and, through her professor Dr. Louise DeSalvo, was published in the December 1980 issue of *Media and Methods*. She is currently working on a book for teachers that expands her TBWAP presentation of using writing to heal.

CAROLYN T. ROYALTY, ACSW (Academy of Certified Social Workers, national) and LISW (Licensed Independent Social Worker, Ohio) has recently retired after over 32 years with the Hamilton County Department of Human Services in Cincinnati. She worked in several different areas: Income Maintenance, Workforce Development, and Child Welfare and Health Services. She has supervised the foster home adoptions and launched and supervised the At Risk Pregnancy Services Program for almost 10 years. The last three years of her service, she represented the agency by monitoring some of the Workforce Development community contracts, which included some highly innovative programs, and served on a number of committees and boards related to improving the delivery of health services to the medically underserved.

NICOLE SCHAEFER-FARRELL is a high school English teacher and journalism advisor at Ridgewood High School in New Port Richey, Florida.

DR. SUE STREET is an Associate Professor in Counselor Education at the University of South Florida. She has worked professionally with adolescents for 35 years, both as an English teacher and as a counselor. Her publications include a number of articles focusing on adolescent self-concept and self-esteem. Dr. Street considers her strength to be resiliency building with at-risk students, and her approach includes a strong literacy-development component. Over the past few years she has worked with Hispanic girls at the elementary, middle, and high school levels.

ｻｫｻ

618.928582 U85 2004

Using literature to help
 troubled teenagers cope
 with abuse issues.

GAYLORD F